The Hill Fights

The Hill Fights

The First Battle of Khe Sanh

Edward F. Murphy

PRESIDIO
PRESS

Ballantine Books • New York

Dedicated to those who fought at Khe Sanh and those whose names are on panels 16E, 17E, 18E, and 19E at the Vietnam Veterans Memorial

A Presidio Press Book
Published by The Ballantine Publishing Group

Copyright © 2003 by Edward F. Murphy

Library of Congress Cataloging-in-Publication Data is available from the publisher upon request.

ISBN: 0-89141-810-5

Manufactured in the United States of America
First Edition: May 2003
1 3 5 7 9 10 8 6 4 2

Contents

Acknowledgments

A book of this nature and scope could not have been written without the assistance and cooperation of a wide variety of people. I would like to express my sincere thanks to those who helped bring this project to fruition:

Bob Kane and E. J. McCarthy at Presidio Press not only believed in the project but recognized the importance of adding the story of the Khe Sanh Hill Fights to the collection of Vietnam War literature.

The Rev. Ray Stubbe, of Wauwatosa, Wisconsin, was a Navy chaplain with the 26th Marines during the Khe Sanh siege in 1968. Since that time he has devoted untold thousands of hours to research that battle and other events relating to Khe Sanh and has earned a well-deserved reputation as *the* authority on the subject. His hard work resulted in the publication of the definitive *Valley of Decision,* which not only covers the siege but also provides considerable background material on the United States military's involvement at Khe Sanh, including the Hill Fights. Ray is also the founder of the Khe Sanh Veterans Association, a veterans group with an annual meeting open to anyone who ever served in and around Khe Sanh. From the first time I contacted Ray about my project, he unselfishly provided every bit of help and assistance I needed. He supported my efforts and encouraged Hill Fights veterans to respond to my request for interviews. Ray routinely provided documents from his archives that even the Marine Corps Historical Center could not. When I needed a photograph, Ray provided it. He devoted some of his rare spare time to reviewing the manuscript and helping me over rough spots. Without his support, help, and encouragement, I could not have written this book.

Retired Marine gunner Dick Shoemaker, a former platoon commander in Kilo 3/3 at the Hill Fights, also read the manuscript. His unparalleled assistance not only helped keep the events straight, it also aided in the usage of proper terminology and nomenclature.

Retired Marine Corps colonel George Navadel, who served during the Hill Fights time period as the S-4 of the 9th Marines, provided background information on that unit and Kilo and Mike 3/9 that gave me considerable insight into the command structure.

Retired Marine Corps major general Matt Caulfield, the S-3 of 3/26 during the siege, graciously consented to review my chapter on the siege to ensure that I had not made any mistakes.

Cathy Leroy, the famed combat photojournalist, unhesitatingly volunteered to let me use the famous series of photographs she took on 30 April 1967.

My wife, Kay, who devoted long hours to typing the manuscript from my handwritten drafts, and never complained about all the corrections, additions, deletions, and changes that followed, deserves the highest accolades for her support and understanding.

Mostly, though, I extend my thanks, deepest gratitude, and appreciation to the veterans of the Hill Fights whom I contacted. All but one of them immediately agreed to revisit and recount the events they experienced more than thirty years ago, even though doing so was painful and emotional for many of them. They not only shared their personal stories, they sent me letters they had written home about the Hill Fights, provided copies of personal accounts of the fight that they had composed over the years, copied photographs, and gave me the names of buddies who had fought with them. I cannot thank them enough for sharing so much with me.

The fighting around Khe Sanh in the spring of 1967 has long been overshadowed by the highly publicized siege of Khe Sanh during the following year. As a result, this battle is rarely mentioned in accounts of the war. Very few Vietnam War historians are aware of the significance and brutality of the battles; fewer still knew of the scandalous failures of the newly issued M16 rifle that caused so many casualties.

I am proud and honored to be the one to tell this story. Any errors or mistakes in the account are mine, and mine alone.

Semper Fidelis!
Edward F. Murphy

Preface

Lance Corporal Steven Wright moved cautiously up the narrow trail. Behind him the rest of the Marine combat patrol snaked downhill for more than a hundred meters, reaching nearly to the base of the knoll. Dense stands of elephant grass covered the hillside, rising above Wright's head and limiting his view to less than ten meters off the trail. No breeze penetrated the foliage; no wind stirred the sharp-edged stalks of grass. Heavy, humid air hung over the hill. The hill was not high and the trail was not steep, but the effort of walking uphill carrying close to fifty pounds of equipment took its toll on Wright. Though it was only midmorning, dark patches of sweat already stained his utilities. He paused to wipe the sweat from his eyes. A few meters ahead of him, the trail turned sharply before cresting the hill. Wright stepped around the curve and froze. There, not thirty meters away, casually strolled three Vietnamese men. Before Wright could react, he heard a rustling sound to his left. He glanced over and caught a fleeting glimpse of a slightly built man wearing a khaki-colored uniform who disappeared into the brush. Nervously shifting his 12-gauge shotgun to his left hand, Wright turned and whispered hoarsely to the patrol leader behind him, "Gooks!"

Sergeant Donald E. Harper stopped in midstride. He hastily signaled the members of his thirteen-man patrol to get down. In the three weeks that he and the rest of Bravo Company, 1st Battalion, 9th Marines (Bravo 1/9) had been at Khe Sanh, he had led more than a half dozen patrols into the surrounding mountains. They had not spotted any enemy soldiers before.

With his heart pounding rapidly, Harper crept forward. He found Wright kneeling in the thick elephant grass alongside the path. In hurried whispers Wright told Harper what he had seen. No, he responded to Harper's questions, he didn't think he'd been spotted. Yes, they were definitely Vietnamese. No, he hadn't noticed if they were armed.

Harper looked around. He knew the area well. The hill they were on sat less than 2,000 meters straight out from the western end of Khe Sanh's airstrip. He had led several earlier patrols across it. In fact, he and his men had eaten their lunch rations near this spot just a few days earlier. Not more than 150 meters high, the little hill guarded the approaches to the larger hill masses rising to the northwest. The closest one, Hill 861, which was perched ominously less than two kilometers away, looked straight down on the Marines' base. If there were enemy soldiers here, Harper reasoned, they must have come from there. He decided they had probably been reconnoitering Bravo's perimeter positions around the base.

Sergeant Harper rose to one knee, then signaled to his fire team leaders to put their men on-line. They would continue up the hill to find out what was going on.

As the riflemen spread out in the tall grass, Harper radioed a situation report to Capt. Michael W. Sayers, the commander of Bravo 1/9, back at the Khe Sanh Combat Base. Sayers instantly approved Harper's actions and told him to report back when he knew more.

Harper stood up, and motioned his patrol forward. Wright and an M60 machine gun team took the point. The Marines moved wordlessly through the elephant grass, their eyes carefully searching the ground in front of them. Then one of the riflemen stopped. Harper quickly made his way to the man. On the ground in front of them, in a shallow depression, were three neat piles of leaves and grass. They had found where the three soldiers had spent the night.

On Harper's command the patrol continued. Still on point, Wright crested the hill. Suddenly, there they were: three North Vietnamese soldiers just twenty meters away. Instinctively, Wright pulled the trigger of his shotgun. The blast caught one enemy soldier full in the head, slamming him to the ground. The M60 machine gunner squeezed off a quick burst at the other two. They squealed in pain but fled into the dense elephant grass. Seconds later came the sharp report of an M14 rifle off to the right. Corporal Hughes hollered out that he had shot a man.

Before the other Marines could react, the forward slope of the hill to their front erupted in a violent blaze of AK-47 rifle fire. Enemy rounds snapped through the air. Harper shouted, "Pull back! Pull back!" The Marines retreated, sending bursts of rifle and machine gun fire in the general direction of the enemy as they fled. They did not stop until they crossed a small stream that meandered along the little hill's eastern slope. After Harper placed his men in defensive positions, he radioed Sayers.

Captain Sayers ordered Harper to return to the site of the contact. Sayers wanted Harper to collect any and all intelligence information.

Harper asked for volunteers to return with him. Only five of his men stood up. With this small band in tow, Harper started back up the trail. When they had the enemy corpse in sight, the others spread out while Harper grimly approached the bloody remains. He searched the dead man and found several documents, which he shoved into his pants pockets. Harper next pulled the man's web belt free and tied it around the corpse's feet. "Let's go," he ordered. Another Marine stepped forward to help him pull the body down the hill. The others walked backward, nervously glancing into the dense elephant grass around them.

They had covered less than ten meters when a burst of enemy fire shattered the air. Harper abandoned the corpse and raced back downhill with the others. When he was safe, he again radioed Sayers to request artillery fire on the reverse slope of the hill. When the fifteen-round barrage of 105mm shells ended a few minutes later, Harper took his volunteers back up the slope. They reached the corpse without incident. As soon as they started to move the body, the enemy again opened fire. This time their rounds hit Marine flesh.

The machine gunner on the right whelped in pain as a slug from a North Vietnamese AK-47 tore into his lower right arm, knocking the M60 from his hands. Another round slammed into Lance Corporal Wright's shotgun, shattering its stock and sending that weapon flying, too. The Marines turned and ran back down the hill to the stream. Harper again radioed Captain Sayers.

Sayers listened to Sergeant Harper's latest report. Alarmed at the turn of events, Sayers ordered reinforcements to move out to help Harper.

First Lieutenant David L. Mellon commanded the Sparrow Hawk team, or quick-reaction force, at Khe Sanh that day. Composed of the 1st Squad of his 1st Platoon, the ten-man unit was strengthened by the addition of a four-man M60 machine gun team, an M79 grenadier, two radiomen, a corpsman, and the platoon guide. Although they had manned bunkers along the base's perimeter, within ten minutes of Sayers's call the Sparrow Hawk members stood assembled at the company command post.

"Here's the situation," Sayers told Mellon, then briefed him on what he knew. "Get out there, recover those weapons and that body, see if there are any more enemy dead, then secure and police up the area," Sayers continued. "Any questions?"

"Negative, sir," Mellon responded crisply. Then, with a nod to SSgt. Kendell D. Cutbirth, the platoon right guide, Mellon led his twenty-man force out of the base. It was about 1300 on 25 February 1967.

The Sparrow Hawk team moved down the dirt road that headed west out of the base. After a kilometer they turned off the road and picked up a trail that would take them right to Harper. Mellon walked at a quick pace, nervous and excited at the same time. Though he had led his platoon for eight months, he had experienced only minor combat with Viet Cong guerrillas. The prospect of finally tangling with regular North Vietnamese Army (NVA) soldiers pumped adrenaline into his veins, which heightened his tension.

Mellon found Harper and his men clustered along the trail at the base of the hill. All of them were excited, several talking at once about what they had seen and experienced. Mellon silenced them, then, while Hospitalman Daniel W. Polland treated the casualties, Mellon pulled Harper aside.

The sergeant drew a map of the action site in the dirt. The lieutenant had not patrolled this sector before, so the terrain was new to him. When Harper finished his report, Mellon called for another fire mission. The lieutenant wanted the artillery rounds to hit the east side of the hill, then advance at fifty-meter increments as his Marines moved up the hill behind the protective barrage. After the first shells slammed into the earth, Mellon motioned his men forward, leaving Harper and his patrol behind. Mellon's team splashed across the stream, then passed through a thick bamboo grove. The lieutenant put his men on-line, and the riflemen spread out right and left into the elephant grass. On Mellon's command the artillery fire shifted forward. The Sparrow Hawk team started up the hill. By moving slowly in measured bounds as the high-explosive shells preceded them up the slope, they reached the hill's crest without incident.

Doc Polland knelt by the body of the enemy soldier. The man's skull had been laid open by Wright's shotgun blast, exposing his brain. Polland pointed to the organ's convolutions and remarked to a nearby Marine, "Christ, it looks just like they taught us in school."

Farther forward Mellon stood in the center of the line with his radioman, LCpl. Frederick A. Westerman, at his side. Corporal Wright pointed to where his weapon had disappeared in the elephant grass. Just as Mellon ordered several men to search for the shotgun, someone called out, "I got movement!"

Below them, the elephant grass swayed in several places as if men were crawling through it. Mellon turned to Cpl. Kenneth D. Vermillion, the M60 machine gunner. "Spray down that grass," he ordered. To several others he yelled, "Get some grenades down there."

As Vermillion triggered short bursts of heavy 7.62mm slugs at the invisible foe, Mellon sent Cpl. Harold Tucker and his fire team out to a lone tree standing about a hundred meters to the left and fifty meters downhill. From there Tucker would be in a good position to flank the advancing enemy.

Seconds after Tucker departed, a tremendous blast of enemy small-arms fire hit the Marines. AK-47s, carbines, and grenade launchers erupted from the hillside in front of them. Mellon and the others scurried for cover. But before Mellon could get down, a carbine round tore into his right knee and sent him spinning. In the next instant a grenade exploded behind him. Westerman caught most of the blast. The radioman fell heavily, his back and side shredded by shrapnel.

A hundred meters away, on Mellon's right flank, Staff Sergeant Cutbirth spotted an enemy soldier slithering through the grass. Cutbirth rose, fired off-hand, and yelled excitedly, "I got him. I got him!" Another enemy soldier heard Cutbirth's yells, turned, and fired. The twenty-three-year-old Texan fell in a heap, three enemy rounds embedded in his chest.

Doc Polland rushed forward, oblivious to the enemy fire. He instantly saw that Cutbirth was dead. A few feet away Sgt. Robert A. Chapps writhed in pain, his stomach ripped apart by enemy bullets. Chapps wailed, "Hail Mary full of grace . . . don't let me die! Holy Mary, mother of God . . . I don't want to die!" Polland patched him up, then directed some nearby Marines to carry Chapps to safety. As Polland paused to catch his breath, his heart pounding heavily, he heard the call: "Corpsman up! The lieutenant's hit. Corpsman!"

Polland sprinted through the elephant grass toward Mellon. A rifle grenade exploded nearby in a deafening blast. Though hunks of shrapnel tore into his left leg and chest and put a big dent in the front of his helmet, the corpsman barely paused in his dash to aid the wounded. Polland first patched up the badly injured radioman, then he turned his attention to Mellon.

By this time the enemy fire had slackened noticeably; only a few stray rounds snapped across the Marine line. Still, Polland felt nervous; he fully expected hordes of enemy soldiers to pour out of the tall grass at any moment. His hands shook as he wrapped Mellon's wound.

Mellon didn't notice the doc's nervousness; he was too busy talking on the radio to an airborne forward air controller (FAC). The FAC had a pair of F-4 Phantoms on station overhead whose pilots were eager to unleash their lethal five-hundred-pound bombs on the enemy. The FAC radioed Mellon, "Dig a big hole, boys. We're coming in."

"Pull back. Get over the hill now," Mellon yelled. "The fast movers are comin' in. Move out now!" Hobbling and hopping on his good leg, the gutsy officer joined the retreat. He heard the whine of the jets' engines as they began their run. He dove and rolled into a ball, trying to make himself as small as possible.

Polland sprinted a short distance, then dropped into a shallow depression. Still convinced that the enemy was going to launch a ground assault, he grabbed an M14 rifle from a casualty and took up a firing position.

"Get down!" "Hit the dirt!" "Incoming!" "Here they come!" The screams of the Marines warned of the approaching Phantoms.

Scant seconds later, the jets raced in with an ear-shattering roar. Skimming the earth at treetop level, the two silvery blurs dropped their bombs. As the jets pulled up in a steep, climbing turn, the five-hundred-pound bombs exploded in four simultaneous blasts, sending thick columns of dirt and shrubbery skyward. The planes made two more passes, blasting the enemy with another two tons of explosives. Then the jets flew off, and quiet slowly returned to the scene. The aerial bombardment had either killed the enemy soldiers or driven them away.

Mellon wasted no time in radioing Sayers. "Send a medevac. I've got several casualties."

"It's coming," Sayers assured him. Sayers also told Mellon that the 2d Platoon commander, 2d Lt. John M. Kramer, was on his way out with two more squads.

By the time Kramer arrived, bringing Sergeant Harper and his men with him, the medevacs had come and gone, carrying the dead and wounded back to Khe Sanh. Mellon, lucid despite his painful wound, briefed Kramer. Then, his mission completed, he limped off to a waiting helicopter.

Kramer assembled the remaining men and started them down the hill's forward slope. Despite the tall, dense elephant grass, it did not take them long to locate the enemy dead. In all, nine NVA bodies were found. One, an enemy officer, had several hand-drawn maps stuffed in his pockets. These showed, in remarkable detail, Bravo Company's defensive positions around the Khe Sanh airstrip. The Marines also found numerous backpacks stuffed with rice, clothing, and shelter halves, as well as an 82mm mortar tube, three mortar base plates, three mortar bipods, nearly four hundred rounds of mortar ammo, a carbine, a submachine gun, several grenades, and a scattering of other documents. The North Vietnamese were certainly up to something, but no one knew exactly what.

While Kramer and his men scoured the hillside, Corporal Tucker brought in his fire team. True to his orders, he had kept his men in position throughout the firefight and air strikes. Only when he saw the other Marines searching the area did he feel he could pull back. In all the excitement, Lieutenant Mellon had completely forgotten about Tucker.

At Khe Sanh, Captain Sayers debriefed Mellon. What he heard deeply concerned him. During Bravo's three weeks at Khe Sanh, its patrols had seen many signs of the enemy but nothing to indicate the presence of a large force.

As the casualties were loaded aboard a C-130 cargo plane for evacuation, Sayers turned an apprehensive glance to the cluster of hills overlooking Khe Sanh. What the hell is out there? he wondered.

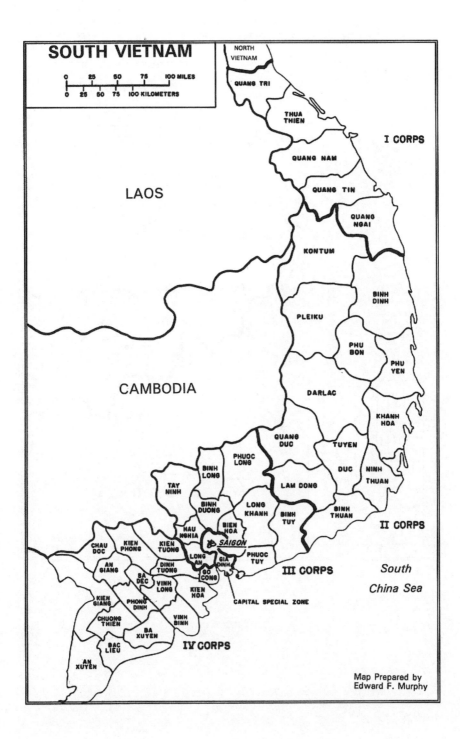

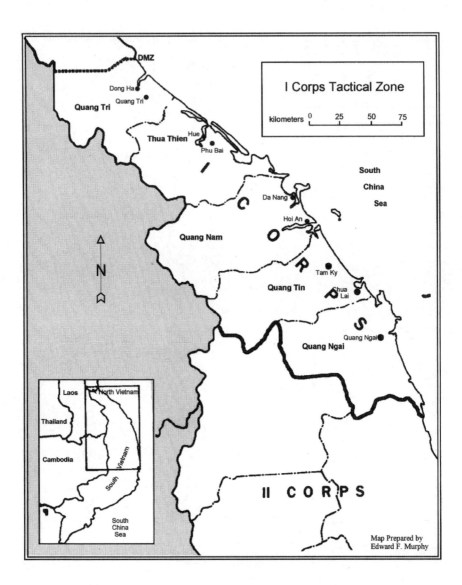

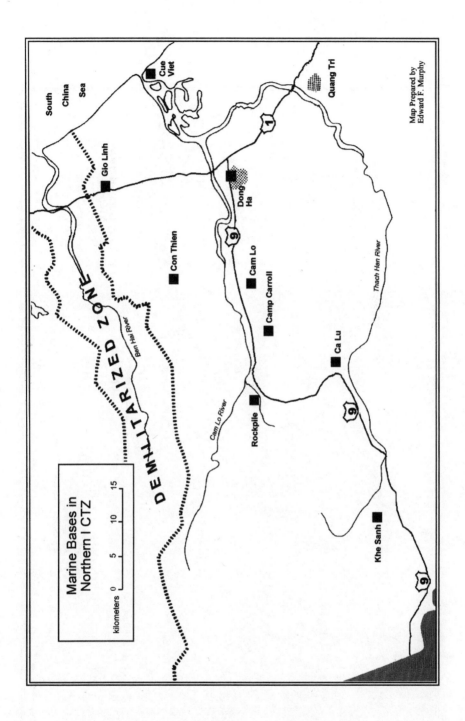

Marine Bases in Northern I CTZ

kilometers
0   5   10   15

South China Sea

DEMILITARIZED ZONE

Ben Hai River

Cue Viet

Gio Linh

Con Thien

Dong Ha

Cam Lo

Camp Carroll

Ca Lu

Rockpile

Cam Lo River

Khe Sanh

Quang Tri

Thach Han River

Map Prepared by
Edward F. Murphy

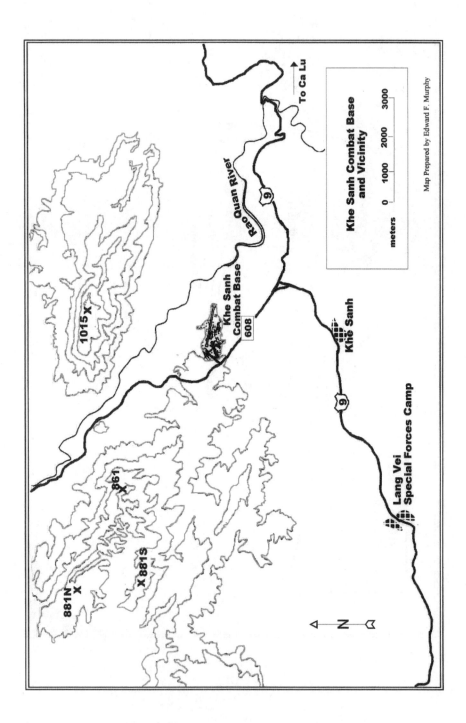

Khe Sanh Combat Base
and Vicinity

meters

0   1000   2000   3000

Map Prepared by Edward F. Murphy

Part One: In the Beginning

Chapter One

O n a hot, humid day in late September 1966, Lt. Gen. Lewis W. Walt wore a deep scowl across his broad face. The commander of the III Marine Amphibious Force (MAF), which incorporated all Marines in South Vietnam, Walt held strong opinions on how his troops should be used to win the war. When that did not happen, the barrel-chested, volatile head of III MAF got angry. Walt's subordinates at III MAF's headquarters in Da Nang had no doubt the old man was in a foul mood that day. They trembled as he barked into his telephone, snapped orders to his aides, and demanded instant answers to complex questions. Those who served under Walt knew all about his temper. They knew that it did not take much to set him off. Recently, the most frequent catalyst for Walt's fury was his superior, U.S. Army general William C. Westmoreland, the head of the Military Assistance Command, Vietnam (MACV). Westmoreland had his own plans for using the Marines to fight and win the war in South Vietnam. All too often these clashed with Walt's.

The conflict between the Marines and their Army superior had been simmering for more than a year. Although trained since before World War II as a hard-hitting, beach-storming, amphibious force, the Marines took a different approach to the war in South Vietnam. Ever since they landed at Da Nang in March 1965, the Marines had supported pacification efforts as the best way to win this war. Walt fully concurred with the statement made by Marine Corps commandant Gen. Wallace M. Greene, Jr., shortly after the Marines' initial landings. "The real targets in Vietnam are not the Viet Cong or the North Vietnamese but the South Vietnamese people," Greene had declared.

So strongly did Walt believe in this strategy that he approved a number of innovative programs to rid the native villages of their insurgent infrastructure and make the South Vietnamese people feel safe in their homes. But this emphasis on pacification programs did not mean that Walt possessed an unwillingness to engage the enemy in full combat. Indeed, quite the contrary was true. A Marine since graduating from Colorado State University in 1936, Walt was one of the Marine Corps' most experienced combat leaders. He commanded a Marine raider company during the D-day landings at Guadalcanal in August 1942 and earned a Silver Star for his heroism. A year later, as a battalion commander, he earned a Navy Cross fighting in the dense jungles of New Britain. He picked up a second one in 1944 battling the Japanese on the fiercely defended coral island of Peleliu. He commanded a Marine regiment during the Korean War, where his aggressiveness and personal valor added more luster to his reputation. If anyone in the Marine Corps knew how to battle with an enemy, it was fifty-three-year-old Lewis William Walt. But he recognized that the civil war in South Vietnam would not be won by the Marines' historic method of wresting terrain objectives from the enemy's armies. In his view, if the Viet Cong and the North Vietnamese Army were to be vanquished, it would happen only if the people wanted it to happen. And the only way to get them to want that was to allow them to feel safe in their villages.

Walt's strategy had the full backing and enthusiastic support of his immediate Marine Corps superior, Lt. Gen. Victor H. "Brute" Krulak. As head of the Fleet Marine Force–Pacific (FMF-Pac), Krulak provided administrative and logistical support to Walt's Marines, but he had no authority over their operational deployment in South Vietnam; that was General Westmoreland's business. Commissioned in 1934, Krulak served two years in pre–World War II China. It was there he began his study of guerrilla warfare and counterinsurgency. As commander of a Marine parachute battalion in World War II, he earned a Navy Cross in October 1942 during the raid on the island of Choiseul. He also saw combat in Korea during that war's later years. Throughout his career he continued his studies of guerrilla warfare. By the 1960s General Krulak not only wielded a tremendous amount of influence as one of the Marine Corps' top officers, he was also a recognized expert in counterinsurgency doctrine. In fact, he had served the Joint Chiefs of Staff as special assistant for counterinsurgency and special activities from 1962 to 1964.

Because 80 percent of South Vietnam's population lived an agrarian existence and raised their own rice crops, both Krulak and Walt recognized that by protecting these peasants and their crops, the insurgents, as well as the infiltrating NVA, would be denied a major food source. The enemy would be forced to depend solely on supplies moved manually from the ports of North Vietnam down the five-hundred-kilometer-long network of paths and roads known collectively as the Ho Chi Minh Trail. Obviously, they could not last long under these circumstances.

General Westmoreland, however, had different plans for fighting this war. Although he acknowledged the benefits of pacification, as a West Point graduate (class of 1936), an artillery battery commander in World War II, and a parachute regiment commander in the Korean War, Westmoreland had focused his entire career on conducting conventional warfare. Indeed, he yearned for a major land battle where his superior firepower would decisively defeat the NVA and send them packing back to Hanoi. And the only way to achieve the traditional victory he had trained his whole life for was to send his troops where the enemy was: South Vietnam's rugged, mountainous interior border regions. But with his limited manpower resources, Westmoreland knew he could not protect the people and battle the enemy's main-force units. He had to make a choice. His 1966 battle plan revealed that choice.

According to his master plan for conducting the war, American troops, better trained and with greater firepower than the Army of the Republic of Vietnam (ARVN), would conduct major "search-and-destroy" operations in the rural, unpopulated areas. Here the combat units could "find, fix, and destroy" the enemy and his base areas. The ARVN would follow up with "clearing operations" designed to ferret out any surviving guerrilla forces. Then the local militia units, or Popular Forces, would move in to provide a permanent defense for area villages. As far as Westmoreland was concerned, the Marines' preferred strategy for winning the war had been seriously downgraded.

But neither General Krulak nor General Walt was easily persuaded. In fact, so strongly did Krulak support the pacification approach that he wrote a seventeen-page appraisal of the situation in South Vietnam and set out to get it reviewed at the highest levels of the U.S. government.

Krulak's appraisal concluded with four recommendations:

• Emphasize the security of the indigent population from guerrilla oppression; fight the enemy's main forces only when the odds are overwhelmingly in our favor.
• Destroy North Vietnam's rail lines, power plants, and fuel storage centers, and mine the entrance to her seaports.

• Put all applicable U.S. resources into the pacification process.
• Force the South Vietnamese government to institute land reform programs.

Krulak secured audiences with everyone up to and including Secretary of Defense Robert S. McNamara and President Lyndon B. Johnson, but his effort failed. His second point, specifically the mining of North Vietnam's harbors, proved anathema to America's foreign policy strategy. President Johnson and Secretary McNamara were completely convinced that this particular action would result in a major global war with the Soviet Union and/or China. Both men lived in fear of such a prospect. Thus, the war in South Vietnam would be fought Westmoreland's way—essentially by sending combat troops to fight a war governed by politics rather than by sound military strategy.

Although assured by McNamara that his strategy would prevail, Westmoreland was politically astute enough to be concerned about accusations of interservice rivalry. Thus, he trod softly when dealing with General Walt. Rather than force the Marines to comply with his strategy for massive infantry campaigns in the hinterlands, Westmoreland preferred to issue orders for specific operations that would eventually pull them out of their coastal enclaves. Opportunities for such orders came sooner rather than later.

Evidence of an increased NVA presence in South Vietnam's northern provinces emerged in early 1966. On 28 February, U.S. Army Special Forces soldiers from the isolated outpost at A Shau, located in a wide valley adjacent to the Laotian border ninety kilometers west of Da Nang, captured an NVA soldier. According to the soldier's diary, the 95th Regiment of the NVA 325 Division planned an attack on the camp on the night of 11 March. As a result of this information, reinforcements in the form of indigenous troops were rushed to the camp. Unfortunately, they were of dubious quality and loyalty.

The enemy soldier's information proved wrong by two days. His comrades launched their attack in the early morning hours of 9 March. A two-and-a-half-hour mortar barrage blasted the camp from end to end, causing more than fifty casualties among the four hundred defenders. The NVA then hit the camp's southern perimeter with a two-company force. They were repulsed after heavy fighting.

The NVA commander had timed his attack well. Low, monsoonal clouds blanketed the valley, limiting retaliatory air strikes and keeping all but a few helicopters out of the A Shau Valley. The NVA continued their attack on the camp throughout 9 March and into the early morning of the tenth. At 0400 that morning the NVA launched their final assaults on the besieged camp. The defenders fought heroically but were badly outnumbered. At 1730 the camp's U.S. Army commander reluctantly ordered it evacuated. A few daring Marine pilots brought their helicopters through the cloud cover and pulled out 69 of the camp's surviving defenders. The remaining defenders fled into the surrounding jungle. In all, 250 of the camp's 400 soldiers were killed or listed as missing. The fall of A Shau opened the way for the NVA to increase its infiltration of men and materiel into South Vietnam's northern provinces.

The loss of A Shau shocked General Westmoreland. He viewed this attack as the first phase of a major enemy assault on Hue, South Vietnam's ancient imperial capital, located sixty kilometers north of Da Nang. Capturing Hue, highly regarded for its wide, tree-lined boulevards, elegant shops, excellent university, and sophisticated residents, would not only give the NVA a major military victory by cutting off South Vietnam's two northern provinces, it would also give them a large moral and political victory. Westmoreland could not let that happen.

Two weeks after the fall of A Shau, Westmoreland received even more disturbing news. His J-2 (intelligence) officer reported that the NVA 324B Division had crossed the Demilitarized Zone (DMZ) that separated the two countries. Then, in early April, MACV learned of the establishment of a major enemy field headquarters near Hue. Identified as the Tri-Thien-Hue Military Command, this headquarters reported directly to Hanoi. To Westmoreland these were sure signs that the enemy planned a major offensive.

General Walt, however, interpreted this information differently. Though he acknowledged the presence of additional enemy forces in the I Corps Tactical Zone, neither he nor his staff believed they posed a major threat. In fact, instead of a full NVA division located south of the DMZ, Walt's intelligence officers reported but a regiment. The differences became apparent at a commanders' conference at Chu Lai on 24 March. Westmoreland bluntly asked Walt if he doubted the accuracy of MACV's reports on the number of enemy units in I Corps. Walt responded that his long-range reconnaissance patrols could not confirm the presence of any large enemy formation. He told Westmoreland, "If they are there, they are hiding in the mountains not far from the Laotian border."

Regardless of how Walt interpreted the intelligence data, Westmoreland was still the boss. He ordered the Marines to send a full battalion to Khe Sanh and look for the enemy.

Khe Sanh sits near the western end of national Route 9, the only east-west road that traverses northern South Vietnam. Route 9 begins at Dong Ha, a once sleepy village located ten kilometers inland on a tributary of the Cua Viet River. A crossroads town, Dong Ha also straddles Route 1, South Vietnam's only north-south road. Sixty kilometers separate Dong Ha and Khe Sanh, but they were sixty of the roughest and most isolated kilometers in all of the war-torn country.

Route 9 had been paved, if it could be called pavement, by the French for about twelve kilometers west of Dong Ha to the village of Cam Lo. From there the road deteriorated rapidly into a two-lane cart path. Fifteen kilometers beyond Cam Lo, the Rockpile, a two-hundred-meter-tall jagged peak, dominates the road. It is here that Route 9 jogs south for twelve kilometers before returning to a westerly heading at Ca Lu. It then became not much more than a wide dirt path, crowded by jungle growth on both sides as it begins to climb into the rugged Annamite Mountains. Sharp turns, steep drop-offs, towering cliffs, and deteriorating bridges characterized Route 9 as it wound its way for eighteen more kilometers to the village of Khe Sanh. From Khe Sanh the road meanders west another fifteen kilometers before it crosses into Laos and continues to Tchepone and beyond. No allied troops had used Route 9 west of Cam Lo since 1964.

Khe Sanh's location near the borders of the two Vietnams and Laos made it an ideal site to set up a camp to monitor North Vietnamese activity on the nearby Ho Chi Minh Trail. A team of U.S. Army Special Forces, sporting their famed green berets, first arrived in the isolated village in the summer of 1962. Their mission: recruit and train local Bru tribesmen for a militia force that could patrol the mountains that hid the Ho Chi Minh Trail.

Though occasional supply runs into Hue were made by truck, the Green Berets depended upon a nearby airstrip for regular resupply. Situated on a long, narrow plateau a few kilometers north of the village, the airstrip had originally been hacked out of the jungle by French colonial troops in 1949. Soon after the Americans arrived, ARVN engineers lengthened the runway so it could accept larger cargo planes. The Green Berets relocated their camp to the airstrip in the fall of 1964.

Unfortunately, several nearby mountain peaks gave enemy observers an excellent view of the airstrip and the soldiers' new camp. Hill 1015, or Dong Tri Mountain, sits four kilometers directly north, rising sharply in a distinctive shape that earned it the nickname Tiger Tooth Mountain. One kilometer to its west is Hill 950 (on military topographical maps, hills are identified by their height above sea level in meters). Four and a half kilometers northwest of the airstrip sits Hill 861, actually one of three peaks that make up a major hill mass located off the west end of the runway. The other two peaks rise to the same height and were known as Hills 881N (north) and 881S (south).

The Green Berets and their indigenous troops spent the next six months constructing a number of permanent buildings, including a large central command bunker, four corner bunkers, and about fifteen other buildings that included a dispensary, mess hall, and barracks. By the time they finished, Khe Sanh had become the largest allied base in far northern South Vietnam. And none too soon.

Once America became fully committed to the war in South Vietnam, the importance of Khe Sanh as an intelligence-gathering focal point increased significantly. As the camp closest to both Laos and North Vietnam, Khe Sanh attracted a multitude of intelligence forces. Not only the regular Green Berets, but Central Intelligence Agency (CIA)–sponsored spy teams, MACV's Special Operations Group, the Special Forces' ultrasecret Project Delta, the Marines' 3d Reconnaissance Battalion, and even the Air Force's aerial reconnaissance project, Operation Tigerhound, sponsored covert activities from Khe Sanh.

Each of these intelligence teams had different objectives and reported to different commanders, creating a real hodgepodge. Sometimes as many as a dozen different recon teams operated in the same area at the same time. Despite their confusing and redundant missions, the teams' activities did provide a steady flow of intelligence information to both Saigon and Da Nang, information that was interpreted very differently by MACV and III MAF.

Responding to Westmoreland's edict, Walt issued orders on 27 March 1966 for a full battalion to conduct a search-and-destroy mission around Khe Sanh. The 1st Battalion, 1st Marines, then operating near Phu Bai, received those orders the same day. Although 1/1 commander Lt. Col. Van D. Bell, Jr., planned for his Operation Virginia to begin on 3 April 1966, bad weather at Khe Sanh grounded the transport planes. They could not take off until 17 April.

Bell set up his command post adjacent to the Special Forces camp. He planned a three-phase operation around the airstrip. His battalion would scour the quadrant northeast of Khe Sanh, then move into the northwest quadrant, and finally work the southwest sector. A battalion of ARVN would search the southeast quadrant.

On 18 April helicopters ferried the men of Charlie 1/1 to blocking positions approximately six kilometers north of the base. The following day Bell's two other rifle companies, Alpha and Bravo, were airlifted to a landing zone nine kilometers east of Charlie. For the next three days, these two companies hacked their way westward through dense vegetation and over rugged terrain. They reached Charlie without encountering the enemy. Based on this and the negative reports of his long-range recon patrols that had already searched the northwest quadrant, Bell canceled the rest of Operation Virginia.

Bell's reports to III MAF gave Walt's staff an excellent opportunity to prove to Westmoreland that no NVA were operating in the area. III MAF ordered Bell to march his battalion east out of Khe Sanh along Route 9 all the way to Cam Lo. It was part tactical maneuver and part publicity stunt, but mostly it was Walt making his point.

In an attempt to beat the oppressive heat and humidity, the battalion began its march at midnight on 26 April. It did not work. The rugged terrain and enervating temperatures so sapped the troops that instead of covering the fifty kilometers in three days, they took five. Not until 30 April did the column of Marines stagger into Cam Lo. Generals Westmoreland and Walt were on hand to greet the weary men. The Marines took full advantage of the event, proudly and loudly proclaiming Bell's battalion to be the largest force in eight years to hike all the way down Route 9.

Unfortunately, Bell's efforts proved inconclusive. The Marines had not seen any North Vietnamese, but that did not mean they were not there. And although Walt felt vindicated, upcoming events would temper his feelings of satisfaction.

Upon Bell's return, Walt turned his attention back to improving his pacification programs. However, in mid-May intelligence sources reported an enemy buildup in the eastern DMZ area, primarily north and east of Dong Ha. They were right. On 19 May strong NVA forces attacked two ARVN outposts, Gio Linh and Con Thien, both just a few kilometers south of the DMZ. Additional evidence indicated that another enemy force operated close to Dong Ha. Once again Westmoreland directed III MAF to insert a battalion in the area and check it out.

This time the 2d Battalion, 4th Marines, drew the assignment. On 30 May the battalion flew into Dong Ha. It spent the next week patrolling all around Dong Ha. The Marines killed three NVA stragglers but saw no sign of a large enemy force. The battalion flew out of Dong Ha on 8 June.

Despite this, Westmoreland still believed that the NVA planned a major move on Quang Tri Province, so he ordered III MAF to conduct extensive reconnaissance patrols in the rolling, heavily vegetated region lying between Dong Ha and Cam Lo, and Route 9 and the DMZ. III MAF organized Task Force Charlie, composed of elements of the 3d Marine Reconnaissance Battalion, a supporting artillery battalion, and Echo 2/1, and sent it to Dong Ha on 22 June. While Echo 2/1 provided security for the artillery battalion, the recon Marines went to work. The recon teams searched a variety of locations from the Rockpile in the west to the low hills north of Dong Ha. Over the next ten days, fourteen of eighteen patrols collided with the enemy. Major Dwain A. Colby, commander of TF Charlie, said every recon insertion "encountered armed, uniformed groups and no patrol was able to stay in the field for more than a few hours, many for only a few minutes. . . ." Even so, a couple of patrols snatched a few prisoners. The prisoners of war (POWs) told their interrogators that the entire NVA 324B Division had indeed crossed the DMZ. According to one, an officer, the division's mission was to liberate Quang Tri Province.

General Walt now had no choice. Faced with this overwhelming evidence from his own men, he had to respond. In a command briefing on 12 July 1966, he advised General Westmoreland that he had authorized a multi-battalion operation south of the DMZ that would drive the NVA back across the border. Westmoreland enthusiastically endorsed Walt's decision, telling Walt to use the entire 3d Marine Division if necessary.

The new mission, Operation Hastings, began on 15 July when a fleet of helicopters deposited two battalions of Marines into landing zones at opposite ends of a wide valley just three kilometers south of the DMZ. The insertion at the eastern end of the valley went smoothly; the one at the western landing zone (LZ) did not. Early in the day three troop-laden helicopters collided and crashed, killing two men and injuring seven. That afternoon enemy gunners shot a CH-46 twin-rotor helicopter out of the sky, resulting in thirteen dead and three injured. The sardonic Marines quickly dubbed the area "Helicopter Valley."

Attacking outward from their respective LZs, the two battalions found the enemy almost immediately. The western battalion, 3/4, took heavy casualties in a fight with NVA soldiers just a few hundred meters south of their LZ. The eastern unit, 2/4, although itself battling the enemy, received orders to reverse direction and help its sister battalion. Struggling through the heavy vegetation, 2/4 completed the linkup on the afternoon of 16 July.

The next day one of 3/4's rifle companies attempted to push south out of the LZ. Almost immediately it ran into a large force of determined enemy soldiers. The Marines fought on and off that day and well into the next before being ordered to withdraw. On 18 July, the two battered battalions received new attack orders, but before these could be carried out the NVA launched an attack of their own. Intense hand-to-hand combat raged most of the day before Marine air support drove the enemy away. Along with reinforcements airlifted in the next day, the Marines spent the next few weeks chasing the NVA across the steep, knife-edged mountain ranges that lined the DMZ. The crafty foe avoided another big battle. Instead, they fought a series of rear-guard actions that delayed and frustrated their pursuers while allowing the main NVA force to slip away.

Whether the Marines liked it or not, Operation Hastings committed them to the DMZ region. Even when the border fighting broke off in late July and four of the five infantry battalions were withdrawn, Walt knew he had to keep an eye on the area. As a result, on 3 August, the day Operation Hastings officially ended, he began Operation Prairie. With recon teams and regular infantry units constantly patrolling the mountainous area, it did not take long for the Prairie units to find the NVA. Throughout the rest of August and well into September, intense fighting raged all around the Rockpile. Eventually, elements of five Marine infantry battalions were fed into the brutal battles for one jagged ridgeline after another. They drove the enemy defenders from the ridges but at a frightful cost.

This increased combat action did not escape Westmoreland's attention. In fact, it worried him a great deal. He saw the NVA feeding even more troops across the DMZ, increasing the pressure on the already strapped Marines and further threatening the security of Quang Tri Province. The MACV commander conceived a worst-case scenario: The NVA would try to outflank the Marine strongholds at the Rockpile and Dong Ha by slipping a force into the mountains straddling the border between Laos and South Vietnam. Once again Westmoreland viewed Khe Sanh as the key to the defense of Quang Tri Province, so he started to put pressure on Walt to reinforce Khe Sanh.

As before, the III MAF commander resisted. He and most of his staff interpreted the recent action along the DMZ as "fruitless" attempts by the enemy to bog them down. So convinced were the Marines of the validity of their opinion of the enemy's intentions that Krulak wistfully cabled Westmoreland that III MAF had evidence that the NVA 324B Division had retreated back across the DMZ and no longer posed a threat to Quang Tri. Not so, retorted Westmoreland. He told Krulak, "The reverse is the case and the NVA forces are not fleeing, they are just licking their wounds and rebuilding before returning to the fray." Further, he told Krulak that two more NVA divisions, the 304 and 341, were camped just above the DMZ, ready to drop into Quang Tri Province at any time.

III MAF still did not buy it. Indeed, its staff members openly criticized MACV, deriding its use of phrases such as "massive buildup," "significant serious threat," and similar terms. And as far as Khe Sanh itself was concerned, III MAF still thought it too isolated to be of any practical use. In fact, Brig. Gen. Lowell E. English, the 3d Marine Division assistant commander who headed the task force that controlled the battalions operating in Operation Prairie, did not think Khe Sanh had any military value. Even though Khe Sanh stood at his west flank, English declared, "When you're at Khe Sanh, you're not really anywhere. It's far away from everything. You could lose it and you really haven't lost a damn thing."

The conflict between the two strong-willed commanders intensified. As Westmoreland's worries about the enemy's intentions to launch a major offensive operation across the DMZ grew, he directed Walt to prepare a contingency plan to handle such a scenario. In mid-September, Westmoreland attended a III MAF briefing in Da Nang to review the results. Walt's plan had the Marines pulling back from their outlying positions and holding defensive positions along the eastern edge of the Annamite Mountains around the Rockpile.

Westmoreland could barely conceal his displeasure. He asked testily, "I notice you haven't made any comment about putting a force at Khe Sanh. What's your reason for this?"

"We think it's too isolated" came the response. "We think it would be too hard to support." To the Marines, Route 9 offered, at best, a dubious link to Khe Sanh while frequent bad weather made aerial resupply of any forces holding Khe Sanh a hit-or-miss venture.

"Nevertheless," Westmoreland responded, "I think we ought to have a larger force out there." He wanted a battalion based at Khe Sanh.

The Marines continued to resist. A few days after the briefing, while Westmoreland visited the Marine air base at Chu Lai, Krulak boarded Westmoreland's plane to plead III MAF's case. He argued that occupation of the Khe Sanh plateau would require not one but two entire battalions, because the hills surrounding the airstrip had to be held if the base was to be secure. Marines in the hills meant a deployment of helicopter assets, because the troops on the hills could not be supplied and supported by ground. Krulak further noted that a large presence at Khe Sanh would not deter enemy infiltration into Quang Tri Province; the NVA would simply hike a little farther down the Ho Chi Minh Trail before turning east. He also reminded Westmoreland that every Marine at Khe Sanh was one less available to carry out III MAF's pacification programs in the coastal area, where 95 percent of Quang Tri's population lived.

Westmoreland remained unconvinced. He patiently explained to Krulak that holding Khe Sanh allowed reconnaissance teams to monitor the enemy's north-south movement along the Ho Chi Minh Trail. Plus, possession of Khe Sanh prevented the NVA from using Route 9. Khe Sanh also anchored the western end of the DMZ defensive line. And perhaps most important to Westmoreland, Khe Sanh provided a logical and strategic jumping-off point for his long-hoped-for invasion of Laos.

"One more thing," Westmoreland pointed out. "Every enemy soldier diverted to Khe Sanh is one less to threaten the population."

Krulak left the command aircraft knowing he had failed to sway the MACV commander.

Krulak was right. General Westmoreland directed III MAF to reinforce and extend Khe Sanh's runway so it could handle the big, four-engine C-130 airplane. Walt reluctantly complied and ordered a detachment of U.S. Navy Seabees to Khe Sanh. The Seabees worked feverishly for nearly two weeks, tearing up the old runway matting, replacing it with newer, stronger plating, and lengthening the strip to more than twelve hundred meters.

III MAF's resistance to Westmoreland's directives ended with a 26 September 1966 MACV intelligence report. That report contained an account of a recon team's encounter with an NVA company just fourteen kilometers northeast of Khe Sanh. It was this report that had caused the scowl on Walt's face. Now he knew he could no longer put off Westmoreland; he would have to send a battalion to Khe Sanh. But even more infuriating was knowing he had been forced to do it.

Colonel John R. Chaisson, Walt's G-3 (assistant chief of staff for operations), put it succinctly when he later admitted, "We were not interested in putting a battalion at Khe Sanh, but had we not done it we would have been ordered to do so. We put it [the battalion] out there just to retain that little bit of prestige of doing it on our own volition rather than doing it with a shoe in our tail."

Even though General Walt spent that late September day in a foul mood, making life miserable for his subordinates, he did order a battalion to go to Khe Sanh and sniff around.

Lieutenant Colonel Peter A. Wickwire had been in South Vietnam just eight days and in command of the 1st Battalion, 3d Marines, for just a week when he received orders to report to 3d Marine Division headquarters at Da Nang. His battalion, one of the first to land in South Vietnam, currently patrolled the vital Hai Van Pass, that ran across the rugged mountains north of Da Nang. But 1/3 had experienced considerable combat in its eighteen months in the war zone, fighting both Viet Cong (VC) around Da Nang and the NVA along the DMZ in Operation Hastings. Many of its junior officers and noncommissioned officers had more than six months in-country, making it a well-seasoned outfit.

At Da Nang, Wickwire learned he would be taking his battalion to Khe Sanh. According to the G-2 briefer, the Special Forces team and other recon units working out of the airstrip were constantly bumping into the NVA. The enemy appeared to be positioning their forces to launch a major assault on the base. Wickwire's mission was to secure the airstrip and keep it secure. The briefer made it sound so serious that Wickwire had the impression his troops would be fighting as soon as they jumped off the planes.

But Wickwire had only one question, "When do we leave?"

"Tomorrow morning" came the answer.

Wickwire headed back to his battalion. He had a lot to get done in the next twelve hours.

Transport planes flew 1/3 to Khe Sanh on 29 September 1966. To Wickwire's relief, he found that the tactical situation was not nearly as dire as he had been led to believe. But the condition of the base shocked him. "I couldn't believe American soldiers lived this way. It was filthy. The Bru camp, in particular, was appalling. Rats were everywhere. I forbade my men from entering the Special Forces camp because of the threat of disease."

Wickwire immediately put his Marines to work building new defensive positions adjacent to the airstrip; he ordered them to dig deep. If the NVA held the nearby hills, they had a perfect view of the base; he did not want his men to be easy, aboveground targets for the enemy's mortars and artillery.

The next day Wickwire started an aggressive patrol schedule. The rifle companies moved off the base to set up in the hills. From there platoon- and squad-size patrols went out. These typically remained in the field three to four days at a time while the patrol searched a specific area. At night each patrol sent out ambushes.

The vigorous patrol activity uncovered evidence of an NVA presence nearly everywhere the Marines went. They found freshly constructed base camps, newly cleared trails, rice bags, discarded canteens, and other pieces of equipment either lost or tossed aside by NVA soldiers.

Lance Corporal Joseph W. Ascolillo, a nineteen-year-old engineer from Boston attached to Alpha Company, went on several patrols around Hill 881S that turned up abandoned enemy equipment. "We found a lot of evidence that somebody was out there, including an NVA's pack with a lot of personal papers," he said. And sometimes, but not often, they found the enemy.

A few weeks after arriving at Khe Sanh, Ascolillo's platoon was moving along a narrow trail near the rock quarry west of the base when a brief but intense burst of rifle fire broke out at the front of the column. Because he was near the rear, Ascolillo could not see anything, but word quickly filtered back along the line that the point man had surprised some enemy soldiers. They fled after firing at the approaching Marines. "We searched and found a blood trail," Ascolillo said. "Another platoon came out from the base and together we followed the blood trail. It took us right to the French coffee plantation just south of the base but we lost it there. We hunted around but never did find the wounded enemy soldier."

All of Wickwire's companies experienced some enemy contact as they patrolled around the base and its environs. Most were brief exchanges of rifle fire, which drastically raised the Marines' anxiety level but offered little in the way of tangible results.

Although Wickwire had no knowledge of it, the high-level controversy that prompted his battlion's deployment resulted in frequent visits from senior officers. General Walt flew out often, and even General Krulak dropped in several times. In fact, on his first visit Krulak hopped off his helicopter, strolled around while gazing at the nearby hills, then turned back to Wickwire. "This looks just like Dien Bien Phu," he said, referring to the North Vietnamese village where the French were soundly defeated in 1954 to end the First Indochina War.

"Thanks a lot, General," Wickwire said wryly.

General Westmoreland visited soon after 1/3 arrived at Khe Sanh. He bore down on Wickwire. Fixing his subordinate with a steely gaze, he demanded, "Do you know why you're here?"

"Not really," Wickwire replied truthfully, "but someone must think it's valuable."

"Do you know about the A Shau Valley?"

"Yes, sir." Even though that debacle had occurred before Wickwire arrived in-country, he had heard about it. Everyone had.

"Well, I'm not going to have another A Shau Valley up here. That's why you're here."

Brigadier General English, an old friend of Wickwire's, also visited frequently. Because Wickwire did not report to English (Wickwire reported directly to III MAF in Da Nang), he wondered why the general came out so often. One day Wickwire jokingly said, "You must really like it out here, sir."

English responded with a serious tone, "You don't belong to me, but when the shit hits the fan up here I'll be the one to deal with it."

The comment chilled Wickwire.

Conditions at Khe Sanh were difficult enough for Wickwire's Marines, but they worsened when the monsoons began in mid-October. Khe Sanh's altitude meant it could be sweltering hot and humid during the day and cold and foggy at night. But when the monsoons came, it turned cold, rainy, damp, and cloudy day after day, night after night. Dense rain clouds hugged the mountaintops all day, then dropped to blanket the valley floors in soggy grayness. The fog and clouds cast a surreal pall over the entire area.

The French had coined a word for this constant rainy, misty weather; they called it *crachin*. The Marines called it many other things.

Life for the troops at Khe Sanh went from miserable to terrible. They were wet all the time, their clothing rotted, and their boots decayed. The simplest of injuries refused to heal in the persistent dampness, quickly leading to festering infections. Khe Sanh's red clay soil, the dust of which shrouded the base and permeated everything, turned into a gooey red muck that also permeated everything.

The adverse weather severely reduced aerial resupply. More than once the battalion had less than a day's rations on hand before the weather cleared enough for a plane to duck in, unload, then fly out with the clouds closing behind it.

Still, Wickwire's battalion had a mission to accomplish. His Marines continued their patrols, as did all the other intelligence-gathering teams operating out of Khe Sanh. A half dozen or more recon missions would launch on the same day. Besides the ground troops, the Air Force operated a number of O-1 Bird Dog observation planes from Khe Sanh as part of their top-secret Operation Tigerhound. These single-engine aircraft flew around Khe Sanh and into Laos and North Vietnam looking for signs of the enemy. When they found a target they would call for a B-52 bomber raid, code-named Arc Light, on the site. Sometimes the Bird Dogs flew right over Wickwire's Marines as they humped through the boonies. Why, Wickwire often wondered, did his men have to be out there if the planes could see the same thing?

Indeed, the rabble of intelligence efforts caused varied problems for Wickwire and his men. Conflict constantly raged among the different teams. The Army troops did not like the Marines, the recon Marines did not like the line company Marines, and the Air Force crews did not like anyone. The Special Forces soldiers and their Bru militia answered to no one. The CIA-sponsored teams were particularly secretive. No unit ever coordinated its activities with another. This failure led to several instances in which Wickwire's troops fired on men they took to be enemy troops but who turned out to be Bru. On at least one occasion the Marines held their fire to avoid ambushing what they thought were friendly troops. Later they learned that no other allied patrols had been operating in that area.

To help straighten out the mess, III MAF sent Col. Thomas A. Horne to Khe Sanh to be the senior officer present. Horne's responsibilities as SOP included the airstrip and base, the coordination of recon patrols, and logistical support; plus he was given operational control over the Special Forces and Marine units at Khe Sanh. Wickwire worked closely with Horne to improve the base. He even loaned some of 1/3's Marines to Horne to help build up the base's defenses. Horne had barbed wire perimeter fences erected, bunkers dug, and fortifications built.

Unfortunately, cooperation from the Green Berets remained almost nonexistent. They considered their efforts to be top secret and took orders only from their direct superiors. Wickwire reacted by announcing that outside the base his Marines would shoot anything that moved. Shoot first and ask questions later became the Marines' new watchword.

For their part, the Green Berets found it difficult to operate from the increasingly busy airstrip. Under pressure from Horne they finally left in December. They set up camp just outside the village of Lang Vei, about halfway between Khe Sanh and the Laotian border.

Lieutenant Colonel Wickwire felt ambivalent about his Marines' role at Khe Sanh. "At times I felt frustrated," he said, "because we weren't engaging the NVA. But at the same time I felt relieved because I knew my single battalion couldn't hold out for long if the enemy attacked. If they came in any strength I figured we'd last three, maybe four days." Wickwire went so far as to tell his company commanders to avoid any major contacts.

The line company grunts shared Wickwire's frustration. Lance Corporal Ascolillo said, "We knew the enemy was out there, but we couldn't figure out what we were up against. We knew someone was watching us all the time, getting ready for something, but exactly what remained a mystery."

Every time a 1/3 patrol stumbled upon some evidence of an enemy presence or experienced a contact, no matter how light, the battalion S-2 (intelligence officer) dutifully prepared his report. After Wickwire approved it and signed it, he forwarded the report to III MAF. And that would be the last that Wickwire would hear of it. Week after week he sent the reports to Da Nang but never once did a staff officer make a comment about or question anything in the intelligence summary. If only they had, Wickwire would have felt that his battalion's efforts were serving a useful purpose. Eventually, Wickwire realized that III MAF was ignoring him. He also concluded that the NVA, although they were stockpiling supplies for some operation, had no plans to attack Khe Sanh at this time.

Thus, Wickwire welcomed news in late January 1967 that 1/3 was headed for Okinawa. Following a period of rest and retraining there, the battalion would assume a role with the Special Landing Force, FMF-Pacific's seaborne reserve.

Soon after he received his orders, Wickwire learned which unit would take over his mission. What he heard stunned him. "I had always thought our tactical area of responsibility was too big for our battalion," he recalled. "When I found out we were being replaced by a single rifle company I thought that was absurd. There was no way one company could patrol all that ground. And, if the enemy hit, they wouldn't last a day."

Actually, they would last four days.

Chapter Two

Captain Michael W. Sayers leaned forward with a start. His briefer's earlier statement that Sayers's Bravo 1/9 would be temporarily detached from the battalion came as no major surprise; it happened all the time. Chopped opcon, the Marines called it—being under the "operational control" of a headquarters unit other than your own. That Bravo would be guarding an airstrip did not seem unusual either; most missions for the Marines in South Vietnam were defensive in nature. And although Sayers had no idea where Khe Sanh was, it did not matter; he would go wherever his orders sent him. The briefer's last comment, though, definitely got Sayers's attention.

"My company's taking over a battalion's TAOR [tactical area of responsibility]?" he asked, a shade of incredulity in his voice.

"That's affirmative, Captain," the operations officer replied. "But One Three's been up there for three months and they've had no trouble. It's been quiet. All the action's east of there. Three MAF can't afford to keep an entire battalion out there when the gomers are hitting all around Dong Ha. You'll be up there about ninety days chopped opcon directly to the Third Marine Division, then we'll get you back."

"Where exactly is Khe Sanh, sir?" Sayers asked.

The S-2 gave him the grid coordinates. Sayers scanned the new map he had been handed. There it was. And just north of the village of Khe Sanh sat the clearly marked airstrip. Sayers's finger traced the nearby area. The clusters of tight contour lines indicated numerous mountains and hills. A line just west of the base identified the Laotian border. Not too far north another line marked the DMZ. To Sayers, Khe Sanh looked to be a long way from anywhere.

"Good luck, Captain," the operations officer said to end the briefing.

Sayers gave a hearty "Aye, aye, sir" and left the briefing room. He needed to get with his people and pass the word; they had a lot to get done in the next few days. But still, the wisdom of his single rifle company taking over from a four-company battalion eluded him. Thank God it's quiet out there, Sayers told himself. He would have a chance to get to know his men better.

Twenty-nine-year-old Mike Sayers had taken command of Bravo Company less than a month before, in early January 1967, while it underwent routine retraining and refurbishment on Okinawa. A Marine since 1959, the Arkansan arrived in South Vietnam in October 1966. He served his first three months as 1/9's supply officer (S-4); Bravo was his first combat command.

Sayers's arrival in Bravo did not initially inspire many of the company's veterans. To them the short and somewhat overweight Sayers hardly fit the image of a hard-charging, gung-ho Marine Corps rifle company commander. But as platoon leader 1st Lt. David Mellon figured, he was the hand they'd been dealt and they'd play it the best they could.

Soon after Sayers took command of Bravo 1/9, it and the rest of the 1st Battalion, 9th Marines, became part of the Special Landing Force (SLF). A floating reserve force, the SLF consisted of a reinforced battalion landing team (BLT) and a helicopter squadron assigned to Fleet Marine Force–Pacific. Though officially not a part of the Marine Corps' forces in South Vietnam, the SLF functioned in reality as a quick-reaction force available to respond to and reinforce any onshore tactical situation. Nearly every Marine battalion that served in South Vietnam pulled at least one tour with the SLF.

BLT 1/9's first assignment as part of the SLF took place not in northern South Vietnam, the Marines' normal area of operation, but far to the south in the Mekong River delta.

Although the American military took control of the fighting in South Vietnam in 1965, responsibility for the Viet Cong–riddled delta region southeast of Saigon remained in the hands of the Army of the Republic of Vietnam. Notoriously inept, the ARVN troops could barely hold their own base camps let alone a tract as vast and rebellious as the delta. But manpower shortages limited MACV's ability to respond to VC threats there. Nevertheless, as the VC's influence grew and threatened the approaches to Saigon, General Westmoreland recognized he had to do something. He called in the Marines.

BLT 1/9, under Maj. James L. Day, steamed south with the rest of the SLF to coastal Kien Hoa Province. On 6 January 1967, Day's troops, along with elements of two Vietnamese Marine battalions, made a combined heliborne and amphibious assault on an area long considered a VC stronghold. Lasting two weeks, Operation Deckhouse V proved to be a major disappointment. Only twenty-one Viet Cong were killed, forty-four small-arms weapons were captured, and a small rice cache was uncovered at the cost of seven Marines killed in action. Intelligence officers later learned that the landings had been badly compromised. Forewarned of the assault, the VC had simply vanished into the trackless swamps.

Pleased with its performance but frustrated with the operation's results, the SLF turned around and headed back north. It had no sooner reached the I Corps area than Major Day received orders to release one of his companies for detached service at Khe Sanh. He sent for Captain Sayers.

At midmorning on 6 February, three C-130 transport planes circled slowly above Khe Sanh's airstrip. They descended one by one to begin the landing approach. As 1st Lt. David L. Mellon's plane turned in the sky, he eagerly gazed out one of its windows. He marveled at the maze of mountains jutting upward from the lush, multihued green jungle. Some mountains sported sharp, jagged edges whereas others were as thin as a knife blade. Towers of serrated limestone stood sentinel-like along the banks of rushing rivers. His eyes found few signs of civilization, however. Only an occasional cluster of thatched huts perched on a mountainside or squatting beside a stream revealed a human presence.

Mellon stared in amazement at the numerous double rows of large bomb craters, each running for a mile or more through the jungle. His stomach churned as he realized these were the results of high-altitude B-52 Arc Light bombing raids. God, he thought, there must be NVA everywhere if they're running that many Arc Lights out here. How's our puny little company ever going to cover all this ground? he wondered as his C-130 chopped power and dropped to begin its approach.

Once on the ground, Mellon and his platoon set up by the side of the runway to await further orders. All the hustle and bustle surprised him. Based on the shipboard briefing the platoon leaders had attended, he expected to find a little dirt airstrip with not much going on. Instead, the Khe Sanh Combat Base swirled with activity. Passing trucks and jeeps kicked up thick clouds of red dust. Arriving and departing planes and helicopters added noise and more dust. A variety of troopers—some Army, some Marine, some American, some South Vietnamese, and others of an ethnic background that Mellon did not recognize—moved across the base. Pilots strolled across the ramp on their way to the air operations center. Mechanics scurried over, under, and inside a variety of aircraft. Groups of well-armed nondescript soldiers huddled by the runway, waiting to board helicopters.

Mellon had not expected such a large complex, either. The base stretched as far as he could see. Numerous aboveground wooden buildings and sandbagged bunkers dotted the landscape. Defensive bunkers lined the north edge of the runway. No doubt we'll soon be manning these, he said to himself.

More than anything, though, the nearby mountains impressed Mellon. Most of the twenty-three-year-old Nashua, New Hampshire, native's six months in-country had been spent in the rice paddies south of Da Nang. There the flat land extended for miles with only a few small hills to interrupt the monotony. At Khe Sanh, mountain peaks reaching seven hundred to eight hundred meters or more above sea level dominated every view. Mellon saw that the sides of the closer mountains were covered with tall, thick elephant grass interspersed with bamboo clumps and thick groves of hardwood trees. A forbidding series of steep, cloud-tipped ridges dominated the far horizon.

"The combat base sat at the bottom of a bowl," Mellon recalled. "Anyone on the hills overlooking the base had a perfect view of every move we made. Thank God it was quiet up there."

While Lieutenant Mellon surveyed his new home, Captain Sayers concluded his briefing with the commander of the remaining 1/3 company; the rest of Lieutenant Colonel Wickwire's battalion had flown out several days earlier. The outgoing captain briefed Sayers on 1/3's patrol activity and the dismal results. As far as he was concerned, the NVA had no sizable forces in the area. Then he was gone, joining his men aboard the C-130s that had carried in Bravo 1/9.

Sayers told his executive officer, 1st Lt. William F. Delaney, to set up the platoons in the positions vacated by 1/3. There would be a platoon leaders' briefing that evening to assign patrol schedules. Then Sayers went to pay a courtesy call on Khe Sanh's senior officer present (SOP).

The SOP still had no tactical control over any of the units at Khe Sanh. His mission remained primarily administrative and logistic. But he did hold frequent debriefings to help coordinate the activities of the various recon teams. Based on the information garnered in these debriefings, the SOP could suggest a mission, such as more extensive patrolling of a certain area, but it would be only a suggestion.

Besides observing proper protocol in his visit to the SOP, Sayers had a more practical mission in mind. Bravo 1/9 carried only the limited-range PRC-25 radio. Sayers needed the SOP's more powerful unit to transmit his daily situation reports to the 3d Marine Division's forward headquarters at Dong Ha.

The original SOP, Colonel Horne, had been replaced by Lieutenant Colonel McGee just a week earlier. Friends from previous stateside assignments, Sayers and McGee enjoyed a cordial meeting. Sayers simply advised McGee that he had assumed responsibility for the base's security. The SOP had little to add to Sayers's limited knowledge of the situation. He concurred with his senior commander's view that the enemy had only a minor presence in this remote segment of Quang Tri Province. Sayers hoped McGee was correct.

At his platoon commanders' briefing that night, Captain Sayers laid out his plan for the patrol schedule. Two of the three rifle platoons would always be in the field, operating from separate platoon patrol bases (PPBs), while the third guarded the airstrip. All three platoons would dispatch squad-size patrols each day to search a specific area for any signs of the enemy. Nightly ambushes and listening posts near the PPBs were a given. The maximum range of the two 155mm howitzers at the base limited the patrols to a fifteen-thousand-meter radius.

Sayers rotated the patrol duty so that each platoon spent two weeks in the field and then a week back at the combat base. The base platoon would not only guard the airstrip but also provide a Sparrow Hawk team to respond to any crisis. A routine plan, it not only accomplished the mission but spread the duty fairly among the platoons.

Bravo's four platoon leaders left the briefing to prepare their men for the mission. Although they were a varied lot, they had quickly earned Sayers's confidence. The most experienced, First Lieutenant Mellon, a tall, lean man, had more than six months in the bush. Second Lieutenant John M. Kramer had taken over the 2d Platoon on Okinawa. Small and plump with a clerkish appearance, Kramer looked less a Marine officer than Sayers. Although Kramer was not viewed as a hard charger, Sayers still considered him to be a good officer. The executive officer, Lieutenant Delaney, temporarily doubled as the 3d Platoon commander because its previous commander had just rotated back to battalion headquarters to take a staff job. Sergeant Larry J. Pratt, a twenty-two year old from Collinsville, Illinois, with five years in the Corps and five months with Bravo, led the Weapons Platoon but did not really have any troops to command. His three weapons squads, each consisting of an M60 machine gun team, a 3.5-inch rocket launcher team, and a 60mm mortar team, were parceled out to the rifle platoons. As a result, Pratt normally attached himself to Mellon's 1st Platoon. That way everyone knew where he was.

The patrols began the very next morning, 7 February, as the two platoons humped out to their respective sectors. Once set up in their PPBs, each platoon leader sent out individual squad patrols. Bravo's mission of searching for the enemy had begun.

"I enjoyed operating independent of the company," Mellon said. "Opportunities to command your own troops in your own little world came rarely to a lieutenant. I took full advantage of it by giving my squad leaders a great deal of independence, too. And, as long as it remained quiet, it was a great training exercise for the new troops."

It did not take long for Bravo's patrols to find signs that someone shared the area with them. Nearly every day at least one of the squads found evidence that the enemy had patrols in the area, too. The Marines found fresh footprints, discarded equipment, and newly constructed bunkers. On a few occasions a sniper's round would snap over a column of Marines. The Marines would hit the ground, eyes frantically searching for the enemy rifleman, but they would never see him. At times antipersonnel Claymore mines placed around a squad's night bivouac would be found in the morning turned around so their lethal steel pellets would erupt toward the Marines. Even at the combat base, Claymores outside the wire would be found rotated inward. The ghostlike foe caused an eerie feeling among the Marines. Although they were trained to fight, and fight hard, they could not fight phantoms.

Even patrols that did not find the enemy could produce stressful moments. Soon after coming to Khe Sanh, Cpl. Kenneth D. Vermillion's patrol moved through dense elephant grass north of the base. As the lanky, twenty-year-old Washington, D.C., native shifted his heavy M60 machine gun for the thousandth time that day, the patrol suddenly stopped. The point man had heard a noise up ahead. Slowly, the Marines inched their way forward. The noise grew louder. Unable to see more than a few meters into the grass, the Marines proceeded cautiously, their mouths drying in anticipation of the looming danger. Suddenly, the point man stepped into a small clearing. The men behind him heard him exclaim, "Holy shit!"

In the middle of the clearing stood a tall elephant. Vermillion and the rest of the patrol crowded around the beast. "Son of a bitch." "Look at that mother." "Goddamn, it's big."

Obviously domesticated, the animal stood unimpressed at the sight of a group of armed Marines; indeed, a large plank tied between its rear legs tethered it. Whether the elephant's master was a local tribesman or an NVA soldier, the Marines would never know, for he had taken off at the sound of the approaching column. At a signal from the patrol leader, the men moved out. In minutes the tall grass enveloped them.

Captain Sayers dutifully reported this and all the other sightings in his daily sitreps. He also attended as many of the debriefings of the different recon teams as he could. Their roamings deep in the mountains along the Laotian border put them in frequent contact with the enemy. Most ended in a brief exchange of rifle fire, but sometimes the recon patrol came under such heavy fire that it would have to request air support and an emergency extraction.

"Right from the start I found the situation very frustrating," Sayers said. "I knew something was up, but when or where it would happen I didn't have a clue. I worked hard to keep the patrols sharp. I knew sooner or later the enemy would hit and Bravo would be ready."

On Saturday morning, 25 February, Lieutenant Mellon's 1st Platoon guarded the airstrip. Their turn back at the base had started the day before. Though some of his men expressed their pleasure at returning to the relative civilization of the combat base, Mellon did not. He still preferred to be out in the field, minding his own show. But, he admitted to himself, the week back at the base would give him time to catch up on his paperwork and letter writing. At midmorning he settled himself in front of his bunker, the papers in front of him and his radio tuned to the company frequency. Several kilometers away, Sergeant Harper's squad began its patrol northwest of the base.

A few hours later Harper's anxious voice crackled over the PRC-25 radio. Mellon jerked upright. As he listened to the fight unfold, he knew what was coming. Sure enough, the word soon came from Sayers: "Saddle up the Sparrow Hawk team."

Within minutes, Mellon and his men stood outside Sayers's command post (CP). Sayers quickly briefed Mellon on the situation. Then the Sparrow Hawks headed out on the double from the base.

Less than three hours later, Mellon lay on a stretcher along Khe Sanh's runway, his wounded knee swathed in blood-soaked bandages. While he waited to be loaded on a C-130, he briefed Sayers on what had happened. "As far as I could tell," Mellon remembered, "the initial contact was strictly accidental, probably a team of NVA sent to observe the base who had gotten a late start getting out of there. I think the enemy had been as surprised at the meeting as Harper was."

Minutes later a pair of Marines carried Mellon aboard the aircraft. As the plane headed east, Sayers could not help but gaze out toward Hill 861. The phantom war in this supposedly quiet section of the DMZ had suddenly become real.

The tension around the combat base rose several notches after Sergeant Harper's fight. A palpable fear hung in the air, coupled with a sense that the enemy was observing the Marines' every move, patiently waiting for another chance to strike. Sayers kept the pressure on his men to be alert and vigilant, but he could do only so much. His company was stretched thin already. A platoon from the division's Headquarters and Service Company arrived one day, but because they were mostly rear-echelon types with little or no combat experience, Sayers used them to man some of the perimeter bunkers.

Sayers took other steps to improve his situation. Whenever he received a high-ranking visitor, he laid out his case for reinforcements. No matter who it was, Sayers pressed the issue. To be successful in his mission, he told them, he had to have more men, more firepower. "I didn't relish Bravo being the sacrificial pawn in this game being played between Three MAF and MACV," he said.

An old friend from stateside duty proved to be a sympathetic visitor. Brigadier General Michael P. Ryan had been Sayers's boss at Parris Island, South Carolina, just before both of them headed to Vietnam. Now, as the 3d Marine Division's assistant commander, Ryan ran the division's forward headquarters at Dong Ha and frequently visited this appendage to his TAOR. In his briefings Sayers stressed the futility of Bravo's situation. He knew that Ryan understood difficult tactical situations. During World War II's bloody battle for the Pacific atoll of Tarawa, Ryan's personal gallantry helped swing the desperate battle in the Marines' favor. Ryan not only earned a Navy Cross but helped put the name Tarawa high on the list of the Marine Corps' great victories.

At the end of each of Sayers's briefings, Ryan asked, "Mike, what do you need to fulfill your mission up here?"

Sayers whipped out his shopping list. "More men. Quad 50s. Searchlights. More helicopters."

"I'll see what I can do," Ryan always promised. Then he would be gone. Sayers could only hope his old friend would come through.

In the meantime, enemy contact increased both in frequency and intensity. Hardly a day passed without one of Bravo's patrols clashing with the NVA. On 1 March an enemy soldier tossed a grenade into the middle of a squad-size patrol. Everyone hit the deck immediately. The missile exploded harmlessly, but no one saw where it came from. The patrol continued without further incident.

The next night, from a ringside seat atop his bunker, Sergeant Pratt watched Air Force jets bomb targets south and west of the base. "They're really kicking some ass tonight," he remarked to some other observers.

"Yeah," another Marine replied. "I'd hate to be on the receiving end of that shit."

They watched the flash of explosions on the horizon for more than thirty minutes. Then word came of an unspeakable tragedy. The Air Force planes had mistaken the friendly village of Lang Vei for an NVA-occupied town twenty miles inside Laos. Hitting the village of two thousand with napalm and deadly cluster bombs, the jets killed more than a hundred innocent civilians and wounded more than two hundred.

Marines from the combat base rushed into the night to help the villagers. Green Berets from the nearby Special Forces camp pitched in, too, treating the wounded and digging through the wreckage of the town in a frantic hunt for survivors. Helicopters ferried the wounded to Khe Sanh, where a special flight of C-130s waited to carry them to hospitals.

The sight of hundreds of horribly wounded Bru refugees who flooded onto the base sobered many of the Marines. It was one thing to see wounded and dead NVA, quite another to see innocent civilians torn by the random violence of war. The Marines gave what first aid they could and helped the injured into shelters. Few of the men would ever forget that terrible night. For Sergeant Pratt this incident, more than anything else he had experienced, drove home the stark realities of war.

To add to the night's tragedy, at 0445 the following morning the enemy dropped seventy-five mortar rounds on the west end of the combat base. Two Marines died and seventeen were wounded, seven badly enough to be evacuated. A dawn sweep of the perimeter revealed an eight-foot-wide gap blown in the wire by a command-detonated mine.

Two days later, just before dawn, a listening post set up southwest of the base spotted an enemy soldier slinking through the elephant grass toward its position. One of the Marines triggered off several rounds from his M14. The NVA blasted off a clip of AK-47 ammo, whirled, and disappeared into the night. One of the enemy's slugs grazed the Marine who had fired at him, inflicting a minor wound. Another patrol a kilometer farther west also suffered a casualty when an unseen enemy soldier flipped a grenade into its position. At the same time, a band of a dozen NVA attacked the northern edge of the combat base. Firing AK-47s and throwing grenades, the small but determined force wounded two Marines before fleeing into the darkness.

The very next night, 6 March, the enemy attacked another Bravo ambush site west of the base. The fight lasted only a few minutes before the NVA pulled back into the safety of the surrounding brush. None of the Marines were hurt, but they were wide-awake for the rest of the night.

Captain Sayers kept busy writing up these contacts and submitting them along with his daily situation reports. Each afternoon he would trudge over to the combat base's operations bunker and drop off his report. When he could, he continued to attend the SOP's debriefing of the other recon teams. Sayers learned from them that they were making more frequent sightings of large enemy units.

"With all this increased activity," he said, "I couldn't help but wonder why my repeated requests for reinforcements were being ignored. I questioned whether anyone was reading my sitreps."

His suspicions increased when a new SOP took over in early March.

Lieutenant Colonel James H. Reeder arrived at Khe Sanh after a stint as the executive officer of the 4th Marines. His former commander there, Col. Alexander D. Cereghino, took over as the 3d Marine Division's chief of staff on 3 March. Keenly aware of the political and military sensitivity surrounding Khe Sanh, Cereghino and his new boss, division commander Maj. Gen. Wood B. Kyle, recognized the need for someone at the base who could not only serve as their eyes and ears but was politically astute enough to balance the command conflict and the increasingly unstable tactical situation. They sent for Reeder.

Reeder sensed that something unusual awaited him when General Kyle opened the meeting by stating, "Your wife's going to kill me for this."

"General Kyle and I and our wives were good friends who socialized frequently when we were stationed together at Marine headquarters a few years earlier," Reeder recalled.

"Colonel Cereghino told me it was a hairy situation up there at Khe Sanh, with a lot of enemy movement throughout the area. There was a single rifle company up there and several different recon units. I was to run the base and help these units in whatever way I could. That was it. They didn't tell me much beyond that."

Kyle and Cereghino could not have picked a better officer for the thankless job as Khe Sanh's SOP. A native Hoosier, Reeder had received his commission at age twenty-two in 1944. His first combat experience came during the bloody, brutal battle for Okinawa. Five years later he was in the thick of things again as a rifle company commander in Korea.

Reeder's career shifted after Korea. He became an aide-de-camp, serving several successive tours as the chief aide to the commanding general of the Fleet Marine Force–Pacific. He even did a stint as a senior aide at the White House, where social protocol ruled. He became known to other officers as a "political" Marine, who had earned his promotions more through whom he knew than by performance in the field.

In the early 1960s, Reeder shifted gears again when he was detailed as a staff officer to CIA headquarters in Langley, Virginia. While there he helped write an analysis of the situation in South Vietnam.

In May 1966 he arrived in the war zone. Ten months later he eagerly accepted the opportunity to go to Khe Sanh. "The prospect of being the commander of two dozen men was far more attractive to me than being the second-in-command of two thousand," Reeder said.

The conditions at Khe Sanh shocked Reeder. A prim, formal, well-mannered, gentlemanly officer, Reeder hated dust. And Khe Sanh was nothing but red dust. Between jeeps and trucks racing down the dirt lanes, helicopters coming and going, and the constant wind, billowing clouds of red dust shrouded the base. The camp area abandoned by the Special Forces was particularly filthy, overrun with huge rats. Reeder had his work cut out for him.

He immediately imposed speed limits on the base. The young, devil-may-care recon Marines could no longer tear along in their jeeps at forty to fifty miles per hour trailing columns of dust. Per Reeder's orders they had to drive slower and safer to keep the hated dust to a minimum. Several times Reeder personally chased down recalcitrant drivers and administered severe tongue-lashings. Eventually the drivers caught on and started obeying the speed limits.

Reeder brought other amenities to the base, too. He ordered construction of a mess hall and a club. "One of my proudest days was when the shower tent opened," he remembered. "Now the troops could get an occasional hot shower and wash away that infernal dust."

Not all of these changes endeared Reeder to the troops. Many felt he spent too much time on area beautification programs and not enough on assessing the intelligence information brought in by Captain Sayers's platoons and the recon units. Even when the debriefings included reports of an enemy presence, Reeder would state, "Bring me proof. Bring me more proof."

"I didn't know what additional proof Reeder wanted or why," Sayers said. "I thought what I included in my daily sitreps to Third Marine Division headquarters accurately portrayed my situation. I didn't think I could make them any stronger without being insubordinate. I began to believe that either they weren't being read or they were being altered prior to transmittal."

Despite his doubts, someone read his reports, for Sayers finally received help. Echo Company, 2d Battalion, 9th Marines, arrived at the combat base on 7 March.

Echo 2/9 had been operating south of Hue when the commanding officer, Capt. William B. Terrill, received a radio message that helicopters were flying in to return them to the base at Phu Bai. Once there, Terrill and his platoon leaders received a briefing from the battalion S-3, Maj. M. K. Sheridan, who explained that Bravo 1/9 had been reporting frequent contacts with the enemy around Khe Sanh for more than a month. Echo was heading to Khe Sanh to reinforce Bravo. Sheridan mentioned that two NVA regiments were reported to be in the Khe Sanh area.

Staff Sergeant Spencer F. Olsen, the twenty-four-year-old commander of Echo 2/9's 1st Platoon, scoffed at that remark. "It seemed every time we were briefed about a new operation, there were two NVA regiments waiting for us," he recalled. "All of these briefings seemed canned." After six years in the Corps and nine months in South Vietnam, most of it as a platoon leader, Olsen carried an aura of cynicism with him. He did not worry about going to this place called Khe Sanh. It was just another assignment, another day in paradise, as he put it.

Captain Terrill, a taciturn, balding, twenty-six-year-old Texas A&M graduate, did not put much faith in the briefings either. To him the staff people always overreacted to situations. With nine months in-country and nearly five months commanding Echo, he, too, approached the war with a certain amount of fatalism and cynicism.

When the C-130s carrying Echo roared onto Khe Sanh's airstrip, Captain Sayers felt relief. Now his Marines would not be stretched so thin. It also meant that someone was paying attention to his warnings of an NVA buildup around the base. He met Terrill at the airstrip and led him away to brief him on the situation. Although neither captain reported to the other, they both quickly agreed to divide the TAOR between themselves, thus not only increasing the patrols but reducing the workload for each company.

It did not take long for Echo to get indoctrinated. Almost immediately its patrols began uncovering more evidence of the NVA. Hardly a day passed without some sign of the enemy coming to light.

On the afternoon of 15 March, Staff Sergeant Olsen received orders for his next patrol. This would be his second excursion out of the combat base. The first had taken him and his platoon south of Hill 881S. Besides being impressed with the sheer beauty of the place, they had an unusual experience on that patrol: a futile attempt to track down an elephant they had heard trumpeting. The jungle and hillsides bounced the sound around so much that the Marines could not tell where it was coming from. After a frustrating afternoon of searching, Olsen gave up and allowed his platoon to bathe in a fast-moving stream that ran past Hill 881S. For the rest of that day, these battle-hardened warriors became boys again, having fun splashing and dunking one another. They forgot the war for a few hours.

On Olsen's second patrol, Terrill wanted him to scout the north side of Hill 881S. Following the well-used trail west out of the base, Olsen was to go up and over Hill 861, then recon the area north of Hill 881S and west of Hill 861. He was to head out that afternoon. The platoon was to set up for the night on Hill 861, then continue the next morning. They would be in the field about a week. With a brisk, "Aye, aye, skipper," Olsen went to round up his men.

Olsen's platoon left the base several hours before dusk. Composed of four rifle squads of six to eight men each, plus the attached corpsmen, engineers, an M60 machine gun team, an 81mm mortar forward observer and his radioman, a 3.5-inch rocket team, a 60mm mortar team, and a platoon radioman, Olsen's patrol numbered about forty men in all. Keeping the proper distance between each man, they formed a staggered column stretching nearly half a kilometer along the trail. Olsen took a position behind the lead squad about a third of the way back. From there he could keep an eye on almost everyone and not be too far from any developing action.

Olsen halted about one-fourth of the way up Hill 861. In case the NVA were watching, he wanted to wait until after dark to set up a defensive perimeter. While he waited he took his radio's handset to report in. What he heard startled him like nothing else he had encountered on his tour. "Vietnamese voices filled every frequency," he said. "No matter how I tuned the radio I couldn't pick up anything but the sing-song jabbering of Vietnamese talking. It was unbelievable. I knew right away this wasn't an attempt to tap into my frequency. There was just so much NVA radio traffic in the area that it was bleeding over onto all my frequencies."

The mortar forward observer, LCpl. James L. Chase, heard the enemy voices on his radio, too. He had taken the handset from his radioman, LCpl. Roger DeWitt, to call in some registration rounds from the 105s at Khe Sanh (although technically assigned to the battalion's 81mm mortar platoon, Chase routinely functioned as an artillery forward observer). "I heard the NVA, so I called the base for some rounds and they didn't believe me," Chase recalled, "so they blew me off."

After dark Olsen attempted to move his platoon to a different position, but the brush proved too thick to navigate. The Marines covered only a few dozen meters before Olsen ordered everyone to halt.

Few of the patrol members slept that night.

The next morning, 16 March, the 1st Platoon resumed its trek. Sergeant Donald Lord of Silver Springs, Maryland, led the point squad that morning. His point fire team leader was twenty-year-old Cpl. Julian A. McKee. Private First Class George D. Johnson stepped off as point man. Private First Class Ivory Puckett, a twenty-year-old draftee from Burbank, California, with four months in-country but little actual combat experience, should have been on point, but he was slow getting his M14 back together after its morning cleaning. Johnson, his buddy, casually offered to take the lead. "No sweat," the Naples, Florida, nineteen year old told Puckett.

The patrol advanced up the hill. Because this was virgin territory for all of them, and the thick vegetation greatly reduced visibility, the Marines moved slowly, cautiously. At one point Johnson reported he heard Vietnamese voices somewhere to his front. Olsen halted the patrol. He radioed back to the base for artillery. Within minutes a brace of 105mm shells whistled overhead to explode with a loud roar out of sight on the far side of the hill.

Olsen signaled the patrol forward. As the Marines neared the top of Hill 861, the elephant grass gave way to thicker stands of trees, and dense underbrush covered the ground. The trail leveled off briefly below the crest before it began its descent down the west side of Hill 861. Lord's squad started down the trail and disappeared from Olsen's sight.

Private First Class Johnson led the way, followed by Corporal McKee, Private First Class Puckett, and LCpl. Gordon Brewer. About fifty meters down the trail, Johnson came to a fork. He stopped, turned around, and whispered to McKee, "Which way?"

McKee pointed to the left fork. "That way," he said.

Thirty meters farther on, Johnson came to a second fork. He turned to ask directions and froze. Behind him, at the first fork's junction, he saw several NVA hunkered down in bunkers. Without a word he swung his M14 around and ripped off two rounds.

The hidden NVA responded with a furious blast of small-arms fire. McKee dropped, killed instantly. Johnson fell in a heap, thrashing wildly in his death throes.

Puckett threw himself down, unhurt, but he landed such that his rifle was trapped beneath him. "It seemed like it took forever to pull the rifle from under me without raising up any higher," Puckett said. "Then when I pulled the trigger all I heard was a 'click.' I'd forgotten to chamber a round." While he struggled with his weapon, he saw Johnson flailing around in the dirt. Puckett could not tear his eyes away. Johnson was his best friend. Why did he have to be dying? Why? Why? Tears coursed down Puckett's cheeks as he finally pulled his M14 free and returned fire.

Back up the trail, Olsen and the others hit the deck and clawed their way to the first shelter they could find. But before Olsen could send Lord any help, the firing stopped. An eerie, unnatural silence followed. Then the hillside above erupted in a deafening riot of gunfire. Dozens of AK-47s fired at the same time, sending sheets of lead zinging downhill. Olsen sought a target but could not see anyone to shoot at because the NVA were well dug in, hidden from view. Suddenly, enemy concussion grenades dropped among the platoon members. Their sharp crashes erupted all along the trail. One landed just three feet from Olsen. It exploded before he could turn away. The blast stung his face with dirt and pebbles but did not hurt him badly. "It was then I realized the enemy was probably trying to take prisoners, and that's why they weren't using fragmentation grenades," Olsen said. "I swore I wouldn't let them get me, no matter what."

Lance Corporal Chase had been in no hurry to get going that morning. By the time he was ready to move out, most of the patrol had passed by. He, DeWitt, and LCpl. Lloyd Kurtz brought up the rear of the column. Kurtz was one of the few grunts Chase allowed himself to get close to. A Marine since his eighteenth birthday in September 1965, Chase had been in South Vietnam for more than a year. In that time he had learned the intense pain of losing friends, so he made few new ones; the fewer he knew, the less sorrow he suffered.

At the first sound of firing, the three men hit the dirt. After listening for several minutes, Chase realized this was no ordinary ambush. He turned to DeWitt. "We're going up front. They'll need us."

The pair left Kurtz and dashed forward, hitting the dirt several times as they drew closer to Olsen. "Slow down, will ya?" DeWitt admonished. "I'm a married man and I'm in no hurry to die."

By the time they linked up with Olsen, the enemy fire from higher on the hill had increased substantially. Above the din Olsen told Chase to bring in artillery. Chase started the rounds on the eastern slope of Hill 861, then walked them up over the top.

As the rounds exploded with a satisfying *KABOOM!* Olsen made contact with a flight of Marine jets. He had to scream into the mike to be heard over the roar of the firefight. At one point he glanced up and his heart stopped. "I couldn't believe what I saw. The gooks were charging right down the hill at us," Olsen said. Yelling and firing their AK-47s, the North Vietnamese soldiers assaulted right into the Marines. Olsen shoved the handset at Chase. "Tell him where we're at," he yelled as he turned back to the fight.

One determined NVA, spraying fire with his assault rifle, headed straight for Olsen. The enemy rounds hit Olsen's weapon, tore into his flak jacket, and struck the ground all around him. Undaunted, the gutsy Coloradan stood his ground, firing back. He shot the enemy soldier at least six times, but the man kept coming. Finally, the NVA dropped. His momentum, though, propelled him farther downhill until he rolled out of the brush right on top of Olsen. The sergeant wriggled his way from underneath the corpse, then calmly resumed firing back at the enemy.

Lance Corporal Chase, who had never directed an air strike before, had given the jets their position. Under his direction they circled wide to make their way in from the west. Chase carefully guided them in. "Come on. Come on. Come on," he urged. Just as the F-4s reached the drop point, Chase screamed into the mike, "ABORT!" They looked too close for comfort.

Chase talked them around again. He spotted them off in the distance as they dropped low, threading their way through the nearby mountaintops. "Come on. Come on. Come on." Then, again, "ABORT!" They still looked too close.

The Phantoms roared overhead.

While the jets lined up yet again, Olsen glanced up the trail. A horrifying sight chilled him. Up and down the trail, enemy soldiers darted and dashed around, shooting Marines in the back and dropping grenades right on the helpless, wounded men. Olsen fired at them when he could but was afraid he would hit one of his own men.

Suddenly, the roar of the incoming jets grabbed Olsen's attention. He turned and saw two planes at treetop level coming right at him. They were going to hit him and his men. "Get down!" he screamed to those around him.

Chase had brought the jets in for a third time. "Come on. Come on." He led them in. This time, though, when they neared, he yelled, "Drop 'em!" Then he froze. The glistening napalm canisters were coming right at him. I've really fucked up, he thought as he curled into a ball.

But the jet jockeys were good. The pilots, who now rushed by in a deafening blur just feet above the desperate Marines, had released their napalm at precisely the right moment. Tumbling end over end, the silvery pods landed smack in the center of the NVA. One second the hillside was green jungle filled with firing NVA; the next, oily black-laced flames engulfed everything. The NVA did not even have a chance to scream. It ended that fast.

The intensity of the blast stunned Chase. "I'd never been closer to napalm than five hundred meters before," he said. "This was like fifty." He and a few others stumbled downhill to escape the heat.

As the enemy firing died out, a new, unexpected danger developed. Spreading fires from the napalm threatened wounded Marines lying in the underbrush. Squad leader Sgt. Stephen P. Bodie rushed forward with his men and beat out the flames before any Marines were burned.

With the battlefield now quiet, Sergeant Olsen focused his efforts on getting the wounded out. He called for his two corpsmen. Someone told him that both had been hit. In fact, Doc Jackobsen lay among the seriously wounded. Corpsman Francis A. Benoit had taken shrapnel in both arms and legs in the opening moments of the attack but had ignored his considerable pain to continue treating the others. Olsen organized his unwounded men into litter teams to carry the casualties uphill to a spot on the crest where the napalm had fortuitously cleared an area big enough for a helicopter to land.

Soon a steady stream of men moved uphill, some limping, some lugging ponchos holding the casualties. Among them Private First Class Puckett struggled to carry the poncho bearing the limp form of his buddy, George Johnson. Puckett just wanted to get his friend out of there to someplace where he could get help.

Lance Corporal Chase, who had taken a grenade fragment in the shoulder, joined DeWitt in helping some of the seriously wounded Marines up and over the hill to the LZ. Once there they learned that Kurtz had been killed when the NVA rolled over the rear of the column.

News of Olsen's contact ignited a flurry of activity at the combat base. Captain Terrill readied a quick-reaction team and ordered up the medevac choppers. Sayers also rounded up a squad from the base's garrison Marines to fly out to help. By coincidence Lieutenant Kramer and his 2d Platoon of Bravo 1/9 were returning from a patrol and were just a few kilometers east of Hill 861. Captain Sayers ordered them to move immediately to Olsen's aid.

Kramer and his men dropped their packs. If they were going to do any good, they would have to get to Olsen soon. They set off through the brush and trees as fast as they could, their hearts pounding in anticipation of a fight.

On Hill 861, Sergeant Olsen had collected most of the casualties around the makeshift LZ. He had already called for medevac choppers, so it was simply a matter of keeping the wounded alive until the aircraft arrived. Doc Benoit continued to ignore his wounds as he moved around the perimeter treating the others. A young man of great compassion, he offered words of encouragement, assuring the injured, no matter how badly hurt, that they would survive their wounds.

When Chase saw Benoit, he good-naturedly congratulated him on his wounds. "You got a John Wayne," Chase teased him. "You're going home." Benoit grinned broadly as he continued to help the wounded.

Thirty minutes later, with a pair of Huey gunships hovering protectively overhead, a CH-46 medevac landed. Able-bodied Marines rushed toward it, the most seriously wounded slung between them on blood-spattered ponchos.

Sergeant Olsen, who held one corner of a poncho, had almost reached the chopper's ramp when a mortar shell went off with a tremendous blast right behind him. He flew through the air and landed in a heap twenty feet down the hill. Slowly, he staggered to his feet. "Wide streams of blood were running down both my arms. There was so much blood I thought one arm had been torn off," Olsen recalled. He checked himself and found shrapnel holes up and down his arms and in the back of his legs.

Though more than a dozen pieces of metal had ripped through his skin, none of the wounds was serious. "I didn't have a lot of pain. In fact, my arms were nearly numb." He struggled back to the top of the hill. Someone wrapped his arms with T-shirts and slapped dressings on his leg wounds to stop the bleeding. Doc Benoit told him that seven of the more seriously wounded had made it out on the helicopter. However, at least a half dozen more, Benoit added, including several fresh casualties from the enemy mortar barrage, needed help soon or they would not make it. Olsen called for another medevac.

The second helicopter landed a short time later. A crowd of Marines hustled forward carrying their wounded buddies. Private First Class Puckett, who had put his dying friend Johnson on the first helicopter, helped another man aboard this one. Suddenly, more mortar shells crashed down on the LZ. One blast threw Puckett into the chopper's hold. Before he could right himself and exit, the CH-46 leaped into the air, carrying him and the casualties back to the combat base.

Chase and another Marine had been carrying a casualty toward the chopper when he spotted Doc Benoit crouched on the rear ramp, treating yet another casualty. As Chase grew closer, he saw columns of earth erupt from the mortar attack. He dropped his end of the poncho and dove headfirst into a nearby hole. A shell went off right next to him. Hot metal from the round tore into his right thigh, right arm, and side. He slumped deeper into his hole.

"The next thing I knew, two guys were trying to help me. I looked around. The chopper was gone. Doc Benoit lay in a heap where it had been. Several newly wounded guys staggered around the LZ, blood pouring from their wounds. It was horrible. Then I remembered DeWitt."

Shrugging off the two Marines, Chase found his radioman lying at the foot of a tree stump. He still held his radio's handset, a few inches of torn wire dangling from its base. Blood poured from holes in his abdomen and pelvic area. "Check and see if I'm all there, will ya?" DeWitt asked between gasps. Chase did. DeWitt's genitals were intact. Soon one of the remaining corpsmen came up and started to treat DeWitt.

Sergeant Olsen, groggy but still on his feet, faced a dilemma. Both times he had called in a medevac, the enemy mortars came too, causing more casualties. He wanted to move the wounded to a safer, defiladed area, but he did not have enough able-bodied people left to carry them all. He had no choice.

He radioed Captain Terrill. "Echo Six, I gotta stop the medevacs. The gooks are hitting us every time one comes in. I don't have enough men left to carry the casualties. Get me some help out here."

Terrill assured Olsen that reinforcements were on the way.

In the meantime, despite his wounds, Lance Corporal Chase took up a position downhill from the LZ. "I didn't want the NVA sneaking up on us from that side, so I fired downhill wherever I thought they might be."

At about 1500, Chase spotted movement below him. He held his fire. Soon, a green-clad column of Marines came into view. It was Lieutenant Kramer's platoon of Bravo 1/9. Chase stood up and waved. "Over here," he yelled. "Over here."

One of Bravo's men waved back. Thank God, Chase thought, help is finally here. He made his way downhill a few meters to meet them.

As Kramer's men neared him, Chase heard the unmistakable whine of a mortar round.

"INCOMING!" he yelled, then turned and ran uphill. His wounds kept him from scrunching down in a hole, so he sought refuge behind a tree. He covered his head with his hands as the mortar rounds flew overhead. They exploded with devastating effect among Kramer's men.

When the barrage ended, Chase looked downhill. His eyes found a ghastly sight. Dead and wounded Marines lay everywhere. Cries of pain rose from the still smoky ground. Bravo's few uninjured moved about as if in a daze, overwhelmed by the carnage. A few Echo Marines moved down to help them. It took most of the afternoon, but eventually all of Bravo's dead and wounded were moved into a perimeter.

While they worked, a helicopter carrying a Bravo 1/9 rifle squad approached Hill 861. One of those on board was Pfc. David J. Hendry, a member of Kramer's platoon. A newbie, Hendry had arrived at Khe Sanh just a few days before. Suffering from a bad case of bronchitis, he had been sent to the dispensary as soon as he arrived. "I didn't really know anyone in the platoon since they were in the field when I signed in," Hendry said. "But as soon as I heard they were in trouble, I wanted to be with them. They were my platoon, after all."

Hendry fled from the dispensary, grabbed his rifle and gear, and sprinted to the airstrip. He jumped aboard the first available helicopter and settled down for the short ride to the battlefield. Suddenly, the craft shuddered. Holes appeared in the fuselage. Hendry glanced out a nearby window; trees were sliding by sideways. "This isn't gonna be good," Hendry said as he searched for something to hang onto. The CH-46 hit on its nose, flipped over, bounced, and came to rest upside down—a crumpled heap of olive-drab aluminum—about seven hundred meters down the south side of Hill 861.

The collision threw Hendry forward, slamming him against the bulkhead of the craft. His rifle barrel sliced open his forehead, causing rivulets of blood to pour down his face. Dazed and groggy, he inched his way toward an opening torn in the side of the helicopter. He pulled himself outside and joined the others. Amazingly, no one aboard had died, but everyone was injured.

Minutes later another CH-46 swooped in and took the crash victims back to the combat base. Less than thirty minutes after he had left, Hendry walked back into the dispensary. "I'm over my bronchitis," he told the doctor, "but I think I need some stitches."

At the airstrip Captain Terrill and his command group climbed aboard a helicopter and flew out to the battlefield. They disembarked on the side of Hill 700, just to the south of 861, and trudged up the trail. When they reached the top, Cpl. Robert Slattery, one of Terrill's radiomen, recoiled in horror at what lay before him. "Dead and wounded Marines were everywhere. Sergeant Olsen had that thousand-yard stare of a man who's seen too much death and destruction," Slattery said.

Terrill's fresh Marines got to work treating the casualties, then moved them downhill to another, more secure LZ. It took the rest of the evening and well into the night to get the wounded out. The dead would wait until the next day.

Passing in and out of consciousness, Chase arranged for some of the newly arrived Marines to carry DeWitt to the new LZ, then he headed down by himself. Afraid the NVA might mortar this LZ, too, he crouched in the brush a safe distance away. Only when the chopper started to accelerate its rotors did Chase move forward. Hobbling along, his right leg stiff, Chase made it to the back ramp just as the CH-46 started to rise. He collapsed in a heap on the metal floor. For the first time since that morning, a corpsman tended to his wounds.

Terrill and his men spent a nervous night on Hill 861 expecting the NVA to attack at any time. But they did not. In the morning, once the fog cleared, helicopters came in for the dead. When they left, another of Terrill's platoons flew out from the combat base. They spent the rest of the day policing up the ambush site and the LZ, gathering equipment and searching for any overlooked casualties. One Marine remained missing. They finally found his badly burned body on the edge of the na-palmed area. He had apparently been dragged off by the NVA just be-fore the first air strike came in. Despite their best efforts, the Marines did not find any enemy dead. The NVA had policed up their casualties very well.

Captain Terrill then personally took his platoons on a two-day sweep of the area between Hills 881N and 881S in hope of finding some sign of the enemy. But they found nothing—not one shred of evidence, no bloody bandages, no blood trails, no footprints. "It was as if the enemy had vanished into thin air," Terrill said.

Elusive as they were, the NVA had caused terrible damage to the de-fenders of Khe Sanh. In Olsen's platoon alone, ten men were killed and twenty-nine wounded, most of those caused by the mortars. Bravo's pla-toon suffered even worse: eight dead and thirty-four wounded. Among Bravo's dead was Sgt. Donald Harper. Both of his legs had been ripped away by the violent explosion of a shell that landed right at his feet. The same blast had badly wounded Lieutenant Kramer, too, causing his evac-uation.

Chapter Three

The grunts of Bravo 1/9 and Echo 2/9 displayed a new respect for their enemy after the carnage on Hill 861. They knew they were no longer facing the irregular guerrilla-force Viet Cong, or, derisively, Victor Charlie, whom they had fought down south. Instead their foe were well-trained, disciplined, hard-core, main-force North Vietnamese Army regulars, or, respectfully, Mr. Charles. This was not a game of hide-and-seek anymore. This was a full-blown war.

The troops knew what to do about it, too. They avoided Hill 861 whenever they could. Unless specifically ordered to go there, they gave it a wide berth. Bravo's Sgt. Larry Pratt said, "We knew what was there. It wouldn't serve any useful purpose finding it out again and getting more people hurt."

Captains Sayers and Terrill agreed, but they had to continue their assigned mission of protecting the airstrip and sending out patrols to gather intelligence on the enemy, although the reasons for needing more intelligence information eluded them. They knew that the NVA roamed the hills around them, but they could not convince the brass of that fact. Sayers still did not think he could adequately defend the base with the troops he had, and he continued to press General Ryan for reinforcements every time Ryan visited. The general always said he was working on it.

Finally, he came through.

At noon on 27 March, the first "Rough Rider" truck convoy to travel west on Route 9 in nearly two years pulled into Khe Sanh. A true occasion for celebration, the reopening of Route 9 not only provided tangible evidence of Marine control of Quang Tri Province, it also meant the Khe Sanh Marines no longer had to depend solely on air transport for resupply. Indeed, this convoy, consisting of sixty-eight vehicles, brought in more than eleven thousand pounds of supplies.

But most importantly for Sayers, General Ryan had provided everything on his shopping list. Included in the convoy were a pair of ONTOS (though the word is Greek for "thing," an ONTOS is a medium-sized tracked and armored vehicle sporting six 106mm recoilless rifles), commanded by 1st Lt. Philip H. Sauer of Alpha Company, 3d Antitank Battalion; a U.S. Army searchlight team; a U.S. Army section of dual 40mm cannon mounted on a 6x6 truck; and a section of quad .50-caliber machine guns also mounted on a 6x6. These reinforcements bolstered Bravo's strength to more than 350 men, almost double the size of a normal rifle company.

Replacements for those killed and seriously wounded at Hill 861 arrived during this time, too. Bravo got a new platoon leader, 2d Lt. Thomas G. King, to replace Lieutenant Kramer. Fresh from the States, the pudgy twenty-two year old took over the 2d Platoon. Lieutenant Delaney now led the 1st, and SSgt. Alfredo Reyes ran the 3d.

Unfortunately, along with the reinforcements, Sayers received some bad news: Echo 2/9 was leaving. Still badly depleted from the 16 March fight, Echo climbed aboard the trucks and returned to Dong Ha to begin rebuilding its ranks. Once again Bravo was on its own.

The NVA stayed out of sight for two weeks after the fight on Hill 861. Then Bravo's patrols began to find signs of the enemy again. As before, Sayers dutifully submitted his sitreps to Lieutenant Colonel Reeder's operations center for transmittal to division headquarters. He continued to believe, though, that Reeder downplayed the evidence that Bravo's patrols found indicating the presence of NVA. "I remember Reeder telling me more than once, 'You've got no real proof, Captain. There's no more than a platoon of Viet Cong running around these hills playing games with you,'" Sayers said.

The games began anew on 30 March. Sergeant Reyes had his 3d Platoon on patrol in the rugged terrain two kilometers northwest of Hill 861. Private First Class Thomas F. Ryan, a streetwise eighteen-year-old Philadelphian who had joined Bravo late in February, had the point. As he neared a thick grove of trees and bamboo on the side of a ridge, his sixth sense alerted him to nearby danger. He halted the platoon. Alone, he slowly inched his way forward. When he entered the grove, what he saw stopped him dead in his tracks.

"I never expected to find something like that," Ryan recalled. "Inside the grove was a large enemy base camp. A couple of dozen bunkers dotted the area. A covered sleeping area big enough for at least fifty men ran along one side of the camp. There were bamboo-reinforced steps leading downhill to a stream. And the gooks had just taken off, too, because I found several large pots of boiling rice hanging over camp fires."

Ryan signaled Reyes and the others forward. They spread out and quickly uncovered other signs of recent habitation. No doubt the base camp's outposts had seen or heard the approaching Marines and high-tailed it back to the camp with the news. The other NVA had then rushed about, gathered up their gear, and fled into the nearby jungle, for some reason unwilling to ambush the patrol. "Thank God they split," Ryan said. "By the looks of things around the camp there would have been enough of them to have really hurt us."

Reyes ordered the bunkers destroyed while he gathered up documents found in several of the larger bunkers. Just then the Marines heard the faint but distinctive and all too familiar *kathunk* of an 82mm mortar round leaving its tube.

"INCOMING!" several men screamed at once.

Everyone scrambled for safety. They knew they had only a short time before the round hit. Scant seconds later the shell crashed in the middle of the camp. It exploded with a resounding roar and threw dust, dirt clumps, debris, and deadly shrapnel everywhere. Before the dust settled, another 82mm mortar shell whistled in. Then another, and another, and another. The Marines huddled deep in protective holes, ears ringing, eyes teary from the acrid sting of burned cordite.

The pounding barrage continued for nearly fifteen minutes. The NVA gunners expertly walked the shells back and forth across the camp in the hope of catching a Marine out of his hole. In all, eighty-five shells rained down from the sky. (Marines were taught to count the explosions, because doing so not only provided accurate intelligence information but kept their minds occupied during a barrage.)

Sergeant Reyes radioed an aerial forward observer (FO) flying nearby. He described his platoon's plight and asked the FO to try to spot the mortar's muzzle blasts. He did. The FO then radioed two F-4s on station overhead. Soon the roar of their jet engines could be heard. Reyes and his

Marines cheered as the deep explosions of several five-hundred-pound bombs echoed over the hills. Unfortunately, an accurate enemy machine gunner hit one of the jets with a burst of fire. The pilot ejected and survived, but the radar intercept officer could not get out of the plane; he died in the crash.

Despite the bombs, two more enemy mortars unleashed a barrage of shells. Forty more rounds tore into the camp. Still safe in the enemy bunkers, none of the Marines was hurt.

"Can you see the tubes?" Reyes nervously asked the FO in the lull that followed.

"Negative" came the response. "But I got worse news. There's a whole company of little people headed your way."

The news startled Reyes. No way could his platoon handle an entire company. He ordered his platoon to saddle up and move out, now. Within minutes the Marines were on their way. They left the advancing enemy troops for the air jockeys to handle.

In late March, General Westmoreland paid a visit to Khe Sanh. Lieutenant Colonel Reeder did not understand why the MACV would be interested in this remote base, but he knew he would have to have a first-class briefing ready for the four-star general.

A flotilla of more than a dozen escort gunships announced Westmoreland's arrival. Dressed in heavily starched, perfectly creased fatigues, the general stepped off his command helicopter. Reeder presented himself, then took Westmoreland to his operations bunker.

"It didn't take too many of his questions for me to realize that Westmoreland had more than a passing interest in lonely, isolated Khe Sanh," Reeder remembered. "But it wasn't until years later that I learned he wanted to hold Khe Sanh in anticipation of his hoped-for invasion of Laos. At the time I simply assumed it was a routine visit by the theater commander."

The arrival of General Walt's helicopter just minutes after Westmoreland's disappeared on the eastern horizon raised more questions in Reeder's mind. As soon as the machine touched down, the pugnacious III MAF commander jumped off and confronted Reeder.

"Did you know he was coming?" Walt demanded.

"Yes, sir."

"What did he want? What did you tell him?"

For the second time in as many hours, Reeder briefed a senior commander. When he had finished, Walt gruffly barked out a few questions, then climbed aboard his chopper and flew off.

"I knew, of course, there was a conflict between MACV and III MAF over how to conduct the war in I Corps, but up until that day I hadn't been aware that Khe Sanh was a major friction point between them," Reeder claimed. "I can't help but feel I could have done a better job as SOP up there if those two senior officers hadn't always been at odds."

As March gave way to April, an unnerving tranquility descended on the mountains of northwestern Quang Tri Province. Occasionally, a Bravo patrol caught a glimpse of the enemy, but for the most part the NVA stayed out of sight. Indeed, Capt. Glen Golden, an old friend of Sayers's whose Foxtrot Battery, 2/12, replaced India Battery, 3/12, at the combat base on 1 April, described his first three weeks there as "almost like a vacation. There was little indication there were strong enemy forces in the area."

Most Marines welcomed the lull, but a few found it ominous. Sergeant Larry Pratt's diary entry for 13 April recorded his concern: "I have a feeling something is going to happen," he wrote. "We've not had contact with the NVA for several weeks."

Some of Pratt's apprehension centered on the newly issued M16 rifle. The rifle was a drastic change from the trusty M14 carried by the Marines. The M16 had a plastic stock, significantly dropping the weapon's weight (the M14 weighed in at a hefty eleven pounds, whereas the M16 came in at just under seven). The new weapon's light weight and unusual appearance—it even had a carrying handle on top—led to many derisive and humorous comments from the Marines. "It's made by Mattel, so it's swell!" was one of the nicer ones.

The M16 used a smaller cartridge—5.56mm—than the standard NATO 7.62mm round fired by both the M14 and the M60 machine gun. Thus, each Marine could carry more rounds. And they would need them. The M16 fired at a higher rate than the M14, meaning it would burn up rounds much faster. But that was the way it was supposed to be. The designers made the M16 a weapon that sprayed out rounds in a wide pattern rather than the more selective, pinpoint accuracy of the M14.

The situation at Khe Sanh meant Bravo's Marines had only a limited time to practice with the new rifle. All they could do was sight their individual weapons on a makeshift twenty-five-meter range and fire off three or four magazines. Almost immediately the rifle displayed its tendency to jam. Often, after just a few rounds, a spent cartridge stuck in the breech. To remove it, a cleaning rod had to be shoved down the weapon's barrel, but only one cleaning rod was issued for every four men. So a Marine with a jammed rifle could either borrow the pieces of a cleaning rod or try to pry the jammed cartridge loose with the tip of a knife or bayonet. That took time and rarely worked.

Sergeant Pratt, and most of the others, hated to give up their trusty M14s.

Bravo received good news in mid-April. The 3d Marines had just launched a major operation, Prairie IV, in the rugged hill country to the east of Khe Sanh. Because of this, 3d Marine Division headquarters decided to give up direct control of Bravo 1/9 and Khe Sanh. Effective 20 April 1967, both Sayers and Reeder would be chopped opcon to Col. John P. Lanigan's 3d Marines. This did not make Khe Sanh a part of Operation Prairie IV, though. It simply meant that because Lanigan's regiment controlled the adjacent TAOR, it would be easier for it to support Khe Sanh and reinforce the base, if necessary.

None of that really mattered to Captain Sayers, though. The truly good news for him was buried in a back paragraph of the operational order. It read: "On a date to be designated 3d Bn, 3d Mar will relieve with one company B Co, 1st Bn, 9th Mar of the mission as security force for the Khe Sanh Combat Base." Further instructions directed 3/3 to move key personnel to Khe Sanh as soon as possible to become familiar with the area. Bravo 1/9 would be going back to its parent battalion in a matter of days. Sayers could not have been happier.

Lieutenant Colonel Gary Wilder, the commander of 3/3, wasted no time in complying with his part of the orders. The very next day, 21 April, he notified Capt. Bayless L. Spivey, the commander of Kilo 3/3, that his company would assume the mission of securing Khe Sanh. Wilder also told Spivey that he would accompany him to the combat base the following day. There they would get a briefing from the SOP and Bravo 1/9's commander to iron out the details of the transfer. The plan called for Spivey to make the move on 1 May.

No battalion commander operating along the DMZ that spring was better qualified to take over Khe Sanh than Gary Wilder. At age thirty-seven, he had been a Marine since he dropped out of high school in his native Cincinnati twenty years earlier. He earned a commission in 1951 and saw his first combat as a platoon leader during the Korean War. Upon his arrival in South Vietnam in early July 1966, he took command of the 3d Reconnaissance Battalion.

Just before Wilder took over the recon battalion, it had begun extensive patrolling of the region between Route 9, the DMZ, Dong Ha, and the Rockpile as part of Operation Hastings. Fourteen of the eighteen patrols Wilder sent out in early July found NVA, several within mere minutes of being inserted into their patrol area. He learned from other intelligence sources that the North Vietnamese 324B Division had moved south of the Ben Hai River with the mission of conquering Quang Tri Province. When Wilder dutifully reported this to higher headquarters, he unwittingly stepped into the fray raging between General Westmoreland and General Walt.

Within days General Walt, General Kyle, and Maj. Gen. Louis B. Robertshaw, commander of the 1st Marine Air Wing, arrived at Wilder's headquarters at Dong Ha for a personal briefing from Wilder. As soon as Wilder mentioned the presence of the NVA 324B Division, Robertshaw rudely interrupted him. "You're a liar," Robertshaw accused Wilder.

"Nobody calls me a liar," Wilder retorted, "not even a general." He pulled back to punch Robertshaw, but Walt stepped between the two. "Knock if off. Tell me what's going on," he demanded.

After calming himself, Wilder patiently, with great care and detail, presented his information. All the facts were there; the evidence was indisputable. The NVA had slipped a full division across the DMZ, right into Walt's backyard. (Wilder, of course, had no way of knowing that Westmoreland had already given this information to Walt and that the III MAF commander had scoffed at it.) As Wilder spoke, it was obvious his information infuriated Walt. He looked so angry that Wilder thought the general might hit him. Wilder respected Walt for his rank and position, but he also knew him to be a general who enjoyed busting the balls of his field grade officers.

Finally, Walt could not stand it anymore. "Dammit," he blustered. "I want to talk to the recon people who think they've had contact with the NVA."

Wilder left the operations tent and personally rounded up about seventy-five junior officers and enlisted men who had been on recent patrols. When he brought Walt to the assembled men, the general exploded. "Dammit, Wilder," he sputtered, "I told you I only wanted to talk to people who think they've had contact with the NVA."

"I did, sir. Here they are."

Walt turned back to the group. He adopted a completely different demeanor around enlisted men, asking in a calm, almost fatherly tone, "Who believes they've had contact with NVA in the last ten days?"

All seventy-five raised their hands.

Walt stood silent for several minutes. Then he selected a corporal. "Son, what makes you think you've seen the NVA?"

"I don't think, sir. I know."

"Why?" Walt prodded.

"Three days ago I killed three NVA officers." The youngster then described the enemy's uniforms, weapons, appearance, and the maps he had removed from the corpses.

Walt questioned several more of the troops, then dismissed them. "I've heard enough," he announced.

Back in the operations tent, Walt demanded of Wilder, "Why didn't I know about this?"

"Ask your staff, General," Wilder responded, trying to keep the incredulity out of his voice. "Everything I've told you has been in my reports."

Walt then turned to Kyle. "I'm convinced there's an NVA division up here. What are we going to do about it?"

The senior officers in Quang Tri Province then laid the groundwork to expand Operation Hastings into the first American offensive against regular North Vietnamese Army units.

Over the next seven months, Lieutenant Colonel Wilder's recon teams roamed throughout the wilds of northern Quang Tri Province. Wilder read every after-action report, debriefed each team, then briefed his senior commanders. Wilder believed beyond a doubt that the NVA were the opposition along the DMZ. They might be fighting a guerrilla war against a sneaky and elusive Viet Cong down south, but not up north. The Marines' foe in northern I Corps was a tough, well-armed, highly trained regular army soldier who neither asked for nor gave quarter.

In early February 1967, Wilder took over the 3d Battalion, 3d Marines. He established his command post near the Rockpile. His battalion's rifle companies patrolled a broad area from north of the Rockpile to Ca Lu in the south. Contact with the enemy came infrequently, but when it did the combat invariably proved to be intense and deadly. Wilder's Marines maintained a sharp edge, ever ready to meet the enemy.

On 22 April, with an entourage that included his S-3, Captain Spivey, 2d Lt. Curtis L. Frisbie, one of Spivey's platoon leaders, Spivey's gunnery sergeant, and two other Kilo 3/3 NCOs, Lieutenant Colonel Wilder choppered up to Khe Sanh. "What I saw when I got there shook me," Wilder said. "There were all kinds of aboveground structures and tents, with white-washed rocks lining the pathways between buildings. The troops strolling around seemed very casual for being in the middle of a war zone."

As soon as he saw Reeder, Wilder confronted him. "What the hell is going on up here?" he asked, indicating what he saw all around him.

"We get a lot of VIP visitors up here," Reeder explained. "We have to present a good image."

Wilder shook his head. "I'm only ten miles east of here and I'm completely underground. Only my flagpole's above ground. You're gonna get handed your ass if you don't get dug in," Wilder warned.

On that sour note, Reeder began his briefing. When he stated that enemy forces in the area amounted to only a platoon or less of Viet Cong, Wilder exploded. "You're fulla shit," he told Reeder. The briefing went downhill from there. Wilder discounted everything else Reeder told him, because he knew who lurked in those surrounding hills. After all, he had been fighting the NVA for ten months. He knew his enemy.

When the briefing ended, Captain Sayers led the liaison team on a short patrol out toward Hill 861; he wanted them to get a feel for the terrain.

Captain Spivey found the area similar to what he had been working around the Rockpile. "Both were relatively open, hilly, and thick with elephant grass at the lower levels," he said. "Higher up, the hills were dotted with thick stands of bamboo and trees."

Before Wilder left Khe Sanh, Sayers discussed with him the date of the relief. "I've got two platoons north of [Hill] 861 scouting out some caves," Sayers told Wilder. "When they complete that mission I'll pull 'em back here. We should be ready to move out on the twenty-seventh."

Wilder and Spivey agreed. Minutes later they were gone.

Sayers felt no disappointment about returning to 1/9's control. He had had his fill of Khe Sanh. In less than a week, I'll be leaving Khe Sanh for good, he thought.

Captain Michael W. Sayers had no idea how prescient that thought was.

Early on 23 April, SSgt. Alfredo Reyes's 3d Platoon, Bravo 1/9, began a routine sweep of several ridge fingers that ran north and northwest off

Hill 861. The platoon had been running squad-size patrols out of a nearby PPB for several days. None of these patrols had reported any sign of the enemy. In fact it had been so quiet in recent weeks, Reyes believed that the NVA had moved on, heading east where the flatter terrain favored an invader. Late that morning Sayers radioed Reyes to order the sergeant to move northeast and link up with the 1st Platoon. From their night bivouac the platoons would head west the next morning toward the caves. Reyes immediately started his men moving.

At Khe Sanh, Sayers gave the 1st Platoon's orders directly to its new commander. Second Lieutenant James D. Carter, Jr., had arrived in South Vietnam from the United States just three days earlier. Following in-processing through division and regimental headquarters, Carter boarded a C-130 at first light on 23 April. When the fog lifted that morning, the day's first C-130 roared onto Khe Sanh's runway. Carter stepped out of its cargo hold dressed in utilities so fresh, so green, and so free of red dust that anyone could see he was a newbie. If he thought he would have several days of orientation before taking over his first command, Carter could not have been more wrong. He received a briefing for his first combat mission within hours of stepping off the plane. That afternoon he joined the 1st Platoon at its night defensive perimeter northeast of Hill 861. It had been a full day for the twenty-two-year-old Houston, Texas, native.

A personable man, Carter was instantly accepted by his new charges, but not everyone was happy to see him. Lance Corporal Kenneth Lease had heard scuttlebutt that the platoon would return to Khe Sanh and then be relieved. Carter's appearance changed all that. Lease, a nineteen-year-old Fort Myers, Florida, high school dropout due to rotate out of South Vietnam in less than two months, cursed when the new lieutenant announced that they would continue to patrol for several more days. "Fuckin' green machine," Lease cussed. "We never catch a goddamn break."

Sergeant Reyes and his 3d Platoon arrived just before dusk. They set up a perimeter three hundred meters south of Carter. The night passed without incident.

Dawn on 24 April brought low clouds, misty rain, and a milky layer of fog in the valleys, typical of the *crachin* that ruled the region at this time of year. A couple of hours later, when the fog lifted, the two platoons headed west, moving on parallel routes a few hundred meters apart. Some of the men casually munched C rations as they moved. Their objective was Hill 516, a small knoll near where the caves had been spotted.

That same morning, Sgt. Richard Huff, the platoon sergeant for Bravo's Weapons Platoon, returned to the combat base with a patrol that had spent several days sweeping the southern approaches to Hill 861. Staff Sergeant William E. Hilliard, the platoon sergeant for 2d Platoon and a good friend, stopped Huff as he came through the wire.

"Huff, do you mind going back out?" Hilliard asked. "Lieutenant King's taking some eighty-ones out near 861. They're supporting First and Third, and the lieutenant could use some help out there."

Huff said he did not mind. He knew the area well enough to find a good site for the mortars. He rounded up his one working 60mm mortar and its crew and joined King's party waiting near the CP. The patrol consisted of a rifle squad, the two mortar crews, a forward observer team, an M60 team, and, to Huff's surprise, Lt. Philip Sauer. Huff knew that in the brief time Sauer had been at Khe Sanh he had gained a reputation as an overly gung-ho officer. Bored with his routine duties around the base, Sauer had recently been pestering Sayers to let him go on a patrol where he might see some action. Huff looked questioningly at Hilliard.

"The lieutenant wants to see if he can take the pigs up 861," Hilliard explained. "Pigs" was the nickname the Marines gave to the ONTOS.

Huff shrugged.

A short time later the thirty-man force walked out of the base. They followed the well-used road and trail leading to Hill 861, the same route previously used by Sergeant Harper, Lieutenant Mellon, and Staff Sergeant Olsen. Less than two hours later, King's patrol stopped on the eastern slopes of Hill 700, about a kilometer south of 861, near where Captain Terrill had set up his medevac LZ on 16 March.

At about 1000, as the mortar crews set up their tubes, Sauer told King he was going up Hill 861. He wanted to scout a route for his ONTOS and help find a good observation post for the mortars. Going with him were the 81s' FO, his radioman, and a couple of riflemen as security. Minutes later Sauer left.

Huff watched the five men work their way downhill, then kept an eye on them as they started up the opposite hill. He did not like such a small group moving out on its own, especially on Hill 861. Soon Sauer and his little band disappeared behind a thick stand of bamboo.

Two hundred meters from the top of Hill 861, just as the lead man for Sauer's little group approached a tree line, a burst of rifle fire shattered the morning air. The Marine dropped in a heap. "I'm hit!" he screamed.

Sauer and the FO, Pfc. William Marks, dove for cover, landing in a shallow depression along the trail. About five meters behind them, the radioman and the second rifleman hit the dirt, too. Another spray of enemy AK-47 fire raked the air. Marks tried to fire back, but his M16 jammed after a few rounds.

Sauer told Marks, "Make a run for it. I'll cover you."

With that, the twenty-four-year-old officer got up on one knee and began firing his .45-caliber pistol at the unseen NVA.

Marks scurried back to the others. "Let's get outta here!" he yelled.

The three sprinted down the trail, enemy rounds buzzing past them. They hit the dirt again. Seconds later they were on their feet once more, fleeing for their lives. Marks could see NVA moving along their right flank, racing to cut them off. Suddenly, the radioman dropped, his chest torn by enemy slugs. Seconds later Marks lost sight of the other rifleman. Terrified, he ran blindly on, stumbling and falling on the slick trail as bullets hit all around him.

After the first crackle of rifle fire, Lieutenant King tried to radio Sauer. When he did not get an answer, King sent his rifle squad to investigate. They took off on the double. When they approached the thick bamboo grove on Hill 861, Marks stumbled out toward them, exhausted and covered with mud. "They're dead. They're all dead," he muttered. The squad leader sent him back downhill, then radioed King.

King ordered the squad to continue up the trail and recover the bodies. The Marines crept forward slowly. A few meters up the trail they spotted the corpses of the radioman and the rifleman. Just as they started to pull them back, a savage blast of enemy automatic weapons fire cut the air. The squad beat a hasty retreat. They could not get the bodies.

King ordered them to pull back. Then he radioed the combat base for a fire mission. Within minutes Captain Golden's 105mm howitzers were pumping high-explosive shells onto the enemy-held hilltop. The 81mm mortars added their rounds to the barrage.

As soon as he heard from King, Sayers grabbed his radioman and jumped aboard a chopper. The NVA greeted the approaching H-34 with a blast of .50-caliber machine gun fire. Though hit several times, the aircraft still made it in. Sayers and his radioman jumped out before the craft touched down.

After being briefed by King, Sayers ordered the lieutenant to take the squad back up Hill 861 and get the bodies. Sayers then radioed Lieutenant Carter. "I ordered him to abandon the sweep of the cave area," Sayers said. "I told him to turn and head south across the top of 861. I wanted to catch the enemy in a squeeze play."

King's patrol reached the first set of remains without drawing any fire. To the lieutenant's amazement, both bodies had been stripped of most of their clothing and equipment. Several Marines wrapped the bodies in ponchos while King led the others in a search for Sauer's and the point man's bodies. After twenty minutes without success, King radioed Sayers for permission to pull back.

"I didn't like the area," King later said. "It was too quiet. There were no noises whatsoever, but I figured the enemy was still there, watching."

The patrol hauled the corpses downhill to a spot where a helicopter could get in. As the H-34 circled overhead, King popped a smoke grenade. The helicopter spiraled down. When its wheels touched the ground, the whole top of the hill erupted in machine gun and rifle fire. Fortunately, King and his men were defiladed by the slope of the hill. The helicopter was not. In seconds thirty-five heavy slugs ripped through the machine's thin aluminum skin. Amazingly, none hit flesh or any major aircraft systems. A pair of escorting UH-1 Huey helicopter gunships hosed down the hilltop with machine gun fire, allowing King's men to load the bodies aboard the H-34. In seconds it was airborne and on its way back to Khe Sanh.

If the NVA planned to attack the base that night, Sayers wanted as much warning as possible, so he ordered Sergeant Huff and the rifle squad to remain in position as a listening post. Then, after the mortar men broke down their weapons, he led the others back to the combat base. Though troubled by the day's events, Captain Sayers did not consider them unusual. He had no way of knowing that his Bravo Company had just engaged in the opening skirmish of the twelve-day battle that would become known as the First Battle of Khe Sanh, or, to those who were there, the Hill Fights. He also had no way of knowing the tragic ordeal that awaited him and his men.

At almost the same time the NVA killed Lieutenant Sauer, Lieutenant Carter's 1st Platoon, two kilometers to the north, started up a shallow ridge finger leading to the suspicious caves. With the morning fog burned off, good visibility prevailed. The men moved easily, confident in their recent good fortune—not finding any NVA.

Suddenly, the point man signaled a halt. He had spotted four NVA carrying a fifth man on a stretcher in the ravine below them. The Marines dropped beside the trail to seek cover. As the enemy soldiers drew closer, their voices filtered through the foliage. When they were about fifty meters away, one of them spotted the Marines. He shouted a warning, then opened fire while the others ran for cover.

Sergeant Kenneth Vermillion, recently promoted and now a squad leader, watched in stunned amazement as another squad leader suddenly broke from cover and ran down the hill after the enemy, yelling and firing as he moved. Several of Cpl. James G. Pomerleau's men ran after him, pumping out rounds in an attempt to give him covering fire. A flurry of rifle fire raged for several minutes. Then came the muffled pop of a grenade. A horrible, skin-tingling scream followed. Then the frantic cry, "Corpsman. Corpsman up!" rose from the ravine.

Hospitalman Daniel W. Polland, a rock-solid twenty year old from Sterling, Colorado, who had joined Bravo in January on Okinawa, ignored the potential danger and scrambled downhill, his medical bag clutched tightly in his hand. He found Pomerleau badly burned and nearly torn in half by the explosion of a white phosphorus grenade. Doc Polland could not do anything for him. He called for stretcher bearers.

Lance Corporal Lease went down with three other Marines to get Pomerleau's remains. He helped wrap the torn body in ponchos, then started the tough climb back up the hillside. By the time they rejoined the platoon, Lieutenant Carter had been given his new mission from Captain Sayers.

The rookie lieutenant faced a dilemma: What should he do with Pomerleau's body? He did not have time to call for a medevac. He could not carry the corpse with them, because the burden would delay his platoon's move across Hill 861. No amount of training could have prepared him to make such a tough decision on his second day in command. But instinct told him he had only one choice.

Carter radioed Sergeant Reyes. Because 3d Platoon's mission continued to be investigation of the caves, Carter told Reyes he was leaving Pomerleau's body on the trail. Third Platoon would recover it, move to where an LZ could be cut, then call in a medevac. With that Carter gave the order for his platoon to move out.

Thirty minutes later the platoon descended into an open saddle between two small knolls. Lance Corporal Lease, walking behind Sergeant Vermillion's point squad, noticed a number of holes dotting the area. "They were small holes, maybe two by two," Lease recalled, "and obviously freshly dug."

Just as Vermillion's point man started up the barren ridge finger, the world exploded with enemy rifle fire. NVA dug in on the adjoining ridge finger to the west unleashed a storm of small-arms and automatic weapons fire on the Marines. The quick snap of enemy slugs filled the air. There was little cover, so Carter's Marines were easy targets.

Lease felt a blow to his chest. "I staggered backwards, bumping into another man, Private First Class Wilson. 'Are you hit?' Wilson asked me. I told him I didn't know. I didn't see any blood. Everything was happening so fast. It was all a blur."

Lease looked again. This time he saw blood. Enemy rounds had nicked his left knee and elbow. Another slug had ripped a link off the belt of M60 ammo he wore across his chest, embedding a piece of it in his face. Wilson pulled out the hunk of metal and taped a bandage over the wound. Then the pair started to return fire. They clearly saw enemy soldiers across from them, firing from bunkers. Others darted back and forth.

A short distance from Lease, Doc Polland sought refuge behind one of the few trees on the ridge. He felt relatively safe until a nearly spent AK-47 round ripped into his flak jacket. Thank God for it, he thought as he tried to get lower.

One of Polland's buddies suddenly screamed in pain. Private First Class Wayne R. Barth rolled in the dirt, excitedly yelling, "I'm going home. I'm going home." While blood spurted from Barth's wound, Polland started toward him, but Lieutenant Carter grabbed him. "Don't go out there," Carter warned. "There's too much fire." Polland reluctantly lowered himself to the ground. The lieutenant was right. The enemy fire was just too strong.

At the head of the column, Sergeant Vermillion and his men put out rounds. Twenty-year-old Pfc. John A. Moore, a Richmond, California, resident who had just joined Bravo in February, suddenly realized that he had picked a clump of grass for protection. That's not gonna be very helpful, he told himself. "But it was my first firefight and I was scared, so I excused myself," Moore said. "I just rolled over and over until I reached a spot where I was safe."

Farther back in the column, LCpl. Dana C. Darnell watched in horror as the mortar gunner fell, knocked unconscious from a severe bullet wound. Undaunted by the intense fire whipping past him, Darnell crept forward to retrieve the 60mm tube. As he crawled, he yelled at nearby Marines to bring him the mortar ammo they carried. Unfortunately, only a few shared his courage. Darnell, a well-liked youngster with a great sense of humor and a roguish attitude, cursed the reluctant Marines, then ran to them, grabbed their shells, and returned to the mortar. Without a base plate to steady the tube, Darnell sat in the open, plopped his helmet on the ground between his legs, and used it as a plate. Holding the tube in his bare hands, the gutsy twenty year old started dropping rounds down the tube. Surprisingly accurate, his shells fell right on the enemy-held ridge, where they blasted clumps of earth and pieces of flesh skyward. When Darnell had used up his supply of ammo, he again ignored the danger to run up and down the column collecting more shells. He then returned to his exposed position and resumed firing.

Four hundred meters behind Carter, Sergeant Reyes's men fired at the NVA, too. His 60mm mortar team set up their tube and sent rounds flying on the enemy, who turned their fire on Reyes's platoon. In a matter of minutes, six of Reyes's Marines were hit, three of them seriously.

Carter had called for air support as soon as the firing started. Though it took thirty minutes for a pair of jets to report to the airborne FAC, they were a welcome sight. To the cheers of the Marines, the fast movers dumped their bombs right on the enemy-held ridgeline.

Although some NVA died in the bomb blasts and others ran for cover, a few defiantly remained in the open, boldly firing their rifles at the F-4 Phantoms. Even as the jets roared back in for another pass, several of the enemy soldiers kept blazing away at them.

"I saw one enemy soldier stand right out in the open, firing his AK at a strafing jet," Moore said. "Even as a napalm bomb engulfed him he never moved. What kind of men are we fighting, I wanted to know."

The napalm strike broke the NVA ambush. The Marines then turned to getting their casualties out. It would not be easy: 1st Platoon alone had several dead and nearly a dozen wounded. Carter ordered Vermillion to get moving and not stop until he found a spot for an LZ.

Doc Polland patched up the wounded as best he could. There were a lot of them, and his medical supplies were being used up quickly. Other men rigged stretchers from ponchos so the dead and those unable to walk could be carried. Vermillion led a ragged and bloody column of Marines.

A few hundred meters up the ridge, Vermillion entered a flat area wide enough for a medevac chopper to get in. His squad set up security as the rest of the Marines staggered uphill, struggling to get the screaming and moaning wounded into the LZ.

Just before 1700, an H-34 appeared overhead, escorted by a pair of Huey gunships. The NVA waited until the chopper set down before they opened fire. Machine gun fire raked the LZ while 82mm mortar rounds dropped out of the sky.

Carter's Marines put four wounded aboard before the helicopter pulled pitch and flew off. Unfortunately, the platoon took more new casualties than it sent out.

Doc Polland treated the freshly injured. Then Carter ordered the men to move out again. He hoped to find another LZ before it got dark, one out of the enemy's sight. The battered platoon staggered uphill another few hundred meters, straining to carry the wounded and the dead. When they reached an area suitable for an LZ, Carter called for another medevac.

Once again the NVA held their fire until the aircraft—a CH-46— touched down. No sooner had the able-bodied Marines started rushing toward the lowered ramp with their loads than the enemy mortars fell. In quick succession more than half a dozen rounds exploded with a thundering crash on the LZ. Red-hot chunks of jagged steel zinged through the air, injuring more Marines.

Sergeant Vermillion knelt beside the casualty he was helping, waiting for the chopper's ramp to drop. When the mortars struck, he and the others instinctively hit the deck. "I glanced up and saw a row of holes suddenly appear in the side of the helo," Vermillion recalled. "Then the beat of the rotors picked up. The medevac was getting out. I couldn't get my man aboard."

The rotor wash steadily increased, blowing up clouds of dirt and debris until the chopper was airborne. In its hold lay two corpses and two wounded. Four previously wounded men and one corpse remained behind. Several new casualties writhed in the dirt of the LZ. One of them, Pfc. Raymond L. Twomey, died when an errant .50-caliber round from one of the escorting Hueys blew off most of his head.

Private First Class Moore watched Doc Polland move upright around the LZ, guiding the wounded toward the waiting helicopter. "Even when the mortars started falling, Doc Polland never hesitated," Moore said. Humbled by this display of raw courage, Moore choked back his fear and grabbed the corner of a poncho holding a casualty. His team got their man up the ramp and inside the helicopter. As they headed for another casualty, the helicopter lifted off. "I couldn't believe that so few of the others had bothered to help," Moore said. "Only Polland and two or three others pitched in. It really pissed me off. I remember thinking, this can't be true; we're Marines and we're supposed to help each other."

As the CH-46 flew off, Lieutenant Carter realized that no more helicopters would be getting in that night. He ordered the remaining wounded placed in the center of a ragged perimeter. Then the men started scraping protective holes in the dirt. Those who did not have entrenching tools used their helmets or knives to hack a refuge in the hard soil. No one seemed panicked, but there were a few who did not think they would be around to see morning.

Carter's Marines performed well that day, but the actions of a few stood out. One was mortar man Dana Darnell. "I saw Darnell that evening," Lance Corporal Lease remembered. "He was stretched out near Carter's CP, looking absolutely beat. I later learned from a couple of others that Darnell had helped two wounded men walk up the hill. At the first LZ he'd been pulling another casualty to cover when an exploding mortar round blew dirt and rock fragments into his eyes, temporarily blinding him. He could have jumped aboard the medevac but didn't. Instead he used some of his precious water to flush out his eyes. When he could see again, he started helping the wounded again. He was some Marine."

The 3d Platoon suffered terribly that day, too. Besides dealing with Pomerleau's body, Reyes's platoon took six wounded, three of them seriously, while supporting Carter. Because no helicopters could get to their position, the casualties had to be carried.

"That's when it began to hit us," Reyes later said. The improvised stretchers proved difficult to carry in the steep, slippery terrain. "They sapped our strength," Reyes said, referring to the wounded. "And because they were buddies and now lay torn and bloody, they sapped our spirits, too."

Reyes led his platoon across a ridgeline toward lower terrain where a helicopter could land. The ground was slick from the day's intermittent rain, and the men struggled to keep their footing. The stretcher bearers slipped several times, dropping their charges and slowing the trek as they carefully replaced the wounded on the stretchers. The platoon lurched forward in brief spurts.

Private First Class Ryan had the point as the platoon moved down the back side of the ridge. "I'd reached the bottom of a ravine when I heard the roar of an incoming jet. I turned to watch it," he said. "At first I thought he was headed for the ridge the NVA had been on. Then as the F-4 started its run it suddenly dawned on me that it was headed right for me." Somehow the pilot had mistaken the 3d Platoon for NVA.

"INCOMING!" Ryan screamed. "Take cover! Hurry!"

Ryan raced for shelter. As the jet's scream grew louder, he hit, rolled, curled into a tight ball, and desperately tried to crawl into his helmet. The Phantom unleashed a pair of 250-pound bombs. One, mercifully, failed to explode. The second hit right in the middle of Ryan's squad. In a devastating flash, six Marines were cut down.

The acrid smell of cordite hung heavily in the damp air as Ryan crawled from his cover. The carnage he saw stunned him. Bodies lay everywhere. Ryan rushed to help. He found one man, Pfc. Daniel T. Perez, still alive but with one leg horribly mangled. Ryan did what he could to patch up Perez, while all around him the plaintive cry for "Corpsman!" filled the ravine.

Sergeant Reyes frantically radioed the airborne FAC to call off the jet before it caused more friendly casualties. He then set about reorganizing his decimated unit.

Reyes faced a tough decision. In addition to the six dead, more than a dozen Marines were wounded by the bomb. One of them, Perez, lay near death. Reyes did not have the able-bodied manpower to carry both the dead and the wounded. The wounded had priority; he had to get them out. He did not want to leave his dead behind—that violated Marine Corps tradition—but he had no choice.

Ryan's squad leader, Cpl. Harry Montgomery, took charge of handling the dead. A twenty-year-old native of Sandusky, Ohio, who had come to South Vietnam ten months earlier with the 26th Marines but had transferred to Bravo in February, Montgomery had his men wrap the remains in ponchos. Then he hid them alongside the trail. Reyes urged Montgomery to hurry because he wanted to find a site for an LZ before it got too dark. When Montgomery finished, the platoon moved out.

An hour later Reyes found a suitable site and called for a medevac. Soon the staccato *thwack-thwack* of a helicopter's rotors could be heard. As they had at Carter's location, the NVA let the aircraft approach unmolested. Once it settled on the ground, they opened fire. The mortar rounds danced across the LZ, spreading death and injury.

Private First Class Ryan remembered, "I had hold of a corner of the poncho carrying Perez. We'd almost made it to the waiting chopper when a mortar round went off behind us." The blast drove the Marines to the ground. Perez spilled out of his litter. He howled in pain as Ryan helped him back onto the poncho. With a start Ryan realized that Perez's wounded leg had been torn off. It now lay in the dirt. He gingerly picked it up and set it in the poncho, then helped carry Perez aboard the medevac.

Ignoring the enemy fire, the battered Marines put six wounded men on the chopper before it lifted off. When the aircraft flew away, the enemy firing ceased. Sergeant Reyes wasted no time in ordering his men to dig in, and dig in deep.

There were only a few entrenching tools in the platoon, so most of the men hacked away at the dirt with whatever they had, desperate to get below the ground before night fell. At one of the forwardmost positions, Ryan worked feverishly to prepare his hole. He did not have an entrenching tool, so he used his helmet to scrape a protective depression.

"All of a sudden I heard this rustling noise in the elephant grass out in front of me," Ryan said. "No sooner did I look up than this gook soldier stood up."

Ryan stared at the man. The only NVA he had seen before were dead. At first he thought the enemy soldier was the vanguard of a ground assault. Then he realized the man had his arms in the air.

Nervously, Ryan motioned the soldier forward. The man jabbered incomprehensibly but made it obvious he wanted nothing more to do with the war. Other Marines quickly gathered around, anxious to see an enemy soldier up close. Someone sent for the one platoon member who spoke some Vietnamese. That Marine soon learned that the enemy soldier's name was Vu Van Tich. A member of the 4th Battalion, NVA 32d Regiment, Tich said he had deserted four days earlier and had been looking for someone to surrender to ever since.

While others led Tich away, Ryan could not help but smile. The battalion's standard reward for capturing a POW was three days of in-country R and R. Things were looking up, he thought wistfully, then returned to digging his hole.

As darkness engulfed Hill 861, Bravo's 1st and 3d Platoons held separate defensive perimeters about nine hundred meters apart. Though medevac helicopters had made it in to their positions, each platoon still had a number of wounded to care for. Medical supplies were critically low, so the corpsmen could do little to ease the suffering. At both perimeters the moans and wails of the injured filled the night air.

At Sergeant Reyes's position, one badly wounded sergeant cried all night, "We're all gonna die. We're all gonna die!" He made it a long night for everyone.

The day's fighting created a flurry of activity at Khe Sanh. The members of Bravo's 2d Platoon readied their equipment, loaded extra magazines with bullets, and gave their weapons a good cleaning. They would be going out to Hill 861 at first light and wanted to be as prepared as possible. Helicopter crewmen fueled their aircraft, refilled ammunition canisters, and gave their ships thorough preflight inspections. In the medical bunker the corpsmen checked the stock of supplies. The next day would undoubtedly bring a flood of casualties, and they had to be ready to ease the suffering and mend torn bodies.

Captain Sayers sent an urgent sitrep, detailing what he knew to 3d Marines headquarters. Based on the reports from his platoon leaders, Sayers said Bravo had suffered fourteen killed in action (KIA), at least eighteen wounded in action (WIA), and two Marines (Lieutenant Sauer and the point man) missing in action. To him that meant the NVA were in the hills in force. Sayers also advised the headquarters staff that he planned to personally take his 2d Platoon out to join his two isolated platoons the next morning. But that would not be enough; he needed more help.

Lieutenant Colonel Reeder agreed. "As soon as I heard there were heavy machine guns firing on the medevacs, I knew there were regular NVA in the hills. Viet Cong didn't use that type of weapon," Reeder recalled. "The chopper pilots were visibly shaken by the volume of fire thrown at them. Several of them told me it was the worst they'd experienced in their tours." Reeder radioed Colonel Cereghino at Phu Bai. "This is a lot more than we can handle," Reeder admitted. "We need help."

Chapter Four

Fog controlled the activities around Khe Sanh on the morning of 25 April 1967. Thick banks of gray mist filled the valleys, and higher layers shrouded the mountaintops. Although Captain Sayers was anxious to join his two embattled platoons and continue his mission, he knew that no helicopter could get to the north side of Hill 861. Impatient and frustrated, Sayers and twenty-two members of the 2d Platoon waited by the runway for the rising sun to burn off the fog. But the morning hours passed and the fog persisted.

On Hill 861 Lieutenant Carter wanted to continue his attack to the south, but the fog cut visibility to mere meters. Although he was a rookie, Carter realized it made no sense to stumble around blindly. And he still had to deal with all the casualties. His platoon would not be an effective assault force if it could not move fast. Carter would just have to sit tight until the fog cleared enough to allow the medevacs in.

Because of the lower elevation at his location, Sergeant Reyes faced even thicker fog than Carter, but he decided to use it to his advantage. He ordered a squad to return to the scene of the friendly fire air strike and retrieve the bodies the platoon had left behind. The detail had not been gone long before it returned, obviously spooked.

"We heard gook voices ahead of us," the squad leader explained.

Unwilling to risk more casualties, Reyes, too, settled down to wait for the weather to improve.

By midmorning the fog at the combat base had lifted enough to allow inbound aircraft to land. The first helicopter in carried Col. John Lanigan, commander of the 3d Marines. An easygoing, decisive, and normally unflappable veteran of World War II and Korea, Lanigan was visibly concerned about this threat to his western flank. Although Khe Sanh was not a part of the 3d Marines' Operation Prairie TAOR, bad news there meant trouble for Lanigan.

Reeder and Sayers both briefed Colonel Lanigan. When they finished, the regimental commander told them he had ordered Lieutenant Colonel Wilder to bring Kilo 3/3 to the combat base that morning. In fact, they were already in the air. As soon as they arrived they would attack Hill 861 from the south. Sayers putting pressure on the enemy from the north should take care of Mr. Charles, Lanigan said. He then climbed aboard his command chopper and flew off.

Sayers radioed Sergeant Huff and told him to return to the base. "When I got there, Sayers told me I was to guide Kilo Three Three out to Hill 700," Huff recalled. "He figured I knew the terrain as good as anyone and could get Kilo out there okay."

When Sayers returned to the airstrip, he saw General Ryan hopping off a Huey. I wonder what he wants, Sayers thought.

Lieutenant Colonel Reeder wanted to know the same thing. He thought Ryan's frequent visits amounted to meddling and interfering with the tactical situation. And he did not like Ryan. Reeder had been upset since the day several weeks earlier when he returned to his bunker to find the general lying on his cot. If that was not bad enough, Ryan had kicked off the poncho that the fastidious Reeder used as a dust cover and had his muddy boots right on Reeder's clean sheets. Barely able to conceal his contempt, Reeder curtly answered the general's questions. He was only too happy to see Ryan leave.

Now Reeder waited quietly nearby while Sayers updated Ryan. When Sayers finished, Ryan announced, "I'm going with you."

Reeder could not believe what he had heard.

Neither could Sayers. "Oh shit, I remember thinking," Sayers later said. "That's just what I need: a goddamn general with me out in the field with all the lead flying around. I sure didn't want to go down in history as the only captain to get a general killed, but what could I do?"

"Aye, aye, sir," Sayers responded crisply.

Lieutenant Colonel Reeder thought it a foolish gesture on Ryan's part. "He had absolutely no business being out there. He'd just screw things up and confuse everything," Reeder said. "The emphasis should have been getting the wounded out, then removing the troops. At this point I didn't think there was any reason for them to be out there at all."

The two men started toward the waiting aircraft. But before Ryan could board, his aide rushed up. "General, General," the young lieutenant shouted above the rotor noise. "You're needed back at Dong Ha."

"Darn it, I'll have to return, Mike," Ryan said.

"That's too bad, sir. Have a good trip back."

Greatly relieved at his friend's departure, Sayers hopped aboard the waiting CH-46. In seconds it and one other lifted off and banked northwest toward Hill 861.

"Because Lieutenant Carter's platoon was closest to the summit of Hill 861, I elected to be put down by him," Sayers said. "From there we could start the sweep across 861."

Once again the wily NVA waited until the chopper settled on the ground before they opened fire. Enemy rounds pinged through the helicopter's thin aluminum skin as Sayers and his group jumped off. They moved away while a small group of Marines surged forward, struggling with the limp weight of the wounded slung between them on ponchos. Private First Class Moore gripped the corner of one poncho while Doc Polland held another. "The skill of that chopper pilot really impressed me," Moore said. "We had a tight LZ. It sat snugly on a small knoll. Because he couldn't get all the way in, the pilot hovered in backwards. With just his rear wheels on the ground, he had dropped the ramp so Captain Sayers and his Marines could get off. When they did, we got our wounded on board."

By then the enemy fire had increased dramatically, leaving the pilot no choice but to depart. He took off as soon as the litter bearers stepped away.

In the meantime, the second helicopter landed some distance from the 1st Platoon's perimeter. Staff Sergeant Leon R. "Lee" Burns, the 2d Platoon's platoon sergeant, exited with the nine men riding with him. Burns, a stocky thirty year old from Portland, Maine, had ten years in the Corps but only ten days with Bravo. "I expected to see Sayers and the rest of the company right there. But nobody was there," he said. Damn, he swore. Where the hell is everybody? And, more important, where was *he*? Remnants of the morning's fog kept him from spotting any landmarks, so he could not be sure of his position. "I had no interest in wandering these hills with less than a full squad, looking for the captain, so I radioed him. Sayers told me to look around for a dead tree on a hilltop. I did. I saw four hilltops with dead trees on them. 'That's no good,' I radioed Captain Sayers. He had someone toss a smoke grenade outside their lines. That I saw." Soon Burns had his little band inside the perimeter.

The helicopter that dropped Burns and his men continued on to Sergeant Reyes's location. The 3d Platoon loaded several of the severely wounded and the POW before the enemy's mortars whistled in. The pilot lifted off as the first rounds exploded alongside the LZ.

At Carter's position Captain Sayers quickly sized up the situation. Although two wounded men had been evacuated, he still had four others to deal with. With no prospect of another medevac getting in due to the enemy fire and the fog, which had redeveloped, they would have to carry the injured men with them. Other than ammo, Sayers had not brought any other supplies with him. Many of the Marines had no water, and some had not eaten in twenty-four hours. An attack was out of the question; they would need all their strength and resources just to survive.

Sayers ordered stretchers built for the casualties. While Staff Sergeant Burns detailed several men to cut bamboo poles, Sayers radioed Reyes and ordered the 3d Platoon to join up. Sayers wanted as large a force as he could muster for the move back to Khe Sanh; he was worried the NVA might cut off and destroy the smaller group.

Reyes wanted to avoid the trail where he had left the bodies, and where his squad had heard Vietnamese voices, so he tried moving cross-country. That route took them straight into the deep ravine between their position and the next ridge finger. From there they could move up to where Sayers waited. But it did not work. The vegetation in the ravine turned out to be so thick that after an hour of chopping and hacking at the tangled growth they had moved less than ten meters. Third Platoon would have to take the trail.

Reyes's Marines moved cautiously, their eyes and ears attuned for any sign of the enemy. The platoon made it to the scene of the accidental bombing with no contact. After picking up their dead comrades, the platoon members resumed their hike. At first the platoon advanced at a good pace, but the thick foliage and steep terrain soon took their toll on the thirsty, tired men. Reluctantly, Reyes ordered the bodies dropped off once again. As layered fog rapidly built up, the 3d Platoon dug in for a second night away from the main body. The platoon's lone corpsman did his best to comfort the wounded, but his supplies were nearly gone.

Meanwhile, Sayers and his group struggled all day and moved only a few hundred meters up the hill. Sniper fire and mortar shells plagued their march. "I tagged this as harassing fire," Sayers said. "A deadly little reminder that the NVA knew where we were and could hurt us whenever they wanted."

Although they had moved only a short distance, the effort sapped the Marines. Nearly every able-bodied man and most of the less seriously wounded carried or aided a casualty. Lance Corporal Lease, for example, held one corner of a poncho that bore a dead Marine. After just a few minutes of gripping the slippery fabric, his fingers ached so badly they nearly locked up. But he hung on.

Ahead of Lease a sudden outburst of cursing and swearing halted the column. A Marine had slipped on the slick trail and dropped his end of a litter. The body fell out and rolled down the steep embankment. The whole column waited as several Marines scrambled downhill to recover the corpse. They started moving again, but Lease had advanced only about thirty meters before the column halted once more. It was like that all day: stop and start, stop and start.

Frustration plagued the troops. Lease wondered why they could not stay and fight the enemy. Doc Polland worried because he had no medical supplies left. He could not comfort the wounded with anything other than words. Sergeant Pratt sensed a growing feeling of desperation in those around him. "I overheard several men mumbling that we were cut off and probably wouldn't make it out," he said. "I immediately told them to knock it off. There was no reason to be spreading panic."

At the rear of the column Staff Sergeant Burns, who cradled a 12-gauge shotgun in his thick arms, kept a wary eye open for any lurking NVA. He had spent several years as a recon instructor, so he knew that the enemy liked to follow behind a column of troops watching for any chance to hit from the rear. But as the column inched its way up the slippery slope, the fog reappeared. "I couldn't have seen Ho Chi Minh himself if he'd been walking right behind me," Burns said. He radioed Sayers, suggesting they set in for the night.

Sayers agreed; his Marines were worn out and thirsty. He passed the word for everyone to dig in where they were. He then radioed Khe Sanh to register artillery fire around his position. "I knew the NVA probably didn't have my exact position due to the fog. But I also figured they were monitoring my transmissions, and I didn't want to give them any helpful information," Sayers recalled. "So I made up a code to give Captain Golden my location. I had great confidence in my friend's ability to decipher it."

Golden did. His registration rounds landed right on target.

That evening Captain Sayers inspected his company's defensive perimeter. He paused at each position to assure his men they would reach safety the next day. What he did not know was the enemy had no intention of letting that happen. They planned to use Bravo as bait to suck other Marines into a deadly trap. And it worked; they had already chewed up another company with that tactic.

Based on Lieutenant Colonel Reeder's and Captain Sayers's reports to his operations staff, Colonel Lanigan radioed Lieutenant Colonel Wilder late on 24 April.

"All hell's breaking loose up at Khe Sanh," Lanigan told him. "Take your jump CP and a company up there first thing tomorrow. Find out what the hell's going on."

The scrappy Wilder had just one question. Based on his briefing with Lieutenant Colonel Reeder a few days earlier, he wanted to know who was in charge up there. "If it's Reeder, I ain't going," said Wilder.

"Don't worry," Lanigan assured him, "you'll report to me."

"Aye, aye, sir," Wilder said.

Wilder wasted no time notifying Captain Spivey of the change in plans. "Have Kilo at my CP as soon as possible tomorrow morning," Wilder told him. "We're going to Khe Sanh a little early. We've got to take Hill 861, the same one we hiked out to a few days ago."

Spivey responded "aye, aye" and issued the necessary orders to his men. A twenty-six-year-old South Carolinian, Spivey had taken a commission in the Marines upon graduation from the Citadel five years earlier. He had been in South Vietnam for ten months but had commanded Kilo 3/3 for only three weeks. Before that he had run a company in the 3d Recon Battalion for Wilder. When Wilder took over 3/3 on 22 February, Spivey had asked to go with him. As soon as a rifle company became available, Wilder sent for Spivey.

The men of Kilo regarded their new CO as a quiet, competent officer. Gentlemanly in the Southern style, Spivey did not raise his voice unless absolutely necessary. Though respected, he had not seen much combat with Kilo, so despite his extensive recon time, most of his troops considered him inexperienced. During his tenure, Kilo had had only a few brief skirmishes with small bands of NVA around the Rockpile. Most recently it had been riding shotgun for the Rough Rider convoys passing through Kilo's TAOR on the way to Khe Sanh. The prospect of tangling with the NVA at Khe Sanh did not disappoint Spivey.

By 0900 on 25 April, Kilo's platoons had gathered at 3/3's CP at Thon Son Lam, a hamlet on Route 9 just east of the Rockpile. In the long-standing military tradition of hurry up and wait, Kilo's Marines lounged beside the LZ, anxious for the fog to clear so they could board the idle helicopters and take off for Khe Sanh. Finally, soon after 1100, they were able to go.

Lieutenant Colonel Reeder met Wilder at Khe Sanh's airstrip. "Don't worry," the SOP announced, "I've already put five hundred rounds of artillery on that hill. You should be able to walk right up it."

Wilder did not believe him. Barely able to hide his contempt, he responded, "If you say you put five hundred rounds out there, then I'll want my own support."

Sergeant Huff waited to guide Kilo out to the vicinity of Hill 861. He spotted a friend, Sgt. Ivan N. Reiner, who had left Bravo just a few weeks earlier to join Kilo. They chatted while the Kilo Marines formed up. Not far from them, Cpl. Donald G. Bigler and LCpl. Thomas A. Vineyard rechecked their gear while they waited for the company to move out. Soon Cpl. Lindy R. Hall strolled past them. Bigler knew that Hall had served an earlier tour with the recon Marines and had been over talking with some of his old buddies who were now with the recon unit at Khe Sanh.

"Hey, Butch," Bigler called out to Hall, using his nickname. "Whatta ya hear?"

"I got a bad feeling about this," Hall replied. "I hear there's gooks all over them hills. Bravo One Nine's been trapped out there surrounded by Charlie for a couple of days. It ain't good. It ain't good at all."

Vineyard felt the fear grip his stomach. Christ, he thought, if a veteran like Hall thinks it's going to be bad, that's got to mean something. Vineyard nervously shifted his M16 from one hand to the other as Hall moved down the line passing the bad news to others.

A few minutes later Sergeant Huff got the word to head out. He wished Sergeant Reiner good luck and moved to the head of the column. Following the well-traveled dirt road leading out of the combat base, Kilo 3/3 headed toward Hill 700.

In the middle of the long, staggered column of green-clad Marines hiked twenty-one-year-old LCpl. Isamu S. Yoshida, a member of Lt. Curtis Frisbie's 3d Platoon. "Sam" to his buddies, Yoshida was born in Japan but had moved to Las Vegas, Nevada, with his family in 1960 when his Air Force stepfather transferred to Nellis Air Force Base. After receiving his draft notice in the fall of 1965, Yoshida and a similarly notified friend talked about their future. Neither doubted they would soon be shipped off to the growing war in South Vietnam. And, reflecting the influence of just five years of exposure to American culture and lore, Yoshida said he wanted to go to war with the best; he wanted to be a Marine. His buddy agreed. They set off to the recruiter's office.

Now, after seven months in South Vietnam, Yoshida had all he'd ever wanted of war. "I'd seen all the death and destruction I could stand," he said. "I had less than six months remaining in-country and I just wanted to survive and go home." The rapid firing of the 105s pounding the hill up ahead encouraged him. Maybe this won't be so bad, he reasoned. No one could survive that pounding.

Wilder halted the column when Sergeant Huff reached the spot where Lieutenant King had set up his mortars the day before. Wilder established his CP there. He and Spivey laid out a plan of attack, then Spivey went to brief his platoon leaders.

"Since Kilo's Second Platoon was short a squad—it was opconned to Mike Three Three—I told its commander, Second Lieutenant Richard L. Hanson, they'd be remaining there to guard the battalion CP and be the reserve force," Spivey said.

"My most experienced and combat-savvy platoon leader, Staff Sergeant Charles R. 'Dick' Shoemaker, would continue up the main trail with his First Platoon to approach Hill 861 directly from the south. Lieutenant Frisbie and his Third Platoon would follow until they reached an intersecting trail that veered off to the northeast. That trail would take them to a ridge finger that led up to a small knoll a few hundred meters north and east of Hill 861; we called it 861 Alpha. Frisbie would occupy 861A and be prepared to assist Shoemaker as needed. I'd trail Shoemaker with my command group."

As a final word, Spivey told his platoon leaders, "We're going in fast. There's not much up there. Drop flak jackets here so the men won't be slowed down. Good luck."

When one of Huff's men saw the Kilo Marines dropping their flak jackets, he called out a warning: "Hey, you'd better not do that. The gooks're dropping mortars all over the place. The shrapnel will get you for sure."

"We're going light so we can charge right to the top and get this over with," a Kilo Marine called back. The Bravo Marine shrugged as if to say, Don't say we didn't warn you.

As artillery shells blasted the crest of Hill 861, the two Kilo platoons left the CP area at about 1630. Sergeant Huff watched for a few minutes, then started his men back to Khe Sanh.

Lieutenant Frisbie directed his platoon on to the intersecting trail. An Air Force brat who had graduated from the University of Alabama less than a year earlier, Frisbie had joined Kilo 3/3 in January. In the following three months, he and his platoon had tangled with the NVA several times while operating around the Rockpile. The combat experience gave Frisbie the confidence that a good rifle platoon leader needed.

From his position a short distance behind Frisbie, Corporal Bigler, a nineteen year old from the small eastern New Mexico town of Floyd and a hardened ten-month veteran with Kilo, witnessed an unusual event. "As the platoon went up a small knoll, one of our two navy corpsmen suddenly flung himself off the trail into a small ravine," Bigler recalled. "The guy wasn't hurt; he just crawled back uphill and got back in line. From where I was I could see the guy was shaking he was so scared. I knew he was a short-timer and wanted out of the field, but I didn't think he'd go that far." Several more times the corpsman rolled down the hill. Each time he arose uninjured, much to his obvious disappointment.

As the column crossed a steep hillside covered with loose shale, the corpsman did it again. Limbs akimbo, he rolled and tumbled nearly fifty feet before coming to rest. "Oh, my ankle, my ankle!" he cried, grasping the injured joint.

As Bigler, Vineyard, and others watched in disgust, the other corpsman hurried downhill. Soon he announced that his comrade had, indeed, suffered a badly twisted ankle and could not go on.

Lieutenant Frisbie arrived on the scene, unaware of the circumstances behind the injury. Assured by Spivey's earlier words that Hill 861 would be unoccupied, Frisbie ordered the two corpsmen to return to the combat base. He detailed LCpl. Harold A. Croft to accompany them as a guard. Croft picked up the injured corpsman's medical kit and joined the pair as they started back. The rest of the 3d Platoon continued on.

In his briefing, Captain Spivey had told his two platoon leaders he did not expect them to find much left on the hill, because artillery had been pounding it all day. Yet one of the last things Captain Spivey said to Staff Sergeant Shoemaker before he headed out was, "Recon by fire if you have to." This technique of indiscriminately spraying the terrain in front of you with rifle and machine gun fire during an advance was designed to trigger an ambush before getting caught in it. Shoemaker nodded but thought the advice unusual because the Marines rarely used it. And Shoemaker would know. One of Kilo's most experienced vets, he had only a few weeks left on his thirteen-month tour. In fact, a few days earlier he had received orders to his new duty station in the States. He had the papers tucked carefully in his pack.

At age twenty-eight, Shoemaker had already served almost twelve years in the Marines. He had left his family home in Coeur d'Alene, Idaho, to enlist on his seventeenth birthday, in May 1955. In 1966 he was a drill instructor training troops at the recruit depot in San Diego. He fully expected, indeed wanted, to go off to war in Vietnam. After all, he had been training for war for eleven years. The Marine Corps did not disappoint him.

Staff Sergeant Shoemaker arrived in Da Nang on 1 May 1966 and went right to Kilo 3/3. He and the company spent four months chasing the elusive Viet Cong around Da Nang before being assigned to the SLF. After a month's training on Okinawa, 3/3 was sent to the DMZ area.

The war up north proved to be completely different for Shoemaker and Kilo's other veterans. Accustomed to splashing through rice paddies and fighting brief skirmishes with fleeing bands of VC, they now faced hard-core, well-trained, regular North Vietnamese Army soldiers operating in rugged, jungle-clad, mountainous terrain. The dedicated enemy troops fought from well-constructed and fortified bunkers, bombarded the Marines with mortars, and even called in heavy artillery from bases north of the DMZ. Kilo had to learn how to wage war all over again. Fortunately, it learned fast and well.

Shoemaker led his 1st Platoon from Wilder's CP toward Hill 861. After Lieutenant Frisbie's platoon peeled off to the right, the 1st Platoon continued up the hill, its forty members strung out for more than 120 meters. Some 100 meters behind them was Captain Spivey and his compact command group. Shoemaker's practiced eye carefully surveyed the terrain. The trail ran along the top of a 50-meter-wide ridge finger. Elephant grass, thick brush, and dense clumps of bamboo restricted visibility along the downslopes of the finger, but there was no evidence of NVA. "I didn't see any commo wire, abandoned gear, bunkers, or anything that indicated anyone had been here before us," Shoemaker recalled. The artillery support had been put on check fire, so the only noise came from the footfall of his men and the clang of their equipment as they trudged upward.

Near the spot where Lieutenant Sauer had been killed the day before, Shoemaker noticed that his point squad's leader, Cpl. Alfonso R. Riate, was behind him and not up front with his men.

"Hey, Riate, get your ass up with your men where you belong," Shoemaker barked.

Riate reluctantly pushed past Shoemaker. The staff sergeant could not help but notice how frightened the four-month veteran looked. Riate soon disappeared from view as the trail curved sharply and snaked its way toward the crest. It was 1700.

Five minutes later a sustained burst of automatic weapons fire erupted from uphill. "Everyone dropped. I couldn't tell if it was Riate's squad reconning by fire or the springing of an ambush," Shoemaker said. Seconds later he had his answer. The volume of fire increased to a level beyond anything Shoemaker had experienced in more than fifty firefights. Bullets snapped overhead in a dense pattern, indicating that the NVA were firing down well-defined, predetermined lanes. The enemy had simply been waiting for the Marines to enter the kill zone.

Braving the slugs that passed mere inches overhead, Shoemaker crawled forward, repeatedly calling out to Riate. There was no answer. Shoemaker moved another ten to fifteen meters uphill but still could not hear or see his point squad.

Shoemaker radioed Spivey. In clipped phrases punctuated by bursts of enemy fire, Shoemaker briefed his CO on what had happened. From his defiladed position downhill, Spivey ordered Shoemaker to continue the attack.

Easier said than done, Shoemaker said to himself. Because the platoon had been moving in a column along the narrow trail, it had little firepower up front. Also, the point squad was gone, apparently wiped out in that devastating opening blast. But Shoemaker had his orders, so he ordered his 3d Squad to slip down the ridge finger on the left while the 2d Squad moved down the right side. From there they could lay down a base of fire, which would let Shoemaker and the others still on the trail move forward.

No sooner did 2d Squad leader Cpl. Jeffrey R. Maloney make the move than his squad ran into a blistering hail of enemy fire. Shoemaker could not believe how much firing there was. "The noise was nearly deafening," he said. "It was as if we were back on the rifle range at Camp Pendleton and everyone in the training company was firing at the same time and not stopping, just firing and firing."

Then Maloney frantically screamed, "My goddamn rifle. It's jammed. It's jammed!"

Then silence.

Staff Sergeant Shoemaker cursed the new M16. The rifle had been a problem since it was first issued to them a few weeks earlier. No one liked it; almost every M16 had jammed during the break-in period. He and every other Marine on the hill wished they still had their trusty M14s. But they could not do anything about it now.

Not far from Shoemaker, Navy Hospitalman Michael G. Gibbs was oblivious to the danger as he low-crawled uphill to reach a man down with a sucking chest wound. Gibbs sealed and bandaged the gaping hole, then pulled the casualty fifteen meters downhill to a slight depression that offered some protection from the continuing small-arms fire. The gutsy sailor continued on, crawling on all fours to the side of another wounded Marine. Seconds later an AK-47 round tore into Gibbs's back. Momentarily stunned by the blow, he ignored the deep pain and returned to treating the Marine. He slapped a dressing on his own wound before moving off toward a third casualty. Before he reached him, an enemy slug shattered Gibbs's leg. He slumped to the ground, immobilized.

By 1800 Shoemaker's platoon had had it. More than half the platoon was down. As much as he wanted to, Shoemaker could not continue the advance; he just did not have the strength. And there was not any chance of air support, because it would be too dark by the time the jets arrived. Artillery could not be used because his men were too close to the enemy. He had no options, so he radioed Spivey.

Spivey listened to Shoemaker's assessment. The sounds of the battle that drifted downhill confirmed the platoon leader's words. "Sit tight," Spivey told Shoemaker. "We'll get help up to you." Then Spivey radioed Wilder's CP. "We really ran into a hornets' nest," he said. "I need my other platoon."

Within minutes Lieutenant Hanson's platoon was hustling up the trail. The sound of gunfire heightened the urgency. Twenty-three-year-old LCpl. Harold A. Croft moved with them. After escorting the two corpsmen back to Hill 700, Croft had remained with the 2d Platoon. He had no reason to accompany the pair back to the combat base, because enough traffic moved along the trail for them to return safely on their own. Besides, he sensed a fight brewing and figured he belonged with his company.

A native of Malden, Massachusetts, Croft had been a student and track star at Villanova University until the previous April, but had dropped out of school after his father suffered a serious heart attack. That made him a prime target for his draft board; but rather than wait to be drafted, Croft enlisted in the Marines. He proved his worth as a combat Marine soon after arriving in Kilo in late January. During an attack on an enemy-held trench, Croft earned a Silver Star when he killed six NVA with several well-placed hand grenades.

Now, as Croft headed up Hill 861 he felt unsettled. As sounds of the fight carried to him, he tightened his grip on the medical bag. His mouth grew drier as he neared the battleground.

In the meantime, Staff Sergeant Shoemaker wisely ordered his men to pull the casualties back down the trail. As they withdrew, the enemy's rifle fire abated, but NVA 82mm mortar shells dropped on them. At first the 82s were too far off target to do much damage, but the enemy gunners soon found the range. The shells burst among the Marines, and jagged chunks of shrapnel hit flesh. Shoemaker wished they had their flak jackets.

By the time the 1st Platoon pulled back fifty meters, the lead elements of Hanson's 2d Platoon had reached it. Lance Corporal Croft joined a fire team that started toward Riate's missing squad. They made it to the ambush site before the enemy opened fire. A virtual blizzard of AK-47 and machine gun fire surrounded them. Croft dropped into a shallow depression. Hot slugs of lead buzzed overhead in a constant drone. The intensity of the enemy's fire stunned Croft; he had never experienced anything like this. He could not see anything or anyone to fire back at; he could not even see any muzzle flashes. He could only lie there with his head down, frustrated at his inability to act.

When the enemy fire finally stopped, Croft crawled over to give aid to two wounded members of his fire team. They all pulled back to join the rest of the Marines clustered in a tight perimeter.

A short distance away, Staff Sergeant Shoemaker carefully searched along the hillside for any wounded. He did not want to overlook anyone in the growing darkness. He did not pull back until he was satisfied that all the casualties had been removed.

The enemy's fire ceased as the Marines withdrew and night began to fall, but that was small consolation for the many wounded. Medevacs could not get in for them, and there were not enough able-bodied men to carry the wounded out of the area. The casualties would have to spend a long, painful night on the hillside. Lance Corporal Croft helped to make them as comfortable as possible. He applied dressings to ripped flesh, injected morphine into pain-wracked limbs, and offered words of encouragement.

After Staff Sergeant Shoemaker set out his perimeter guards, he tended the wounded, too. He helped one youngster who had a serious neck wound. Then he had another casualty hold a compress against the gaping hole to stop the bleeding. Shoemaker hoped the effort would keep the man alive through the night. When he knelt by Hospitalman Gibbs, the gallant sailor spoke quietly. "Am I gonna die?" he asked.

"No," Shoemaker assured him. "You need permission to die around here and I'm not giving it."

Gibbs smiled weakly at Shoemaker's good-natured comment, and then he died.

Shoemaker moved away, nearly overwhelmed by emotion. The cries and moans of the wounded filled his ears. He hoped the NVA would not come for them. There was no way his battered platoon could survive another attack.

After Lieutenant Frisbie sent Croft and the two corpsmen on their way, his 3d Platoon continued around to the east side of Hill 861. When he reached the jumping-off point, Frisbie radioed Spivey. The captain ordered him to proceed. Frisbie pointed uphill and his platoon started moving. It was 1645.

Dense brush and a scattering of trees covered the ridge finger they followed, but visibility was good. No one saw any sign of the NVA. "I could see a fair distance," Frisbie recalled, "but the hill was steep enough that I couldn't see the crest."

Near him Lance Corporal Yoshida moved forward, his M79 grenade launcher held at the ready. Reassuring blasts of 105mm howitzer shells continued up ahead. Suddenly, a shrill whistling sound signaled a warning to Yoshida. He dove for cover. Scant seconds later a short round slammed into the ground not more than fifty meters in front of him.

Yoshida staggered to his feet, his ears ringing, dust and dirt falling around him. Screams—horrible screams—broke through the din. In front of him, Cpl. Lindy Hall lay curled on the ground with blood pouring from a big hole in his back. As Yoshida passed by, he heard Hall plead with a buddy, "Please don't let me die here. Please! Please don't let me die here."

Lieutenant Frisbie had been just a few meters from Hall when the errant round hit. The blast threw him backward, but he escaped injury. He moved to Hall's side. Hall's wound was serious; most of his lower left back and buttock were gone. Without a corpsman, Frisbie could not do much for him. He ordered his radioman, LCpl. James E. March, to remain with Hall. He then pointed to Lance Corporal Vineyard, the radioman for Cpl. Henry Contreras's 3d Squad. "You're my new radioman," he said.

Slowly, the platoon continued up the hill. The point man, Pfc. John K. Miller, advanced cautiously, his keen eyes alert for any sign of the enemy. Halfway up the hill, Vineyard tapped Frisbie on the shoulder. Spivey wanted him on the radio.

"Hold up. We're taking some fire," Spivey's voice cracked over the PRC-25's little speaker.

Frisbie halted his men. With the artillery fire now on hold, they could hear the distant crackling of small-arms fire. After what seemed like hours, Spivey finally radioed again. First Platoon had been hit, he said. They would regroup and resume the attack in the morning. Spivey ordered Frisbie to halt and dig in for the night. His platoon would also resume the attack in the morning.

"That was okay with me," Frisbie said. "The thought of attacking an unknown position in the dark didn't interest me at all." He passed the word for the platoon to halt where it was. Then he settled on the ground and tried to sleep.

Lance Corporal Yoshida joined his squad mates in a shallow ravine. They set up a watch schedule, then spread out, looking for a reasonably comfortable place to bed down. Yoshida lay there, afraid of what the next day would bring. "I felt for sure that some serious fighting awaited us," he said. "We hadn't taken any enemy fire during the day, but I sensed the enemy was up there, on the top of the hill, waiting for us. Tomorrow was going to be bad; I could feel it." He shuddered, searching for the calming peace of sleep. It never came.

Farther uphill Corporal Bigler knew that the enemy awaited them. "I was less than two hundred meters from the hill's crest and could hear the North Vietnamese soldiers talking," he recalled. "Why the enemy hadn't heard or seen us bewildered me." They would see the Marines in the morning, he knew, and then it would be tough. Too nervous to sleep, he lay there dreading what daylight would bring.

Because of the unexpected heavy resistance on Hill 861, Lieutenant Colonel Wilder altered his plans. "Originally I fully expected the NVA to withdraw from the hill that night," Wilder said. "That's what they'd done in every fight we'd had with them around the Rockpile. I had no reason to think this situation would be any different. That's also why I left Spivey's platoons out there.

"And, with Bravo One Nine wandering around God-knew-where, I couldn't effectively deploy my supporting arms without risking danger to them. I had to get them out before I could continue the attack. I radioed Colonel Lanigan that afternoon. After I briefed him, I asked for

another company. A short time later his S-3 called me back and told me
the division reserve was on its way."

Although greatly concerned about Kilo 3/3, Bravo 1/9's predicament
frustrated Wilder the most. Bravo had been chopped opcon to him upon
his arrival at Khe Sanh, but Wilder could not communicate directly with
it. Captain Sayers did not have and could not get 3/3's radio frequencies or codes. He thus had to communicate with Sayers via Bravo's CP,
back at the combat base.

To make matters worse, Sayers could not tell Wilder where he was; the
fog made it impossible for Sayers to get a fix on any landmarks. At one
point Wilder had his assistant operations officer radio Sayers for an update briefing. When the S-3A asked Sayers for a better fix on his location, Sayers fired back, "Just ask Glen Golden. He's been dropping
rounds near me all day. If anyone knows where I'm at, it's him."

If Wilder or any of III MAF's staff officers had had any idea of the enemy's plans, they might not have fallen into the same trap that had
doomed military operations for centuries: feeding forces into a battle
piecemeal. Three rifle companies had already been dropped, one by one,
into the meat grinder called Khe Sanh. Two were ground up and spit out,
mere skeletons of their former selves.

As later reconstructed by Marine and MACV intelligence specialists,
the North Vietnamese had planned a multi-pronged attack on several
Marine Corps bases in northern I Corps. Besides Khe Sanh, the enemy
had also targeted Dong Ha, Gio Linh, Con Thien, and Camp Carroll for
severe mortar attacks, designed to disrupt the allied fire support and logistical networks. Also, sappers were detailed to blow up key bridges along
Route 9 to further isolate the targeted bases. The NVA threw in a raid
on the airstrip at Phu Bai for good measure, in the hope of hampering
the Marines' ability to provide aerial support to their besieged bases. Successful execution of this battle plan would leave most of Quang Tri
Province's defenses in a shambles and the North Vietnamese victorious
over the Americans.

All of this might have come to pass if Lieutenant Sauer had not decided to look up on Hill 861. By forcing the NVA to prematurely trigger
their main effort at Khe Sanh, Sauer had inadvertently prevented what
could have been a very serious attack.

Captain Mike Sayers, of course, had no idea of Bravo's role in pre-
cipitating the battle. All he knew was that his company was hurt, and hurt

badly. With few supplies and little water, Sayers ordered a search of the dead's gear. The effort uncovered a few canteens of precious water, which Sayers reserved for the wounded. He knew there was not much more that he or the corpsmen could do to ease their suffering. He could only hope that a medevac chopper would get in the next morning with supplies and carry out the most seriously wounded.

In the dark hours before dawn, Doc Polland awoke to Vietnamese voices. Initially alarmed that the enemy had snuck up on them, he soon realized that the voices came from below him, from a nearby valley or another hillside.

Lance Corporal Lease heard the enemy talking, too. They were some distance away, for sure, but they did not make any effort to conceal themselves. "Their lack of concern told me they knew we weren't a threat, so they just calmly went about their business, completely unconcerned about the Marines dug in on the hillside above them," Lease said.

The enemy revealed their intentions at 0500. The sudden blast of 72mm recoilless rifles and the distinctive *kathunk* of 82mm shells leaving their tubes startled the men of Bravo. The weapons' discharges reflected off the fog bank, creating a deadly light show. The Marines watched as the shells flew toward Khe Sanh.

Captain Sayers immediately radioed Captain Golden. Under Sayers's direction, Golden fired a few 105mm rounds in the general vicinity of the enemy weapons. "I listened carefully to the explosions," Sayers said. "In this way I could adjust the howitzers' aim. Sometimes, through breaks in the fog, I saw the flash of the erupting shells." By this crude and unorthodox method, Sayers walked the artillery shells toward the enemy gun positions.

When pain-laden cries and screams followed one barrage, Sayers yelled into his radio, "Fire for effect!"

The subsequent deep-boomed explosions greatly comforted the battered Marines of Bravo.

Chapter Five

Bravo 1/9's third day behind enemy lines began with the unexpected lifting of the protective veil of fog. Captain Sayers immediately issued orders for his men to move out. If they did not get going, they would be easy targets for the lurking NVA. Although without food for the last thirty-six hours, limited to mere swallows of a dwindling water supply, and under enemy fire the entire time, Bravo's Marines never hesitated. They picked up the poncho-wrapped corpses of their buddies, helped the walking wounded to their feet, and renewed their trek.

Near the center of the column Sergeant Pratt, weary but undefeated, struggled to his feet. "I saw the body of a dead Marine along the trail," Pratt said. "Somehow the remains had been overlooked. I reached down, grabbed the back of the man's collar, and started dragging him along the trail. We staggered forward five to ten meters and stopped for some reason, then lurched forward another few meters. That's the way it went. Lurch and stop, lurch and stop." Nearly exhausted, Pratt simply concentrated on putting one foot down in front of the other, pulling the corpse behind him.

Sergeant Vermillion, at the point position, moved cautiously, mindful of the danger of enemy ambushes and the weary Marines strung out behind him. "It seemed like I wouldn't make twenty-five meters before word came to hold up," Vermillion said. "Either a body had fallen out of its poncho and rolled downhill or a worn-out Marine had collapsed. In a few minutes I'd get the word to continue. That's the way it went all morning."

Doc Polland used the frequent halts to collect moisture-laden leaves. They were not for him. Rather, he carefully gathered the minute amounts of water on the leaves' surface, then dispensed the precious fluid to his thirsty patients.

At the same time that the main body of Bravo started moving, Sergeant Reyes sent a four-man fire team to recover the bodies he had abandoned the previous day. Fifty meters from the perimeter, a blast of AK-47 fire ripped through the patrol. One man died instantly, riddled with bullets, and two others fell badly wounded. Private First Class Charles Tranum ignored the intense enemy rifle fire and crawled to the nearest wounded man. He pulled the Marine to cover, then—determined to save the casualty—hoisted him on his back and stumbled back into Reyes's position.

Sergeant Reyes rounded up a few men and went after the other wounded man. They reached him and pulled him to safety. Reyes wanted to recover the dead body, but the enemy fire halted him. Reluctantly, he ordered his men to pull out.

Just then an enemy soldier rose out of the elephant grass below them and sprayed the Marines with a burst of AK-47 fire. Ahead of Reyes a Marine screamed in pain as a slug of lead tore into his calf and shattered a bone. Reyes cursed and tossed a grenade in the general direction of the enemy solder. He and another man grabbed the new casualty and, with the others, hustled up the trail.

Once back at the perimeter, Reyes hurriedly barked orders: "Saddle up, now! We're moving out. Let's move!"

In minutes the 3d Platoon had gathered up its wounded and all its gear and headed out in the direction of Captain Sayers. As the platoon disappeared around the hillside, an enemy machine gun fired a farewell burst at it. To Reyes's immense relief, the bullets flew wide of their mark.

Captain Sayers's group did not fare as well. The rising sun continued to clear the fog banks, which gave the NVA emplaced on nearby hillsides a clear target. Enemy rounds zinged over the column like swarms of angry bees and forced the Marines to hit the deck frequently. In addition, mortar rounds dropped among the battered Marines, inflicting even more casualties. One blast killed the gallant company rogue, Lance Corporal Darnell.

A short time later Sergeant Reyes's 3d Platoon finally caught up with the main column. Sayers took a few minutes to collect excess water from Reyes's men to give to the wounded, then started the column moving. For the rest of the morning, during breaks in the enemy fire, the column lurched forward, slowly closing on Hill 861.

Lieutenant Colonel Wilder radioed Captain Spivey at dawn and ordered him to take the hill. "I didn't think Wilder had a clear picture of the situation," Spivey said. "He apparently thought my two unhit platoons were enough to drive the enemy from Hill 861. I wasn't so sure but I had my orders."

Spivey radioed Lieutenant Frisbie to start his attack on Hill 861A. The captain planned to send Lieutenant Hanson's 2d Platoon and the remnants of Shoemakers' 1st Platoon to squeeze the NVA from the south side as soon as Frisbie established a toehold on the east side.

In the meantime, Staff Sergeant Shoemaker concentrated on getting help for his wounded. Despite heroic attempts by the corpsmen and volunteers, such as Lance Corporal Croft, at least two of his casualties died during the night. He did not want to lose any more.

At first light Shoemaker issued orders: Ponchos were to be used to carry any wounded who could not walk, and ambulatory cases would be helped as needed. When everyone was ready, the 1st Platoon started downhill.

Seconds later the NVA opened fire. Small-arms fire cracked overhead. Mortar rounds exploded nearby as the enemy gunners sought the range. Shoemaker and his men hit the deck, protecting the wounded as best they could. When the firing ceased they started down again. The lead man made all of fifteen meters before the enemy firing resumed. The Marines again sought cover. In this manner, in leapfrog spurts of ten to twenty meters, Shoemaker's platoon headed toward a medevac site below Captain Spivey's CP.

By this time, on the other side of Hill 861, Lieutenant Frisbie's platoon had felt the fury of the determined enemy, too.

Just after dawn Lance Corporal Vineyard took Captain Spivey's call. The skipper wanted Frisbie. Vineyard passed the handset to the lieutenant. Vineyard, a nineteen year old from Pasadena, California, with less than a year in the Marine Corps and not quite four months with Kilo 3/3, overheard Spivey tell Frisbie to attack the hill. His CP and Shoemaker's platoon were still taking fire, Spivey said. He needed Frisbie to get to the top of the hill to take the pressure off them. As he passed the handset back to Vineyard, Frisbie said, "Radio the squad leaders. We're moving out."

Corporal Bigler's fire team led the way. Because two of his men were new, Bigler again put his buddy, Private First Class Miller, at the point position. Miller, a Baltimore native, had joined the company while it was being refurbished on Okinawa. Since arriving in South Vietnam, Miller repeatedly proved himself to be a solid combat Marine. He had Bigler's complete confidence and, more important, friendship.

As Miller started up the hill, Bigler moved into the slack (number two) position, about ten meters back. Fifteen meters behind Bigler came his squad leader, Corporal Contreras. At the rear of the fire team, the two new men, Pfcs. John Diaz and Gerald McLanahan, moved forward, their M16s at the ready.

Farther down the hill, the rest of Frisbie's 3d Platoon spread out to take up positions in order to move on-line up the elephant grass–covered hillside. The platoon stretched over nearly 150 meters of ground as it started uphill.

Bigler's mouth became drier the farther up the hill he moved. After hearing enemy soldiers talking all night, he knew that they would open fire any second. Every nerve in his body tensed in anticipation of taking a round. Though it was hard to keep walking, Bigler was determined and committed to do his duty.

Up ahead Miller entered an area covered with low scrub. He had advanced just a few meters into the thicket before he spotted two NVA in a listening post (LP) a short distance away. Miller turned and in a dead-pan, very deliberate voice stated, "The enemy is in sight."

Bigler turned to pass the news to Contreras. "We got their LP," he told his squad leader.

Contreras left to carry the word to Frisbie; they were too close to the enemy to use the radio.

Suddenly, the hillside erupted in a hail of enemy gunfire; the NVA had seen the Marines. One burst of AK-47 fire stitched three rounds across Miller's unprotected chest. Though stunned, he triggered a burst from his M16 as he fell. His high-powered rounds killed the two NVA in the LP.

At the first blast of enemy fire, Bigler rushed forward to help his buddy. He made two steps before several enemy rounds slammed into his helmet. Those barely registered before another round hit his chin strap swivel and burned across his cheek. Bits of metal exploded into Bigler's face. The force of the hits flung him backward. "As I fell I was sure I was dead," Bigler recalled.

But he was not. He lay there stunned, his ears ringing, his face stinging from the embedded bullet fragments. As he stared upward, dozens of enemy grenades flew overhead to erupt farther downhill with sharp cracks.

At the rear of the platoon, the initial rifle fire startled the command group. "The volume of enemy fire surprised me," Frisbie said. "There were a lot more of them up there than I'd been expecting." Not far from him a rifleman suddenly went down, his chest riddled by a well-aimed burst of AK-47 fire. The Marine screamed in pain as he thrashed in the grass. An M60 machine gunner raised his weapon to fire uphill but took a round in the head before he could get off a single shot. He fell without a sound.

A few meters to Frisbie's right, Lance Corporal Yoshida dropped to one knee and scanned the hillside for a target. He spotted a tree stump pointing jaggedly skyward near the top of the hill, its trunk lying beside it. If I were an NVA, I'd take up a position there, Yoshida reasoned. He cocked his grenade launcher and plopped a round at the stump. It exploded at the tree's base with a reassuring blast. Hoping to get any hidden NVA, he fired several more rounds around the tree.

As the line of Marines continued uphill, the enemy's grenades began to fall among them. Their explosions drove the men to the ground. Lance Corporal Vineyard hit the deck on Frisbie's left side. Six feet away Pfc. Dale Carmichael lay in a prone position, calmly firing his M16 at fleeting glimpses of NVA. An enemy grenade rolled unnoticed alongside his head. Before Vineyard could shout a warning, the grenade went off. Carmichael died instantly.

Overwhelmed by the sight, Vineyard barely heard Captain Spivey's voice coming over the radio. "Attack!" Spivey yelled. "Keep attacking. You've got to take that hill."

Vineyard turned to pass the handset to Frisbie.

At that instant Frisbie became aware of something on the ground in front of him. He could not tell what it was, but it hissed as if a fuse were burning. He scrunched down, instinctively throwing his right arm up to protect his face. The device exploded with an ear-shattering blast. Jagged pieces of metal ripped into his right arm and peppered his face.

The same blast got both Yoshida and Vineyard. Yoshida felt as though he had been hit with a baseball bat. Hunks of red-hot shrapnel tore into his left side, shoulder, back, and eye, blinding him. One small piece of hot metal embedded itself deep under his right thumbnail, causing pain so excruciating he could not even cock his M79.

Vineyard caught a load of shrapnel, too. "It felt as if someone had slammed my left hand with an ax," he said. "For a few minutes I was too afraid to look at the damage. Finally, I opened my eyes. Although several fingers had been blown off, I was greatly relieved to see that my hand was still there."

Through his mental fog, Frisbie heard a voice calling him. "Lieutenant, you're hit," it said. He looked to his right. Yoshida was talking to him. "So are you," Frisbie responded, amazed at the amount of blood running down the enlisted man's face.

"Yeah, I know," Yoshida replied, then rolled over to fumble through his gear for a bandage.

Although he was wounded, Frisbie remained determined to lead his platoon and take the hill. He staggered to his feet. He picked up a discarded M16 from somewhere, fired a few bursts uphill, and shouted words of encouragement to the men near him. As he moved forward, a sharp pain in his right arm stopped him in his tracks. The sight of the jagged end of a bone protruding from the wound stunned him. Gritting his teeth, he shifted his rifle to his left hand and kept firing.

Near the top of the hill, Bigler slowly regained his senses. As his mind cleared he could think only of his buddy. "I didn't know if Miller was alive or dead, but either way I wasn't going to leave him up there," Bigler said. He started crawling uphill through the elephant grass.

The NVA spotted him almost immediately and unleashed a barrage of grenades. Bigler rolled left and right as best he could, avoiding the blasts. In between he fired his M16 at the fleeting glimpses of enemy soldiers moving above him. Then his rifle jammed. "I had no cleaning rod, so I couldn't force the jammed cartridge from the breech," Bigler recalled. "I was helpless. Before I could do anything, three enemy grenades came sailing in. One plunked down to my left. The second rolled past my left side. The third rolled to a stop against my right thigh. I decided to jump away to my right. I was a half second too late."

All three grenades went off at the same time. The triple blasts rocked Bigler. Blood streamed from both his eardrums and a gaping hole in his right thigh. I'm dying, he told himself while marveling at how calm he suddenly felt.

Then he heard Miller calling to him. "I'm hit, Biggy. I'm hit."

"Be quiet, be still," Bigler called back. "They'll hear you."

Then, without a sound, Pfc. Jerry J. Moran, a mortar man, suddenly appeared at Bigler's side. "I was surprised because normally the mortar crews stayed near the CP. I didn't know what Moran was doing this far forward until he started putting a field dressing on my torn leg. Apparently, the mortar men had been detailed as corpsmen."

As Moran worked, Bigler told him where Miller was. "I'll try to get him," Moran said reassuringly.

Just as suddenly as he had appeared, Moran was gone. Bigler never saw him again.

Still concerned about his buddy, Bigler tried several times to crawl up to Miller. Each time, a burst of enemy fire across his back halted him. Frustrated, Bigler pounded his fists into the dirt.

Lieutenant Frisbie, meanwhile, continued to push his men forward. Despite his leadership, despite his shouted orders, the attack faltered. All around him Marines were down. The enemy weapons chattered nearly nonstop. Grenades and mortars exploded all across the face of the hill. The NVA clearly had the upper hand.

Just then Frisbie staggered and fell. Blood gushed from a hole in his right shoulder. "Whether I'd been hit again or just hadn't noticed this wound before I didn't know," Frisbie said. "What I did know was that if we didn't pull out then we wouldn't make it."

"Pull back," he called out. "Pull back."

With that, Frisbie started back down the hill. Lance Corporal Yoshida joined him. Yoshida had tried to wrap a bandage around his bleeding head, but the pain from his injured thumb was so intense that he could not tighten the dressing. As a result, the end of the cloth dangled free, flapping in the breeze, while rivulets of blood coursed down his face.

From his prone position, Lance Corporal Vineyard got the word to pull back at the same time Frisbie and Yoshida, both covered in blood, went by. As enemy rounds snapped through the air above him, Vineyard crawled down Hill 861. Not until an intervening hillock offered some protection did he rise and join the knots of wounded Marines staggering toward a safe landing zone.

Back at the top of the hill, Bigler felt someone pulling at his leg. He resisted, afraid the enemy wanted him as a prisoner. Then he heard Corporal Contreras talking to him.

"C'mon, we're getting outta here," Contreras said.

Bigler nodded. But first he described to Contreras as best he could where Miller lay. "You gotta get him," Bigler demanded. "You gotta get him."

Contreras assured him he would. Then Bigler started downhill. He used his jammed M16 as a crutch, grateful it served some useful purpose. He had to crawl a few times to avoid enemy fire. Along the way he picked up another jammed M16 to use as a second crutch. Near the base of the hill he joined the stream of men scurrying to safety. "I could not believe the number of casualties," he remembered. "We really got our asses kicked."

Lance Corporal Vineyard felt the same way. "I remember thinking, this is a real whipping," he said. All around him wounded men headed away from the hill in search of safety.

Most of them did not know where to find safety. They just kept walking away from the hill. Lieutenant Frisbie felt as though he had walked for miles before he reached a spot where wounded Marines sat in a cluster, waiting patiently for a medevac. Frisbie had no idea who had radioed for a chopper or when it would get there. He simply joined the other wounded.

Lance Corporal Yoshida plopped down on the ground near Frisbie. Though badly wounded, he could not help but feel elated that his part in this ugly war had ended. I'm going home, he thought, and an eye seemed a small price to pay for survival.

After a painfully long wait, a lone CH-46 finally chattered into view. It landed and dropped its ramp. The most seriously wounded boarded first. Vineyard noticed that the aircraft's gunner looked scared to death. What the hell has he got to be scared of? Vineyard wondered.

Corporal Bigler lay sprawled on the ground not far from Vineyard, wracked by pain from his wounds and nearly overcome by guilt for not being able to save his friend Miller. "Every time a new casualty staggered in or was carried into the LZ, I looked to see if it was Miller," Bigler said. "It never was. Soon a couple of Marines carried me onto a chopper. I yelled over to some guys helping other wounded to ask if they'd seen Miller. They hadn't." Then Bigler was inside the aircraft; the ramp closed, the beat of the rotors increased, and he was gone.

Throughout the rest of the day, additional helicopters dropped out of the sky to evacuate the 3d Platoon's wounded and dead. Not until 1900 were the last members of Lieutenant Frisbie's platoon returned to Khe Sanh.

At 0830 Captain Spivey received a radio message telling him that the 3d Platoon's attack had failed. Even worse, the message said Lieutenant Frisbie was down and his platoon had taken heavy casualties. Kilo 3/3 would not be doing any more fighting that day.

Spivey radioed Lieutenant Colonel Wilder's CP. "We've taken a lot of casualties," Spivey reported. "We don't have the horsepower to take the hill."

The news shocked Wilder. "Up until then I hadn't really known just how strong the NVA were," Wilder recalled. "Before, they'd never had the forces to hold a position. I figured if they had enough men to hold the hill and chew up two companies, I needed more help."

Wilder told Spivey, "Hold your position. I'll send you some help."

Wilder ordered his operations officer to bring reinforcements forward from the Khe Sanh Combat Base. Next he radioed the 3d Marines operations center to update them on the situation on Hill 861. "If I was going to clear those hills of the NVA, I'd need more than the one extra rifle company I had," he said.

That one extra company was Capt. Jerrald E. Giles's Kilo Company, 3d Battalion, 9th Marines. The previous afternoon it had been on perimeter watch at Camp Carroll, the Marines' artillery base on Route 9 west of Dong Ha. As the 3d Marine Division's Bald Eagle (company-size reaction force), that was their mission until they were needed somewhere. The word that Kilo 3/9 was needed at Khe Sanh reached Captain Giles late on 25 April.

Giles grabbed his company gunny, GySgt. John C. Hatfield. "Get the men saddled up. We're moving out now!" he told him. Giles then ran to the operations center to learn what he could about his new mission.

Unfortunately, the ops officer did not have much to tell him, only that a couple of companies had run into a large NVA force near Khe Sanh. Giles was to help them as ordered. He would be opconned to 3/3. Choppers were inbound to lift them to Khe Sanh.

By 1800 the men of Kilo 3/9 were disembarking from CH-46s at Khe Sanh's airstrip. Gunny Hatfield barked out orders. In minutes the troops were formed up and headed to their night bivouac site just outside the main perimeter.

Kilo 3/9 was one of the best companies operating along the DMZ, and the main reason for that distinction was Captain Giles. Born in Spokane, Washington, in 1935, Giles took his commission through the University of Idaho's naval ROTC program. One of his early assignments brought him to South Vietnam to survey its beaches. For months he and his eight-member recon team, none of whom wore military uniforms, insignia, or any identifying marks, traveled the coast to map and chart the shore. A tour as a Marine Corps aide at the White House followed before Giles volunteered for service in the war zone, eager to stop the spread of communism.

The gung-ho captain arrived in-country in July 1966 and joined Kilo 3/9 near An Hoa, south of Da Nang. For the next six months, he and

Kilo chased Viet Cong guerrillas through rice paddies and jungled low-lands. In January 1967 the company rotated to Okinawa to be retrained and outfitted with the new M16. When it returned to South Vietnam six weeks later, it joined the rest of the 9th Marines then operating just south of the DMZ.

Eight months of combat had jaded Giles's attitude toward his coun-try's efforts in South Vietnam. He questioned the worthiness of spend-ing American lives to battle insurgents who wanted only to govern their own country. The Americans never held terrain objectives; rather, they fought, died, and moved on. The wasted lives troubled him deeply. Con-vinced that his combat experience could save lives, Giles refused every offer of a job in the rear. He would stay with Kilo as long as he could, de-termined to bring as many of his men home alive as possible. His Marines loved him for his devotion to them. They would follow him to Hanoi if he asked.

Kilo 3/9 spent a quiet morning at the combat base. Giles and Hatfield both began to think that maybe Kilo would not be needed. They might even be back at Camp Carroll in time for chow in the mess hall. Then Wilder's S-3 radioed. They were going forward.

Giles and his company arrived at Lieutenant Colonel Wilder's CP just after noon. Wilder's S-3 gave Giles a quick briefing. His mission was to help Kilo 3/3 disengage from the enemy and bring out its casualties. There was no time to waste. Giles immediately sent one of his platoons to link up with Lieutenant Frisbie's platoon. He led his other two pla-toons up the hill toward Captain Spivey's CP.

Kilo 3/9 took no enemy fire as it moved up the side of Hill 861. As he closed on Kilo 3/3's night position, Giles noticed two Marines towing a bag of gear trotting downhill toward him. Neither of the men carried weapons or wore a flak jacket. As they drew closer Giles saw stark fear on their faces. Then he noticed something else: It was not a bag of gear they pulled behind them, it was a dead Marine.

Too startled to question them, Giles stepped aside as the men rushed past, the corpse's bloated features burning a lasting image into his mind.

"Jesus," he muttered to Gunny Hatfield. "That's a pretty shitty way to bring a Marine down."

"Skipper," responded the hardened Marine noncommissioned officer, "that's just the way it is. This guy is dead, others up the hill aren't. We're here to save the living."

Kilo 3/9 continued upward. Its Marines did not know what they would find. Then, as the company neared the battle site, Pfc. Gordon J. Fenlon, a nineteen year old from Green Bay, Wisconsin, saw bodies in the underbrush, Marine bodies. "I saw several crumpled beside their broken down M16s," Fenlon recalled. A cleaning rod protruded from the barrel of one rifle, grim evidence of the owner's futile efforts to clear a jam.

Another nineteen year old, LCpl. Robert W. Stewart, of St. Petersburg, Florida, saw the bodies, too. Stewart, an artillery FO from Foxtrot 2/12 attached to Kilo, remembered, "First we saw some abandoned gear. Then we continued on up and we could see the bodies in the grass."

Stewart hoped the rescue operation would not last too long. He was near the end of his tour but had recently volunteered to spend another six months in-country. He had a thirty-day leave coming as a result, and he badly needed the break from the war.

A few minutes later, Giles's point man met up with the lead elements of Shoemaker's platoon. The sight of the fresh Marines greatly relieved Shoemaker. His platoon's eighteen-hour ordeal was nearly over. While Giles's corpsmen tended to Shoemaker's most seriously wounded, Shoemaker helped organize carrying parties for the dead. There were no stretchers, so the bodies were rolled into ponchos. Less than an hour later, the two Kilo companies started down Hill 861.

Stewart and his radioman, Pfc. John A. Krohn, a twenty-year-old Chicago draftee, picked up a poncho bearing a bloated body. The corpse weighed so much that they could barely carry it. But they struggled.

Private First Class Fenlon had a hard time, too. Though he had been in South Vietnam since October and experienced a good amount of action, this was the worst he had seen. He could not believe the number of casualties.

Suddenly, a Huey helicopter roared directly overhead, its multiple machine guns blazing away at a target on the top of the hill. Greatly concerned that the aerial gunners might mistake his Marines for NVA, Shoemaker anxiously radioed Spivey. "We're on the gun line of that Huey. Call him off now," Shoemaker roared into the mike. "Have him make his runs east to west."

Spivey relayed the urgent message. Shoemaker breathed a sigh of relief when the Huey changed course.

The movement downhill proceeded slowly. Rain began to fall, turning the well-trod trail into a carpet of slick mud. Marines slipped and fell, dropping the corpses they carried. It was a struggle to recover the bodies, but both Giles and Shoemaker were determined not to leave anyone behind.

Halfway down the trail someone called out, "Gooks!" On a nearby ridge finger a squad of enemy soldiers maneuvered to flank the retreating column. Shoemaker unslung his M16, raised it to his shoulder, and took aim. With an enemy soldier in his sights, he squeezed the trigger. The man crumpled. The other NVA fled. Shoemaker grunted with satisfaction. Although the range was only about three hundred meters, Shoemaker was soon being praised by his men for his "thousand-meter kill." The rest of the trek passed without any action.

A Navy chaplain stood near the casualty collection point at Wilder's CP. The chaplain approached Lance Corporal Croft as he set down the end of the poncho he had been carrying. "Good job, Marine, good job," the priest said.

"That really pissed me off," Croft said. "It wasn't a good job. We'd been whacked pretty good. I took my frustrations out on the chaplain. I guess my tirade surprised him, because he didn't say anything as I cut loose, cussing him out. When I finished I just walked away and joined up with the others waiting to hump back to Khe Sanh."

Staff Sergeant Shoemaker felt great relief at being off Hill 861. The havoc he had witnessed was the worst of his tour. By the looks on the faces of the Marines standing around watching the bodies being laid out, it was the worst that most of them had seen as well. But Shoemaker could not dwell on the losses. And he could not let the surviving members of his platoon dwell on them, either. He barked out orders: "Let's go. Stand tall. Square yourself away. You're still Marines. Get your gear together. I want everyone ready to move out in five minutes. Five minutes. Let's go."

His company's inability to take Hill 861 frustrated and disappointed Captain Spivey. Kilo 3/3 had suffered nineteen men dead, four missing and presumed dead, and forty-two wounded. And what did they have to show for it? Nothing. Not a damn thing, he thought bitterly. Not a damn thing.

But he could not dwell on the slaughter, either. He oversaw the evacuation of the casualties, reconciled rosters with Shoemaker and Hanson, then ordered what remained of his company back to the combat base. It spent the night there before being ferried to Dong Ha for an infusion of replacements and rebuilding.

Kilo 3/3 might have been finished with Hill 861, but Bravo 1/9 was not. At midmorning the column started up a small knoll about five hundred meters west of Hill 861's summit. Lieutenant Carter's platoon had the point, Staff Sergeant Burns's 2d Platoon and the CP group were in the center, and Staff Sergeant Reyes's 3d Platoon brought up the rear.

Just as Carter's platoon reached a ravine along the base of the knoll, an NVA automatic weapon emplaced on a nearby hillside spat out several bursts of fire. The heavy slugs tore into the platoon, wounding five, including Lieutenant Carter. Seconds later enemy fire raked the entire column. Two men in Staff Sergeant Burns's platoon went down; one, Sgt. Kenneth W. Orton, was nearly cut in half by a machine gun burst. Another man, Lance Corporal Puelo, took the enemy gun under fire with his M60. He got three NVA before they turned their fire on him. In an instant Puelo took three hits and his gun was blown away.

Staff Sergeant Reyes ordered Corporal Montgomery, Private First Class Ryan, and Pfc. Shelly Egly forward to take the pressure off Carter's platoon. The trio made it to the edge of the ravine, where they took up firing positions. "I was pointing out targets to Egly when I heard a sound like a bullet slamming into a tree," Ryan said. "I turned to say something to Egly but froze. A round had hit him square in the head. But he was still alive. He kept pushing his helmet back, spilling his brains down his face."

Ryan grabbed his buddy's hand. "Stop it. Stop it," he pleaded. But Egly kept flaying away. Finally, Ryan pinned Egly's hands down.

From their position in the ravine, Carter's men had a hard time bringing fire to bear on the enemy above them. Fortunately, one of the radiomen was able to raise a passing flight of Marine jets. The two aircraft responded to his desperate call for help by roaring earthward and unleashing a cluster of 250-pound bombs on the NVA positions. Then, turning 360 degrees in a tight, ear-splitting bank, they raced back to strafe the adjacent hillside. When they were finished, an Air Force jet lined up to take a swing at the enemy. Unfortunately, one of his rockets went wild; it hit less than a hundred meters from Sayers. A chunk of American metal slashed across the captain's neck.

From his prone position Corporal Montgomery fired a burst from his M16 at the jet.

"Hey, knock it off," a nearby sergeant ordered. "You can't fire at our planes."

"Bullshit," Montgomery snorted. "If they're firing at me, I'm gonna fire back. You'd better get on the radio and call them off."

Someone did. The jet disappeared before it could cause any more friendly casualties.

Despite the errant rocket, the air strikes silenced the enemy. Captain Sayers decided to use the lull to call for another medevac. If the chopper got in before the NVA recovered, he might be able to get several of his most seriously wounded out.

Sayers ordered Staff Sergeant Burns to set up an LZ. While one of Burns's squads went to secure the site, the platoon sergeant assembled several groups of men to carry the casualties. He warned them to move out quickly once the chopper touched down; they would not have long before the NVA dropped mortars on the LZ.

At 1315 they heard the incoming CH-46. In minutes the helicopter hovered over the LZ. Burns popped a smoke grenade and waved the aircraft in. The waiting Marines gripped the ponchos carrying the wounded. As soon as the heavy machine touched down, the litter teams rushed forward. Just one team had dropped its casualty inside the helicopter before the first NVA mortar shell hit. The remaining litter teams raced for cover as more of the powerful shells whistled down from the sky. The chopper lifted off in a cloud of enemy tracers.

Corporal Montgomery struggled with the heavy poncho his team carried as they sought cover. They had almost made it when a brace of mortar shells crashed behind them. The twin blasts threw Montgomery into the brush. When he came to a few minutes later, blood flowed from shrapnel wounds in his right thigh, right hand, left arm, left buttocks, and the right side of his neck.

"I looked around. No one else was there," he recalled. "Mortar shells were still exploding along the ridgeline. I was afraid I'd been out a while and had been overlooked in a withdrawal, so I crawled on all fours to a nearby bomb crater. I hurt too bad to go any farther so I started calling for help. Two Marines hiding in another crater answered. As soon as I told them I was wounded, they crawled over and patched me up."

"Where is everybody?" Montgomery asked. "Where did they go? Are they all right?"

The two Marines told him what they knew, which was not much. Then Montgomery asked them for a favor. The two Marines exchanged puzzled glances, then nodded their agreement. Montgomery pulled a camera from his pack and handed it to one of the men. With mortar shells crashing behind them, the man took Montgomery's picture. What a souvenir that'll make, he thought.

As soon as the mortars stopped, Montgomery's two new friends helped him back to the main body. Minutes later, without a word, everyone began to move out. The few remaining able-bodied Marines grabbed the wounded and dead and started humping. The beleaguered company surged forward, now more a mob than a column of well-disciplined Marines. The men moved with a single-minded goal: get out of the killing zone.

The NVA were not going to let that happen.

About ten men made it safely over the ridgeline before the mortars came again. In rapid succession, more than a dozen high-explosive shells wracked the column. Marines dove left and right, seeking cover on the barren hillside. Still, chunks of hot metal found flesh. Up and down the column men yelped in pain; some were wounded for the second time that day. More than half a dozen freshly injured moaned. Desperate cries of "Corpsman! Corpsman!" echoed across the hillside.

This attack pushed Bravo 1/9 to its limit. Burdened with more casualties than it could carry, without food for two days, with little water, low on ammo, and without any prospect of evading the enemy, the unit saw no sense in continuing. The ambulatory and uninjured might make it to Khe Sanh if the dead and the badly wounded were left behind. But Captain Sayers never considered this. If anyone had suggested it, he would have refused; Bravo Company would succeed or fail as a unit. That was the way it was; there were no other options. Sayers radioed Lieutenant Colonel Wilder's CP. "We can't move anymore," he told Wilder's operations officer. "We'll stay here and fight 'em off as long as we can."

No sense of bravado permeated Sayers's statement. No hint of "John Wayne" Hollywood heroics lay behind the words. He had delivered a simple statement of fact. Bravo had been beaten, but it was not defeated. The survivors would sell their lives for a high price, taking as many enemy soldiers with them as they could.

Lieutenant Colonel Wilder had other ideas. No way would a Marine rifle company be wiped out on his watch. He sent for Captain Giles.

The summons reached Giles just as he was settling in for the evening. He quickly made his way to the CP. Wilder wasted no time in setting out Giles's mission. "Bravo One Nine's trapped out there," he said, jabbing his index finger at his map to indicate Sayers's approximate location. "They're hurt and can't move. You've got to get to them and bring them in."

Without hesitation Giles responded with a strong "Aye, aye, sir" and returned to his company. He called for his most experienced platoon leader, twenty-three-year-old Lt. John B. Woodall. Giles briefed Woodall on the situation, then said, "Get your men saddled up. Have them carry extra water and rations. We'll be moving out in one zero minutes!"

The Marines of Woodall's platoon headed out on their second rescue mission of the day, guided by the last rays of the setting sun. If they avoided the NVA, the linkup with Bravo 1/9 would occur within a few hours.

The news that the rescue column was on the way buoyed Sayers's spirits. If the Kilo Marines made it to him, his wounded would be cared for, the dead tended to, and the living fed, all within a few hours. To guide Giles to Bravo, Sayers ordered Lieutenant Carter to take a small patrol out to meet him. Though in pain from his wounds, Carter rounded up a dozen Marines and set off, with Sergeant Vermillion again at the point.

Carter's little band set a quick pace. They made good progress until they descended into a gully choked with vegetation. As Vermillion started up the far embankment, a burst of enemy fire erupted in front of him. He hit the deck and sprayed a magazine from his M16 at the unseen enemy as he rolled. Behind him, the others dove for cover as enemy bullets cut the air around them. Carter had no choice. "Pull back," he ordered.

The desperate Marines did not need to be told twice. They hurriedly retraced their steps up the back side of the gully. As they fled, Private First Class Moore stopped and turned to cover their retreat by firing off a whole magazine on automatic. He was halfway through a second magazine when he felt someone tugging at his collar. Doc Polland yelled in his ear, "C'mon. You're not gonna die here today."

With that the two men turned and ran up the hillside to join the others. The patrol backtracked for nearly half an hour, anxious to put as much room between itself and the enemy as it could. Not until it had nearly reached its starting point did it halt. The men spent several minutes catching their breath.

Soon they set off on another route. In the growing darkness they hugged the vegetation, moving safely in the shadow of tree stands and bamboo groves. Near the top of one ridgeline, Vermillion's keen sixth sense detected movement ahead. He signaled a halt. An enemy patrol, some of its members pulling a wheeled artillery piece, soon sauntered by. Carter's patrol silently melted into a bamboo grove, unwilling to challenge the enemy force. Fifteen anxious minutes later, the NVA had moved out of range. Vermillion signaled the patrol to continue.

Then a hard, pounding rain began to fall. Although it cut visibility, the Marines welcomed the first fresh water they had had in days. Carter halted the patrol while his men turned their helmets upside down to catch the needed liquid. Once refreshed they resumed their trek. During a brief lull in the rain, Moore spotted a column of men moving toward them. He knew instinctively they were Marines.

Carter guided Giles's column by retracing his patrol's route back to Sayers's defensive perimeter. Once there Lieutenant Woodall's corpsmen and Marines spread out among Bravo's wounded to give aid and pass out water.

Lance Corporal Stewart remembered the look of defeat on the faces of Bravo's survivors. "They'd been through a lot and it showed." And he remembered the bodies. "One was just a torso with a gold crucifix strangely out of place on its chest. Another man had obviously been hit with a .50-caliber, for he'd been torn nearly in half."

The two captains worked on a plan to return to Hill 861. Because of the heavy downpour, Sayers and Giles agreed to wait until morning to start the march out. They radioed their decision to the 3/3 CP.

Wilder exploded. "Absolutely not. Get out now!"

Wilder well knew the hazards of a night move through enemy territory, but leaving the two units out there presented more dangers.

"Get movin' now," he repeated.

Staff Sergeant Burns took a leading role in getting the column organized. He ordered some of Woodall's men to hack down nearby trees and bamboo stalks for stretcher poles while others were detailed to gather up all the extra equipment and gear. It was nearly midnight before the combined group set out. Every able-bodied man except the point and rear squads either carried the corner of a makeshift stretcher, helped one of the walking wounded, or humped extra gear. Private First Class Ryan, for example, slung seven M16s across his back. Even the radiomen, usually burdened enough with their PRC-25s, carried people on stretchers.

Stewart and Krohn each buddied up with a Bravo casualty. Stewart recalled that the man he helped thanked him repeatedly. "Man, thanks for coming. We were nearly out of ammo. Thanks, man."

Lance Corporal Arthur V. Gennaro, a nineteen year old from Passaic, New Jersey, with nine months' combat experience, picked up the corner of a poncho. "It was hard to walk in the mud with all that weight," he said. "It seemed like we only took a few steps before someone called 'Halt' because someone had slipped and fallen, or a body fell out."

Not far behind Gennaro, another Kilo veteran struggled with his burden. Twenty-year-old West Virginian LCpl. William Van Devander carried a body locked into a grotesque position by rigor mortis. As a result, it frequently fell off the poncho. With the others he lifted the decomposing body back onto the makeshift litter, then stepped forward carefully, hoping the body would not fall out again. But it did. Many times.

At the rear of the column, Staff Sergeant Burns listened to some of his men grumble about the rain. He welcomed it. It not only provided much-needed water, it kept the NVA from pinpointing the Marines' position. To be sure, enemy gunners threw a few mortar shells in the general direction of the column, but they landed so wide that it was obvious the enemy had lost track of Bravo 1/9.

The Marines humped throughout the night. With only an occasional break they trudged through thick mud, up and down ridge fingers, across gullies, and along ankle-busting hillside routes. Every step brought them closer to the safety of 3/3's CP on Hill 700. The men moved as robots; nary a word passed among them. Thick, predawn fog cut visibility to just ten meters in any direction, but still the Marines pushed on. Somehow Woodall's point man kept his bearings, skillfully guiding the column through the featureless night.

Finally, at 0500 on 27 April, the column crested a long ridge finger that pointed right at Wilder's CP. Thirty minutes later the Marines of Bravo 1/9 and Kilo 3/9 entered friendly lines. Navy corpsmen rushed to tend the many wounded. As soon as the morning fog burned off, helicopters arrived to carry Bravo's casualties to the evacuation hospital in Da Nang. Kilo's Marines moved over to their company's perimeter. They wanted to down some rations and catch a little shut-eye. They also hoped to erase from their minds the horror they had witnessed. But none ever would.

Bravo's able-bodied members dumped the extra gear and scrambled around looking for food and other needed items. Private First Class Ryan sauntered up to a Marine standing off by himself. "Hey, buddy," he called out. "You gotta smoke?"

"Sure" came the response.

In the match's flare, Ryan realized he had bummed a cigarette from a colonel.

"Sorry, sir," he offered.

"That's all right, son."

The number of Marines encamped around the base of Hill 700 impressed both Ryan and Lance Corporal Lease. To them it seemed that nearly every square foot of ground was covered. The barbed wire surrounding the battalion CP and the dozens and dozens of pallets loaded with supplies caught Lease's attention. Something really big must be up, he thought.

As soon as the wounded were evacuated, Bravo's dead were loaded aboard helicopters for the short flight to the Khe Sanh Combat Base. Someone approached Captain Sayers and told him trucks were waiting to carry Bravo's survivors back to the combat base. He refused the offer. "We walked out and we'll walk back in," he said.

The announcement did not please everyone. It pissed off Private First Class Ryan, for one. After what we've been through, a ride would be nice, he thought.

At the combat base, Bravo Company faced the gruesome task of identifying its dead and reconciling its roster. Doc Polland had tried to identify each casualty with a tag as soon as possible after death, but some of the tags were destroyed in the rain or were lost as the remains tumbled downhill into thickets. Accompanied by Sergeants Pratt and Reyes and Doc Polland, Captain Sayers positively identified every corpse that had been carried out.

Sergeant Pratt approached the horrifying job with the stoicism of a dedicated noncommissioned officer (NCO). Although the corpses were swollen and bloated, their features and skin color distorted, Pratt discovered several buddies among the bodies. He vowed then and there never to make close friends in his unit again.

Only when convinced that he had accounted for every man in Bravo did Sayers turn his casualty report in to Wilder's S-1 (personnel) officer. It was a long list. Twenty-four Bravo 1/9 Marines had died on the slopes of Hill 861. Eight more were missing, and 46 received wounds severe enough to warrant evacuation. Of the 110 Bravo Marines who had been trapped on the hill, less than 40 returned to Khe Sanh uninjured. The devastation hit every platoon. Staff Sergeant Burns, for example, started out with 21; he and 7 others walked back to Khe Sanh.

Late on the afternoon of 27 April, the survivors of Bravo 1/9 boarded a C-130 for the brief flight from Khe Sanh to Dong Ha. From there trucks carried them to Camp Carroll. Conditions at the artillery base were luxurious compared to what Bravo had experienced for the past three months. Although the men still had to pull guard duty, the threat of enemy action was almost nonexistent. Tents provided shelter from the elements. The men could sleep off the ground in bunks. Chow was served in mess halls where the men could eat all they wanted. Sergeant Vermillion, for one, spent some time getting reacquainted with the milk machines in the mess hall.

But it would not last for long. Over the next few days Bravo would get a new CO and dozens of replacements. Within two weeks it would be back in the field hunting the NVA. After only a few weeks, the horror of Khe Sanh would become a distant memory.

The swarm of Marines around Hill 700 that had impressed Lease and Ryan resulted from Lieutenant Colonel Wilder's situation report to Colonel Lanigan on the morning of 26 April. As soon as Lanigan read the message, he knew he had to reinforce Khe Sanh if he wanted to secure the hills around the base. Fortunately, he had a fresh unit to dispatch. The 2d Battalion, 3d Marines, newly assigned to the Special Landing Force, had just started Operation Beacon Hill northwest of Hue along Highway 1, an area known as the Street Without Joy.

Lanigan did not hesitate. "Send them up immediately," he ordered.

In a rice paddy not far from Hue, 2d Lt. Ord Elliott's platoon of Hotel BLT 2/3 maneuvered against a Viet Cong–held village. In the four days since they had come ashore, Elliott's Marines had done nothing but chase an elusive foe who refused to stand and fight. Until this morning.

A flurry of sniper rounds had cracked over the platoon soon after it disembarked from helicopters. The Marines found cover from which they could return the fire. After taking several casualties, Elliott called for a medevac. Soon after the medevac flew off, a Huey gunship came on station over Elliott's platoon. The helicopter fired rockets as it swooped down on the village. For eighteen-year-old LCpl. Wayne L. Ithier, of Hicksville, New York, who had joined Hotel in January, it was a thrilling sight.

"This was the first time I'd seen a Huey in action," he recalled. "It was cool. They hit the gooks with tremendous rocket and machine gun fire."

Eager to tangle with the enemy, Elliott readied his men for an assault. Just then his radioman tapped him on the shoulder. "Hotel Six for you, sir." Elliott took the handset.

"Pull back. Choppers are coming in for you," Elliott's CO, Capt. Raymond Madonna, ordered.

Elliott reacted with disbelief. "Say again, Six," he requested.

Madonna did so.

He should not have, but Elliott asked, "Why? We're in the middle of a firefight." "We're needed elsewhere. Move to the landing zone. Now!"

Elliott immediately began the difficult task of disengaging his platoon. In short order, though, the men had moved to the LZ, about three hundred meters away. While the Marines waited, an occasional sniper round snapped overhead.

Soon a flight of choppers appeared on the horizon. As the aircraft circled overhead, Elliott's men moved into position for loading. Suddenly, there was a huge explosion. "I went flying through the air," Lance Corporal Ithier remembered. "I landed in a heap a few feet away. My ears were ringing badly and I had a lot of pressure in my head."

Ithier slowly rolled over to see what had happened. A Marine sat upright a few feet away, his bloodstained hands gripping the slippery intestines that bulged from his torn abdomen. Lance Corporal Perry L. Peoples lay crumpled on the ground, obviously dead. Ithier did not know it, but Peoples had stepped on a mine.

One of the NCOs helped Ithier to his feet. "My ears were still ringing and I felt like I was in a fog," Ithier said. The NCO helped him aboard a CH-46. Inside, a corpsman pulled a piece of shrapnel from Ithier's hand and wrapped a dressing around it, but he could not do anything for Ithier's concussion.

The helicopters carried Elliott's platoon and the rest of Hotel BLT 2/3 to Phu Bai, ten kilometers south of Hue. A flurry of activity greeted them. Marines rushed back and forth across the assembly area, carrying gear and distributing ammo and rations. Several C-130 cargo planes sat on the runway.

Lieutenant Elliott and his platoon were directed to a line of Marines disappearing into the bowels of a C-130. As Elliott shuffled forward, he could not help but wonder if the day's tragedy was not a precursor of things to come.

Chapter Six

Lieutenant Colonel Earl R. "Pappy" Delong took command of the 2d Battalion, 3d Marines, in the middle of a vicious firefight early on the morning of 1 March 1967. One week earlier he had turned over 3/3 to Lieutenant Colonel Wilder to become the executive officer (XO) of the 3d Marines under Colonel Lanigan. Delong's eight months at the helm of 3/3 had added to his reputation as an outstanding Marine officer who commanded in the style of his mentor, the legendary Lt. Gen. Lewis W. "Chesty" Puller. The command of 2/3, though, would challenge Delong unlike any earlier assignment he had had, and add a third Silver Star award for his personal gallantry in action to the ones he had earned in World War II and Korea.

The 2d Battalion, 3d Marines, landed at Red Beach outside Da Nang in April 1965, one of the first units committed to the ground war in South Vietnam. The battalion spent its first eight months fighting Viet Cong guerrillas around Da Nang. That was followed by two months on "the float" as part of the Special Landing Force before the battalion rejoined its parent unit at Da Nang in March 1966. When III MAF increased the forces along the DMZ in late 1966, the 3d Marines' three battalions moved north.

Combat action against the NVA was light during 2/3's first few months in Quang Tri Province. By the time the battalion was told in February 1967 that it would again serve with the SLF after a month of retraining on Okinawa, many of its members had come to believe that the enemy had withdrawn back across the DMZ. Until 27 February.

On that morning a recon team had become embroiled with a large force of NVA about five kilometers north of Camp Carroll, 2/3's base.

Unable to extract itself, the team called for help. Colonel Lanigan dispatched a nearby rifle company, Lima 3/4, to its aid, but Lima's CO soon reported that he was unable to advance due to the difficult terrain.

Colonel Lanigan now faced a dilemma that would plague Marine commanders throughout the war: a shortage of troops. Lanigan had no real reserve forces; nearly all his rifle companies were already committed. But he had to do something. He could not let the recon team be overrun. He had no choice but to turn to 2/3, then in the middle of its relocation to Okinawa. All of the battalion that remained at Camp Carroll was Golf Company, two platoons of Foxtrot, and a token command group. Lanigan ordered Golf Company to help the surrounded recon team. It took until midnight, but it fought through the enemy and rescued the Marines.

At dawn on 28 February, Lanigan dispatched the battalion command group and the two Foxtrot platoons to link up with Golf. Halfway there the battalion commander, Lt. Col. Victor Ohanesian, a promising field grade officer on the fast track to general officer rank who spoke several languages, received orders that diverted him to Lima 3/4, then under attack. Ohanesian and his small force fought their way to Lima and drove away the NVA. By then, though, Golf Company had been hit, too, and was in a fight for its life.

Ohanesian never hesitated. He took his two platoons and command group and set out to help Golf.

Second Lieutenant Charles P. Chritton's 2d Platoon, Foxtrot 2/3, took the point with two squads; his third squad traveled with the command group, located about seventy meters to the rear. The dense foliage not only drastically hampered visibility but slowed the Marines' progress. About a hundred meters down the trail, Chritton directed his point man to take a fork that veered to the right. A short distance later they crested a small knoll and entered an abandoned NVA camp. By the nature of the camp and the scattered equipment lying around, even the freshest rookie could tell that the enemy had made a hasty and recent departure.

On the flank, Pfc. William A. Ryan, Jr., who had been in South Vietnam for three months but had not yet been under fire, spotted an enemy soldier strolling along a streambed below him. Unsure of what action to take, Ryan passed the word to Chritton: "I got a gook. Should I shoot him?"

"Of course," Chritton snapped back.

But by then it was too late. The enemy soldier had disappeared.

Chritton ordered his platoon forward.

The point man headed up the trail and almost instantly disappeared in the jungle. Six men went before him, then Ryan stepped onto the trail. He had taken two steps when the jungle erupted in a horrifying blast of small-arms fire.

"The rounds seemed to come from everywhere," Ryan said, "and the gooks were close. Just meters away."

Everyone hit the deck. Unbelievably, no one had been killed. There were several wounded but they could still move. Chritton, experiencing his first combat, ordered his men back to the NVA camp.

Behind Chritton, his third squad, just ahead of Ohanesian, took a blast of intense enemy fire, too. Marines fell left and right as automatic weapons fire raked the column. Many Marines never had a chance. With thick jungle growth on either side of them, all they could do was hug the dirt. The wounded cried for help as the NVA flipped grenades among the Marines. The sharp blasts drove shrapnel deep into flesh. One of Chritton's men, Pfc. James Anderson, saw one grenade roll near a wounded man. "Look out!" the nineteen year old yelled, then scooped up the deadly missile and swept it under his chest. The blast killed Anderson but saved the wounded man.

As Ohanesian tried to restore order out of the chaos, NVA mortar rounds started to drop on the trail. Landing with pinpoint accuracy, the bombs tore flesh and killed Marines. One round hit beside Ohanesian, mortally wounding him and injuring four others lying nearby. One was 1st Lt. Richard R. Brammer, the battalion fire support coordinator, who caught a shard of metal in his left shoulder. A twenty-five-year-old Ohioan with nine months in-country as an artillery forward observer for Bravo 1/12, Brammer vividly remembered the blast: "There was a collective groan from the five of us that had been hit by that round. Ohanesian was the worst. He was wounded all along his right side and was bleeding badly. The sergeant major had both his hands torn off. The battalion XO, a Navy doctor, and myself had been hit as well, but at least we could still move."

Brammer ignored the pain from his wound and grabbed his radio's handset. Before he had left Camp Carroll that morning, he had marked several preplanned artillery concentrations on his map. Now he called the battery of 105mm howitzers at Camp Carroll and gave them the coordinates. "Fire for effect," he barked into the mike.

As the shells crashed down protectively around them, the XO, Maj. Robert F. Sheridan, ordered everyone back to Lima Company's perimeter. Brammer commandeered four Marines and helped them rig a litter with a poncho and four rifles for Ohanesian. Sheridan did the same for the sergeant major. Though mortars, grenades, and small-arms fire filled the air, the Marines arose and rushed back to Lima's position.

"We'd been in the kill zone too long," Brammer said. "We had to get out of there before we all died."

Although they had less than a hundred meters to move, it seemed to take forever. Brammer helped and encouraged the other wounded, completely unaware he had been hit again, this time in the left leg. Finally, though, everyone staggered back into the little clearing.

The members of 2d Lt. Patrick G. Carroll's 3d Platoon of Foxtrot 2/3, who had been at the rear of the column and never had a chance to leave the perimeter, did what they could to treat the wounded, but there were just too many casualties. Someone called for a medevac, but by the time it arrived mortar rounds had started to hit inside the perimeter. The medevac was waved off. More mortar rounds struck the tight perimeter. Lieutenant Carroll, another rookie, caught a blast of shrapnel that rendered him immobile.

Brammer called in another fire mission. Soon artillery shells began to drop around the embattled Marines, some as close as twenty-five meters. The few unwounded and the walking wounded fought off several waves of attacking enemy infantry. The Marines faced a long night.

On his little knoll, Lieutenant Chritton relayed his artillery requests through Brammer. Without hesitation, Chritton called the rounds down on his position. He had to; the enemy was too close. Minutes later the high-explosive shells hit mere meters away. Private First Class Ryan remembered the blasts: "They were so intense, so powerful, the concussion literally sucked you right out of your hole. I was terrified but knew the enemy was getting the worst of it."

Several barrages later, Chritton checked fire. The artillery had done its job. The NVA backed off.

Still cut off from the rest of the Marines, Chritton told Foxtrot's XO, 1st Lt. Richard D. Koehler, that he could not pull back. "I had too many wounded," Chritton said. "Besides, there were still NVA between us and the rest of the company. I didn't want to be wandering around in the dark. At least I could defend myself where I was."

Throughout the long night, Lieutenant Koehler radioed Chritton every half hour. "Foxtrot Two, this is Foxtrot Five. If you can hear me, click your handset twice."

Each time, Chritton faithfully clicked twice, reassuring Koehler that he and his men were alive.

In the surrounded perimeter, Marines began to run out of ammunition. Despite the enemy fire, a brave chopper pilot flew in a resupply. His crew chief kicked out several cases of the desperately needed bullets. They fell among the NVA. Another chopper came in a little later. This time the ammunition crates fell in the middle of the beleaguered perimeter. Unfortunately, they contained rounds for the M16, a weapon not yet issued to the 2/3 Marines. The embattled men of 2/3 would have to make do with what little ammunition they had.

"How that screw-up happened, I'll never understand," Brammer said. "Because we were so low on ammo, I brought the artillery rounds in as close as I could. Sometimes I'd hear the enemy moving around and talking in the brush just meters away and I'd call in a concentration. Then all I'd hear would be their screams."

Despite the best efforts of the dedicated corpsmen, the inability of the medevacs to get in resulted in the deaths of several Marines, among them Lieutenant Colonel Ohanesian and Sgt. Maj. Wayne N. Hayes.

At Lanigan's headquarters at Cam Lo, Pappy Delong was monitoring the fight in the communications bunker. When word of Ohanesian's death reached them, Delong turned to Lanigan. "Send me," he said. "I'm ready."

With Lanigan's approval, Delong jumped aboard a helicopter for the short flight to the battleground. Heavy enemy fire drove it off. Delong then had the pilot fly him to Foxtrot 2/9, which was being sent overland to reinforce the battered 2/3 Marines. Delong and the fresh company linked up with 2/3 at 0340 the next morning.

Delong immediately reorganized the perimeter, adjusted the supporting artillery, and prepared the wounded for evacuation. At first light the medevac choppers finally made it in to lift out the wounded. Then Delong sent a strong force to rescue Lieutenant Chritton and his two squads. When they linked up, medevacs were called in to take out those casualties. Chritton and the others then moved back to the main perimeter.

With the casualties evacuated, and now joined by Golf 2/3, Delong sent out patrols to find the NVA. But they were long gone. Only a few stray shots from stay-behind teams bothered the patrols. The next day Delong took the remnants of his two companies to Dong Ha. From there they resumed their interrupted trip to Okinawa.

It became obvious as soon as the transport set out that the entire battalion, but especially the survivors of Foxtrot, Golf, and the command group, suffered serious emotional distress from the beating they had taken and their losses, which included their highly regarded commander as well as the battalion sergeant major and Golf's CO. Delong put a stop to that self-pity. At the end of a shipboard memorial service for the dead, he told his Marines they could not feel sorry for themselves.

Golf's gunnery sergeant, thirty-six-year-old William H. Janzen, remembered Delong's speech. "He told us we were doing our buddies a disservice by hanging our heads. They wouldn't want us to be that way. We were Marines and we shouldn't feel sorry for ourselves. He said we still had a war to fight and had to be ready when we returned to Vietnam. It worked. By the time we got to Okinawa we were all right."

The battalion spent more than a month on Okinawa, most of it at the island's northern training area. The Marines trained intensively, practicing everything from basic infantry maneuvers to amphibious assaults. To bring it to full strength, the battalion received hundreds of replacements. These new troops were quickly integrated into the rifle companies as the veterans passed along the many valuable lessons they had learned during their time in-country.

On Okinawa the Marines of 2/3 turned in their trusty M14s for M16s. The weapons training consisted of a brief lecture followed by the firing of a few magazines at the rifle range. Most of the troops took an instant dislike to the new weapon. Corporal Frederick G. Monahan, a twenty-year-old Philadelphian with seven months' service in Echo Company, was one of them. "Most of the guys thought it was a 'sissy' weapon because of the lightweight plastic stock," he recalled. "But worse than that it jammed all the time. Plus, the magazines had to be individually loaded, we had no 'speed clips.' And then, we could only put seventeen or eighteen rounds in each magazine, not twenty like it was designed for, or else you'd overloaded the spring. We were only issued three magazines each and one cleaning kit for every four guys. The men in the rear were giving their magazines and cleaning kits to the grunts before we headed south so we'd have enough."

Lieutenant Colonel Delong's frequent attempts to inspire and motivate his new charges did not impress Monahan either. "We're gonna attack right into their mortars, if necessary, and kill gooks!" Pappy said at one rally. Easy for you to say, Monahan remembered thinking.

Others reacted differently, however. Staff Sergeant Robert French, a Korean War veteran, served with the battalion's logistic support unit, the rear echelon Marines who serviced vehicles, radios, and weapons; looked after fuel needs; and handled other maintenance items. French attended one briefing for all officers and senior noncommissioned officers that Delong held at their camp's movie theater. Most listened politely as their CO briefed them on how he expected them to operate in South Vietnam.

Then Delong startled everyone when he told them how he planned to use the support troops. "I remember he told us to get our shit together," French said, "because by the time this trip was over we'd be running combat patrols and taking an active role in every operation. You should have heard the whining, and the pissing and moaning from some of our officers and senior NCOs. One gunnery sergeant with more than twenty years in the Corps was visibly shaken."

When none of the sergeants senior to him stepped forward to take command of the provisional rifle platoon that Pappy formed, Staff Sergeant French did. Though it would not see combat at Khe Sanh, French's provisional platoon did provide valuable service at the airstrip.

Delong's reconstituted and highly motivated battalion landing team departed Okinawa on 14 April 1967 as the infantry element of Special Landing Force Bravo. Once it arrived off the coast of South Vietnam, it immediately launched Operation Beacon Star (originally Bo Diddley). The target area for the operation was a major Viet Cong stronghold and supply area along Highway 1 straddling the border of Quang Tri and Thua Thien Provinces northwest of Hue. The first helicopter load of BLT 2/3 Marines touched down at 0809 on 22 April. Over the next four days, BLT 2/3's four rifle companies repeatedly assaulted target areas, but they found only small VC forces and encountered minimal resistance. Casualties were light. In fact, the battalion suffered far more heat stroke victims (sixty) in the first three hours after landing than it did casualties from enemy action (one KIA and ten WIA) in four days. The transition from air-conditioned troop compartments aboard ship to the intense heat and humidity of South Vietnam proved to be too brutal for many of the Marines.

On the morning of 26 April, the battalion launched a combined helicopter and overland assault against an enemy strongpoint held by an estimated 250-plus NVA. Before the operation fully developed, however, orders came that attached BLT 2/3 to the 3d Marine Division and sent it to Khe Sanh.

Four hours after it received its orders, Echo BLT 2/3 was off-loading at the Khe Sanh airstrip. Its commander, Capt. Alfred E. Lyon, was briefed aboard the C-130 that ferried him and his company to Khe Sanh. "The S-3 told me Khe Sanh was 'hot' and that my company would be responsible for securing the airstrip and setting up a perimeter. That news got my heart pumping. Of course, when we disembarked it was instantly apparent that the strip wasn't under attack. I turned the company over to my XO and strolled over to the base's command bunker. There I ran into an old stateside buddy, a major, who gave me a better briefing."

Golf Company, along with Lieutenant Colonel Delong and the 2/3 forward CP, touched down at Khe Sanh at 1320. Delong was briefed with the latest information on the fighting around Hill 861 involving Bravo 1/9 and Kilo 3/3. Before he left the base, Delong issued an order to his men that not only violated one of his basic edicts but also exposed his men to unnecessary danger: "Drop your flak jackets," he ordered. He apparently believed that the heavy protective vests had been responsible for the battalion's high number of heat casualties along the coast, and he did not want a repeat. The jackets were tossed in a pile. The more mobile but now more vulnerable Marines set out for Hill 861, where they linked up with Lieutenant Colonel Wilder at 1620. Hotel BLT 2/3 arrived at Khe Sanh about the same time and immediately headed out to Hill 861.

Delong's arrival pleased Wilder. Not only did he have great respect for his fellow commander, he knew he needed Delong's help to rid the Khe Sanh hills of the North Vietnamese. While BLT 2/3 set up its company perimeters along the southern approaches to Hill 861, Wilder continued with the removal of Kilo 3/3's casualties and organized the relief of Bravo 1/9. He then met with Delong and Colonel Lanigan to plan the capture of Hill 861 and nearby commanding terrain.

"Pappy Delong was senior to me," Wilder said, "but he wasn't the type to get hung up on that. We worked together as equals, each in charge of our own battalion but with our CPs co-located so the attack could be coordinated. Colonel Lanigan gave us the general outlines of an operational plan but left it up to us to work out the details. He didn't interfere much, just let us and our staffs plan who would attack what."

The two commanders agreed that Delong's battalion would seize Hill 861. Wilder's battalion would then attack and seize Hill 881S. In the meantime, Delong's men would screen 3/3 to the north while moving into position to attack Hill 881N, believed to be strongly held by the NVA.

But first, Captain Sayers's Bravo 1/9 had to be moved to safety. After that, replacements for that unit and Kilo 3/3 could be brought into Khe Sanh. When the battalion was up to strength, it could then move into position to execute its portion of the attack plan.

Medevacs completed the evacuation of the Bravo 1/9 casualties by 0730 on 27 April, and Captain Sayers and the other survivors trekked back to Khe Sanh accompanied by Kilo 3/9 and Wilder's command group. Once inside the perimeter, Wilder briefed Colonel Lanigan and General Walt. Recalling his previous encounter with the III MAF commander, Wilder prefaced his comments by saying, "General, I don't think you're going to like this any more than the last time I told you this, but we've got an entire NVA division operating out there."

Walt acknowledged Wilder's observation with a grunt. Wilder continued his brief with a review of the fighting his Marines had experienced in the previous twenty-four hours. He noted that some aerial forward observers had observed groups of elephants in the area. That could mean only one thing, he concluded. The elephants were being used as pack animals, and only battalion-size forces or larger would have a need for such transportation. Walt asked a few perfunctory questions, then approved the attack plan before departing.

While the two battalion commanders ironed out the final details of the attack plan, 3/3's reinforcements arrived. Just after 1600, C-130s carrying Mike 3/3 touched down at Khe Sanh's airstrip. A little more than an hour later, Mike 3/9 flew in. Lieutenant Colonel Delong's last rifle company, Foxtrot 2/3, arrived that afternoon, too. Foxtrot received the dual mission of providing base security and acting as battalion reserve.

Mike 3/3 had experienced considerable combat in recent months, but its commander had not. Captain Raymond H. Bennett, of Columbus, Ohio, actually commanded the Marine contingent aboard the aircraft carrier USS *Enterprise,* then operating off the coast of North Vietnam. He had volunteered for a program the Marines offered that allowed an officer with no combat experience to temporarily command a rifle company while its regular CO was absent. When Mike 3/3's CO, Capt. William Griggs, went on R and R, Bennett offered to replace him. Lieutenant Colonel Wilder reviewed Bennett's records and gave his approval.

On 14 April a helicopter deposited Captain Bennett at 3/3's head-quarters. Wilder briefed him while Griggs boarded a chopper to begin his R and R. A few hours later Bennett, a thirty-year-old Bowling Green State University graduate, joined his new charges in the hotly contested area near the Rockpile. The company's artillery forward observer, 2d Lt. David M. Rogers, a twenty-three-year-old West Virginian who had been in South Vietnam since the previous September but with Mike 3/3 only since 1 April, remembered Bennett as "very gung-ho."

For the next two weeks the company swept the rugged terrain around the Rockpile. It found signs of the enemy but no enemy. Then on 26 April word came to move overland to Route 9. "Trucks picked us up," Rogers recalled, "a Rough Rider convoy. And rough it was. To avoid sniper fire they raced down that bumpy road, knocking us around in the back of the trucks." The convoy carried Mike 3/3 all the way to Dong Ha. There they were hustled aboard C-130s, "packed in like fully combat loaded sardines," Rogers recalled, and flown to Khe Sanh. By 1600 the Marines were on the ground and on their way to join Lieutenant Colonel Wilder and Kilo 3/9 just outside the base.

"I remember passing by another company of battle weary Marines as we left the airstrip," Rogers said. "We weren't allowed to talk to them; there wasn't any contact between us. I thought that rather strange and a good indicator of the seriousness of the situation."

As Mike 3/3 headed away from the airstrip, the Marines they had passed—Captain Sayers and the remnants of Bravo 1/9—boarded the C-130s for their flight to Dong Ha. This time there was plenty of room on the plane.

While Bravo 1/9 flew east, Capt. Robert W. Swigart's Mike 3/9 flew west toward Khe Sanh. Just like the other companies assembled around Hill 861, it had been pulled out of the field and ordered to Dong Ha. The seriousness of the impending operation was impressed upon the veterans when they were loaded aboard the C-130. It was rare enough for Marines to be ferried by helicopters, let alone a cargo plane. Many of them thought something really big must be up.

Unfortunately, a good number of Mike 3/9's Marines wished they were not headed into combat under Swigart. A married thirty-four year old from State College, Pennsylvania, Swigart had taken command of the company in late 1966. Almost immediately it became apparent to the men that he was in over his head. Rather than leading by virtue of his rank or the strength of his personality, Swigart yelled at his men. In his eyes, none of them could ever do anything right. Swigart rarely passed a positive comment to any of his Marines. Rather, he berated and chastised them for even the tiniest infractions.

Hospitalman Randall J. Hoffman had grown up a military brat—his father was a Marine Corps sergeant major—so he had a good idea of how officers should act and perform. "Swigart was aloof and showy," he remembered. "He wasn't a real leader."

Unable to correctly read a map, Swigart often got his company lost. When his more experienced platoon leaders and NCOs tried to point out his error, Swigart would not listen. He frequently blundered off in the wrong direction, greatly increasing the anxiety of his Marines.

When the company (along with the rest of 3/9) went to Okinawa in January for refurbishing, Swigart still did not let up. Regardless of how well the company performed or how well the men behaved, Swigart found something to complain about. Twenty-year-old LCpl. Ira G. "Ricky" Johnson, who had been in the company since the previous August, remembered the time he incurred Swigart's wrath. Although he was normally assigned as the radioman to the 2d Platoon leader, Johnson carried Swigart's radio one day. The captain berated Johnson for carrying too much gear on a training march. "You'll never be able to keep up," Swigart yelled at him. To prove his point, Swigart set an unnecessarily brisk pace on the march. Johnson never gave up despite the cruel pace. "That made Swigart even madder," Johnson said.

Low morale permeated Mike 3/9 as it winged its way to Khe Sanh. Few of its members had any confidence in Swigart. Upon arrival at the remote combat base late on 26 April, the company headed out to link up with the rest of the improvised 3d Battalion, 3d Marines.

While the infantry forces tasked to wrest the Khe Sanh hills from the grasp of the fanatical foe waited patiently, supporting arms blasted the top of Hill 861. On 27 April alone, aircraft hit the enemy with more than 382,000 pounds of bombs, including a dozen 2,000-pounders and nearly 75,000 pounds of napalm. An additional 968 artillery rounds from the batteries at Khe Sanh fell on the hill. To the west and north, B-52 bombers conducted two Arc Light strikes to discourage NVA reinforcements from joining the battle.

It was an awesome display of American firepower. Few of the allied observers who saw it failed to be impressed by this pyrotechnic show. None believed that any of the enemy could survive such an onslaught.

On 28 April, in a classic infantry tactic taught for decades in America's military academies, BLT 2/3 ascended Hill 861 with two assault companies, Echo and Golf, up front and one, Hotel, behind in reserve. Beginning shortly after the noon hour, the anxious riflemen picked their way uphill. Ever cautious, always alert for any sign of enemy resistance, the Marines steadily neared the hill's summit. By 1600 they stood on top. What they found astounded them.

There were no NVA. They had withdrawn sometime between the last contact on 26 April and the day's afternoon assault. Although they had abandoned their positions, the North Vietnamese soldiers left plenty of evidence of their presence. The BLT 2/3 Marines found twenty-five bunkers, more than sixty fighting holes, and more than three hundred spider holes. Although some positions had been destroyed in the pre-attack bombardment, many of the bunkers were so well constructed with multiple layers of logs and dirt that only direct hits had damaged them.

The enemy positions were all mutually supporting and offered evidence of having been well camouflaged. Most were oriented toward the finger that ran up the hill from the south, the same finger on which Lieutenant Sauer and the Marines of Kilo 3/3 had met their demise. Two companies of NVA could easily have been accommodated on the hilltop.

Despite the intense bombardment, the enemy had carefully policed their former positions. The Marines uncovered little physical evidence of their presence and nothing of any intelligence value. That they had suffered casualties was unmistakable; a heavy, nauseating odor of dead and decaying flesh hung over the hill.

Though there were no NVA dead to be found, the men of BLT 2/3 did recover a number of Marine dead. Echo's Marines found the missing members of Corporal Riate's Kilo 3/3 squad but not Riate, and Golf Company Marines discovered the remains of Lieutenant Sauer and his escort. Helicopters flew in just before dusk to evacuate the bodies.

Shortly after the Marines set in for the night, they heard the *kathunk* of an enemy mortar. Veterans scrambled for cover while the novices looked at one another with questioning gazes. When someone yelled "Incoming!" they understood and dove to the ground or sought refuge in enemy fighting holes. Nearly two dozen 82mm mortars slammed into Echo's position over the next ninety minutes.

From his protective position, Echo Company's Corporal Monahan watched with admiration as the artillery forward observer and another officer popped out of their holes after each blast to examine the crater.

Done properly, the exam would allow them to shoot an azimuth to the mortar's position. Monahan was amazed that the pair was not hurt but even more amazed and appreciative when their counterbattery fire silenced the enemy weapon.

Early the next morning, 29 April, LCpl. Thomas E. Rice, a 3.5-inch rocket man assigned to Echo BLT 2/3, accompanied a patrol sent to verify reports of several Marine bodies lying to the southwest of Hill 861. Rice, a twenty-one-year-old native of Pasadena, California, had enlisted in the Marines a year earlier after dropping out of Santa Barbara City College. He joined Echo in October 1966 while it operated near Da Nang. Although Rice was a six-month veteran, his combat experience had been primarily against irregular Viet Cong forces operating down south.

When the small patrol reached the bottom of the draw running along Hill 861, the men found evidence of a fight. Discarded web gear, ammunition boxes, and other debris littered the ground. The odor and the buzz of flies helped them find two dead Marines. The badly decomposed bodies bore signs of having been mutilated by the NVA. Barely able to control their heaving stomachs, the Marines rolled the corpses into ponchos and began lugging them uphill.

After depositing the bodies at the hilltop LZ, Rice and his comrades returned to their positions along Hill 861's southwestern edge. A few minutes later Rice saw what few other Marines in South Vietnam would witness. Below him a full battalion of combat-laden Marines, organized by company, moved past Hill 861. Although he did not know it, he was watching Lieutenant Colonel Wilder's 3d Battalion, 3d Marines, move into position to launch its assault on Hill 881S. The sight of more than four hundred Marines marching to the attack both thrilled and terrified him. He could not help but think there must be a lot of enemy up here.

Suddenly, sharp staccato bursts of small-arms fire shattered the morning quiet. From the next ridgeline, about five hundred meters to the west, a force of enemy soldiers fired down on the lead elements of 3/3. The thought that just minutes earlier he had been under the same guns shocked Rice. He would never know why he had not been shot at; he could only speculate that his patrol had been too small for the NVA to bother with. As he watched dumbfounded, the fight below him continued.

The previous night Lieutenant Colonel Wilder had briefed his three company commanders on their mission for 29 April. He told them the battalion would leave its bivouac positions, located about a thousand meters south of Hill 861, and advance in a northwesterly direction until it reached its intermediate objective, a small knoll about 750 meters north of Hill 881S. The battalion would launch its attack from there the next morning, 30 April. Wilder concluded the briefing by stating that Mike 3/9 would lead the way to the intermediate objective and then spearhead the attack on Hill 881S.

Back at his company's perimeter, Captain Swigart assigned 2d Lt. Edward J. Kresty's 2d Platoon the point position for the next day's advance. At age thirty-five, Kresty was not only older than Swigart and most of the men in Mike Company, but he had been in the Marines nearly as long as some of them had been alive. Born in Dubois, Pennsylvania, on 14 December 1931, Kresty enlisted in the Marine Corps the day after his seventeenth birthday. He saw a year of combat in Korea and steadily moved up the enlisted ranks, his eyes on the three-up-and-four-down chevrons of a sergeant major. Then the Vietnam War began.

Because of a dearth of young college graduates entering the various officer candidate programs, and the high casualty rate among platoon leaders in the ever-widening war, General Greene, the commandant of the Marine Corps, announced a new program in late 1965. Qualified noncommissioned officers would receive temporary commissions as second lieutenants and be rushed to the war zone to command rifle platoons. Although the program solved the officer shortage problem, the rising casualty rate decimated the senior NCO ranks, depriving the Marine Corps of its leadership and experience for years to come.

Kresty pinned on his gold bars in the fall of 1966 and headed for South Vietnam a short time later. His years of experience made him leery of Captain Swigart from the moment the new CO took over Mike Company in December. "Word reached us that Swigart had had some trouble in the 26th Marines and was sent to 3/9 to redeem himself," Kresty recalled. "He came across as overly aggressive but very indecisive." Kresty kept a wary eye on his new commander.

Besides a lack of confidence in its leader, Mike 3/9 also found fault with its new weapon. When Kilo 3/9 left Camp Carroll a few days earlier to move to Khe Sanh, Mike 3/9 moved in behind it to take over as the Sparrow Hawk quick-reaction force. Immediately upon arrival the troops were relieved of their M14s and issued M16s. Mike 3/9's Marines had the same reaction their comrades in other units had had when they got the new weapon: They were angry.

"I was given one magazine to practice with," Lance Corporal Johnson said. "After just one round the weapon jammed. I was furious. I couldn't believe they wanted us to go into combat with these things."

Johnson concluded that the bolt of his weapon was the culprit and set off to get a good one. It took a heated confrontation with the armorer before Johnson got a new bolt. After that he had no trouble with his rifle.

Armed with the untried weapon, Mike 3/9 received orders to Khe Sanh on 27 April. To Lieutenant Kresty the brief he received on their new mission was the typical "doom report."

"They told us there'd be VC all over the place; we'd be fighting as soon as we left the planes," Kresty remembered. "But, of course, when we arrived at the airstrip there was no fighting there."

The briefing Kresty received from Swigart on the night of 28 April was not much better. "Captain Swigart didn't give me any information about any of the earlier contacts around Khe Sanh," Kresty said. "I was just given some map coordinates and told that was my objective for the next day."

The members of Mike 3/9 and 3/3's other two companies spent a quiet night in their perimeter. Kresty's platoon headed out at 0800 on 29 April, followed by Mike 3/3, then Kilo 3/9. The first two hours of humping passed uneventfully. After a short break, the column recommenced its movement. About an hour later, Kresty's platoon approached the mouth of a wide draw that ran north and south along the west side of Hill 861. His point squad had just started up a small hill when Kresty noticed abandoned Marine gear scattered about.

"I saw several helmets, packs, and a shot-up sixty-millimeter mortar," Kresty said. Because he had not been told of any earlier contact in the area, he decided to halt his platoon and radio back to Swigart for instructions. He signaled Johnson forward as the point squad crested the small rise. That's when the NVA opened fire.

Lance Corporal Gregory Chapin, the platoon's eagle-eyed sniper, took three hits immediately and crumpled to the earth. A Marine behind Kresty and Johnson fell. The lieutenant and his radioman both dove for cover, going in opposite directions as a spray of enemy bullets snapped overhead.

Johnson's radio crackled. Swigart wanted a situation report from Kresty.

"Lieutenant," Johnson called out, "the six is on the radio for you." Unwilling to expose himself, Johnson wanted Kresty to come to him. Kresty had a different idea.

"You're coming to me!" Kresty yelled back.

Swallowing his fear, Johnson low-crawled to Kresty's position, where he gave the lieutenant the handset.

Kresty reported to Swigart that his point squad was pinned down ahead of him and under heavy fire from enemy bunkers in a tree line across a ravine and that his Marines were returning fire as best they could. Then he signed off. He had no time to waste. He had a squad in trouble and had to get it out.

In the meantime, some of Kresty's Marines had already risked their own lives to bring in casualties. Corporals Vincent M. Kowalski and Wayne Krelter both ignored the enemy fire to rescue one of the wounded. Lance Corporal Johnson spotted a wounded man lying in the open, completely exposed to the enemy's fire. Without concern for his own safety, Johnson sprinted to the man's side, bandaged his wound, then carried him out of the line of fire. He then saw a corpsman struggling to bring in another casualty. Once again Johnson braved the enemy fire to help the corpsman carry the wounded man back over the little rise.

Kresty focused on the pinned down point squad. The enemy had it under deadly fire. Determined to remove it from harm, the lieutenant crawled to the top of the small rise. From there he spotted an escape route through a nearby gully invisible to the earth-hugging squad members. He radioed directions to the squad leader, who had his men inch backward until they could drop into the gully. From there they were able to make their way to safety.

But Kresty still had to recover Chapin.

"The NVA were using Chapin as bait," Kresty said. "Every time I tried to send a fire team out to get him, the NVA opened up. And they had several good snipers working us over. They must have shot Chapin five or six times. Not enough to kill him but enough to taunt us."

A pesky sniper had Lance Corporal Johnson pinned down, too. The enemy marksman would fire three quick bursts and then stop, a tactic that made it extremely difficult to pinpoint his position.

"A Marine I knew as Woody crawled up to me and said he was going home in two more weeks and wanted to get some more action," Johnson said. "I pointed out where I thought the sniper was. 'You can try for him,' I said. Woody slowly raised himself up. POW. POW. POW. Three quick shots rang out, drilling Woody in a tight pattern right in his temple." Johnson scrunched down as low as he could.

Still focused on Chapin, Kresty motioned an M60 gunner forward.

"You John Wayne it," Kresty ordered him, "and when the gooks are down we'll pull Chapin back." Kresty gave the signal, and the machine gunner let loose with a sustained blast of fire. Then Kresty ordered a fire team to get Chapin. Under the accurate covering fire, they pulled him to safety.

With all his men safe, Kresty now turned his attention on the enemy. He ordered LCpl. Lance Vanderhoff to fire white phosphorus rounds from his 3.5-inch rocket launcher at what he determined to be the enemy's key position. With the target thus marked, Kresty directed his platoon's rifle fire against the enemy. He then called the artillery forward observer forward. A sniper dropped the man before he reached Kresty. Determined to soften up the enemy before he launched an attack, Kresty called in the artillery himself and pounded the enemy's hillside positions.

As Kresty started to maneuver his squads into position for the attack, Johnson took a radio call from the battalion CP.

"Pull back" came the order. "Pull back."

Johnson could not believe it. They were just minutes from attacking the NVA and they had to give up. It was not fair. But he dutifully passed the word to Kresty. The lieutenant and nearly everyone else was angry because they knew they could have taken the positions. But orders were orders. They started withdrawing.

What Kresty and his platoon did not know was that they were much farther north than they were supposed to be. Somehow, through a mistake or poor map reading—no one ever knew for sure—the company had gotten off course and stumbled into the waiting NVA, who were actually in Lieutenant Colonel Delong's TAOR. The mistake infuriated Wilder. The firefight had not only caused unexpected and unnecessary casualties, it had disrupted his plan of attack. Now, instead of Mike 3/9 leading the attack against Hill 881S, Wilder had to realign his forces. Mike 3/3 would lead the attack the next day, with Kilo 3/9 backing it up.

None of this information reached Kresty, or would have mattered to him if it had. After he had moved his casualties—two dead and ten wounded—to an LZ near the battalion CP, he saw Wilder, whom he did not know, barking out orders to his subordinates and complaining loudly about Mike 3/9's action. That apparent insensitivity angered Kresty.

While Mike 3/9 tangled with the NVA, Mike 3/3 pressed forward to the intermediate objective. Just before 1900 it secured the little hillock. Seven hundred meters south of them, Hill 881S rose ominously in the dusk. A few hundred meters to the east, Captain Giles halted Kilo 3/9 and had his men dig in for the night. He knew the next day would be rough.

Part Two: Hill 881 South

Chapter Seven

As evening descended on the Khe Sanh hills, the Marines of 3/3 settled into their night perimeters. Captain Bennett's Mike 3/3 was positioned closest to Hill 881S, about eight hundred meters away. Lieutenant Colonel Wilder set up his CP several hundred meters to the east. Captain Giles's Kilo 3/9 and Captain Swigart's Mike 3/9 dug in around the CP for the night.

The area in which Mike 3/3 had set in had once been covered with tall, thick stands of elephant grass. Days of pounding with artillery shells, aerial bombs, and napalm, however, had severely scorched it. The smell of burned vegetation and the acrid aroma of cordite and burned petroleum lingered over the area.

Lieutenant Dave Rogers, the artillery forward observer attached to Mike 3/3, found it easy to dig a hole that night. "The ground was fairly soft and easy to dig up with our small spades," he recalled. "I dug a six-foot-deep hole in about six minutes—a foot a minute."

Rogers had barely finished his digging when Captain Bennett called him over to his hole. Bennett pointed to the top of Hill 881S.

"Look, Dave," Bennett said to him. "There's North Vietnamese on top of that hill. Get some arty up there real fast."

Rogers could plainly see three or four NVA silhouetted against the sky-line. By their movements it was obvious they were setting up mortar tubes. "I think that was about the fastest fire mission I ever called in my life. We got rounds up there within a matter of two minutes or less," Rogers said. "I can still remember real vividly the sound of those rounds coming over our heads."

The artillery did the trick. The enemy mortar crew got off only four ineffective rounds before it broke and ran.

Minutes later a horrible plaintive wailing echoed through the hills. Agonizing moans interspersed with guttural mutterings cast an eerie pall across the area. The Marines soon spotted the source. A delirious North Vietnamese soldier lay trapped in a collapsed bunker on a hillside several hundred meters to the west of Mike 3/3's position. His upper torso protruded aboveground and swayed at random as he wailed and moaned in pain. He was too far away for the Marines to do anything about it in the growing darkness. His cries haunted the Marines throughout the night.

Lance Corporal Donald A. Hossack heard the moaning. "It was weird, very strange," said the nineteen-year-old Kalispell, Montana, college dropout. "But worse than that were the taunts from the NVA." From the dark valley below their hilltop position, NVA soldiers called out to the Marines. "You die, Marine. Get your helmet on, Marine, we're coming for you. We're going to kill you."

Hossack's buddy, 2d Squad leader Cpl. Thomas C. Wheeler, heard the cries also. "It was spooky," he said. "It was worse than those old World War Two movies."

Mike 3/3's executive officer, twenty-two-year-old 2d Lt. Joseph Cialone, thought so, too. A University of Texas graduate, Cialone had joined Mike 3/3 as its Weapons Platoon leader upon his arrival in South Vietnam in January 1967. During the next three months he experienced several firefights with the NVA while the company operated around the Rockpile. By the time Mike 3/3 had boarded trucks for the ride to Dong Ha, Cialone considered himself an experienced combat veteran. While he waited to board the C-130s that would take him and the company to Khe Sanh, he spotted a buddy from basic school, Tom King of Bravo 1/9. The two had time for only a brief conversation, but Cialone learned that King had just left Khe Sanh. Before Cialone could ask King anything else about the situation there, King suddenly grew serious. "Don't let your men talk to mine," he warned before walking away.

What the hell is that all about? Cialone wondered.

Now, as he listened to the taunts and the distant wailing, King's warning sent a shiver up Cialone's spine.

Hossack, the radioman for 2d Platoon commander 2d Lt. Joseph R. Mitchell, received a call from Captain Bennett's radioman, Cpl. Peter J.

Marines of B/1/9 and K/3/9 carry Bravo dead into the 3/3 CP on the morning of 27 April 1967. (Courtesy M. Sayers)

Capt. Michael W. Sayers, B/1/9, (right), on the morning of 27 April 1967 after his four-day ordeal behind NVA lines. Pfc. David Hendry, second from left. (Courtesy M. Sayers)

WO Charles R. "Dick" Shoemaker, K/3/3, after his promotion to Marine Gunner. (Courtesy D. Shoemaker)

Lt. David L. Mellon, B/1/9, displays an M14 rifle equipped with a night vision device. (Courtesy D. Mellon)

LCpl. Thomas R. Ryan, B/1/9, prepares to head out on a patrol after the Hill Fights. (Courtesy T. Ryan)

Pfc. John K. Miller, K/3/3, in a bunker near the DMZ. (Courtesy D. Bigler)

LCpl. James L. Chase (left) and Hospitalman Francis A. Benoit (right), E/2/9, in a South Vietnamese village near Da Nang before moving to Khe Sanh. Benoit would be killed and earn a Navy Cross and Chase would be severely wounded during a brutal fight on Hill 861 on 16 March 1967. (Courtesy J. Chase)

2d Lt. Curtis L. Frisbie, K/3/3, at Camp Carroll before the Hill Fights. (Courtesy C. Frisbie)

LCpl. Thomas A. Vineyard, K/3/3, before the Hill Fights. (Courtesy T. Vineyard)

LCpl. William Van Devander, K/3/9, recovering aboard a hospital ship after being wounded at the Hill Fights. (Courtesy W. Van Devander)

LCpl. Harry O'Dell, K/3/9, enjoys a relaxed moment on Okinawa before the Hill Fights. (Courtesy H. O'Dell)

2d Lt. Edward J. Kresty, M/3/9, after returning home from the war zone. (C. E. Kresty)

LCpl. Donald A. Hossack (second from right), M/3/3, as he is helped down Hill 881S. (Courtesy D. Hossack)

LCpl. Harold A. Croft, K/3/3, earned both a Silver and a Bronze Star for his valor during his tour. (Courtesy H. Croft)

Cpl. Donald G. Bigler, K/3/3, poses in front of his position near the Rockpile. (Courtesy D. Bigler)

Echo 2/3 members Sgt. James J. Marden (left) and Cpl. James Mason (third from left) near the end of their tours in December 1967. (Courtesy J. Marden)

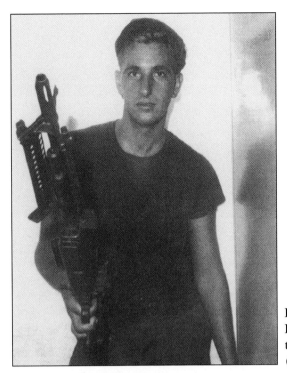

Pfc. George Sternisha, E/2/3, poses during training on Okinawa. (Courtesy G. Sternisha)

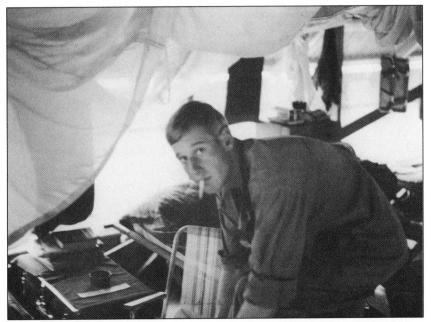

Hospitalman Randall J. Hoffman, M/3/9, at a Da Nang hospital after being transferred there from the field. (Courtesy R. Hoffman)

GSgt. Robert E. French, 2/3 LSU, in his bunker near Highway 1 on Operation Beacon Star before moving to Khe Sanh. (Courtesy R. French)

2d Lt. Charles P. Chritton, F/2/3, (center), and 2d Lt. Thomas Givvin, H/2/3, (right) on the day they were promoted to first lieutenant. (Courtesy C. Chritton)

1st Lt. Richard D. Koehler, F/2/3, known as the "Rock" for his inability to swim, proved to be rock-solid under fire. (Courtesy R. Koehler)

1st Lt. Richard R. Brammer, B/1/12 attached to 2/3, at Camp Carroll before the 28 February 1967 fight that devasted 2/3. (Courtesy R. Brammer)

GySgt. William Janzen (center) and Capt. James P. Sheehan (right), G/2/3, enjoy a laugh after a company party. (Courtesy W. Janzen)

Cpl. Frederick G. Monahan, E/2/3, would earn a Navy Cross for his valor at the Hill Fights. (Courtesy F. Monahan)

Capt. Raymond Madonna, H/2/3, a Naval Academy graduate whose company was hard-hit early in the Hill Fights but later went to the aid of the embattled E/2/3. (Courtesy R. Madonna)

2d Lt. Andrew McFarlane, G/2/3, who good-naturedly referred to himself as the "oldest second lieutenant in the Marine Corps." (Courtesy A. McFarlane)

LCpl. Thomas E. Rice, E/2/3, returns to the USS *Princeton* after the Hill Fights carrying his near useless M16. (Courtesy T. Rice)

LCpl. Tom Huckaba, H/2/3, poses with his M14. (Courtesy T. Huckaba)

Wounded G/2/3 Marine, 30 April 1967. (Courtesy C. Leroy)

G/2/3 Marines await order to attack near Hill 861, 30 April 1967. (USMC photo)

In one of the most dramatic photographs of the Vietnam War, Hospitalman Vernon Wike, G/2/3, tends LCpl. William Roldan on 30 April 1967. (Courtesy C. Leroy)

Hospitalman Wike listens for a heartbeat. (Courtesy C. Leroy)

Hospitalman Wike looks uphill in a vain search for the NVA sniper who killed Lance Corporal Roldan. (Courtesy C. Leroy)

Hospitalman Wike dives for cover before advancing uphill. (Courtesy C. Leroy)

Austen Deuel sculpture portrays a scene from Hill 881. Don Hossack is the radioman depicted in the statue. He is the only radioman to survive Hill 881. (Bud Shannon photo)

Scully. Because the NVA were sneaking around, Bennett wanted Claymore mines set out around the perimeter, Scully said. Lieutenant Mitchell passed the word to his squads to put the mines out.

When the Marines scurried back into their lines, Hossack noticed that Wheeler was grinning. He asked why. "There's no C-4 in the Claymores," Wheeler said. "They're useless." He explained that the troops had been periodically opening the curved antipersonnel mines and removing chunks of the explosive. It made great coffee and C-ration warmers. Now the mines held just the steel balls and no charge.

At 2015, one of the company outposts reported movement to its front. It estimated that a full company of enemy soldiers was moving toward the company perimeter. Alerted to the threat, Lieutenant Rogers called in another artillery mission. This time he wanted variable timed (VT) fuses used. These would detonate the shells in the air and shower lethal shards of steel upon the enemy. Minutes later the shells exploded across the night sky. Those in the outpost reported screams of pain from where they had seen the enemy.

Back at the 3/3 CP, Lieutenant Colonel Wilder put the final touches on the order for the next day's attack. He planned for Captain Bennett's Mike Company to lead the way up the hill. Giles's Kilo 3/9 would move up to Bennett's perimeter and hold there until needed. Swigart's Mike 3/9 would remain near the battalion CP to provide security and a reserve. Normally, Wilder would have put two companies up front, with one in reserve in the classic infantry formation, but he could not do so here because there were only a few routes to the top of Hill 881S. There was no way to move two companies abreast on the steep hillside and have them be able to support each other. Besides, his experience in fighting the NVA had been that they would pull out after the initial contact and bombardment. He did not expect Mike 3/3 to find much up on top.

What neither Wilder nor any of the Marines around Khe Sanh knew was that the 18th Regiment of the battle-tested NVA 325C Division occupied the hills outside Khe Sanh. A full battalion of the 18th occupied Hill 881S and had been busy preparing for the upcoming battle.

Somehow the NVA avoided detection by recon teams, aerial observers, and constant Marine patrols and had turned Hill 881S into a fortress. Dozens of well-constructed, well-camouflaged bunkers that could withstand all but direct hits dotted the landscape. Hundreds of fighting holes and one-man spider holes lay concealed amid the brush. The NVA had carefully cleared avenues of fire, zeroing in on the most likely approaches the Marines would take and crisscrossing them with interlocking fire. Mortars were preregistered so their fire could be brought to bear almost instantaneously. And most of the enemy soldiers were armed with the ubiquitous AK-47 rifle, a weapon that would prove to be more than a match for the newly issued M16.

Soon after dawn on 30 April, Captain Bennett dispatched two patrols from his perimeter. The first patrol searched the draw into which Lieutenant Rogers had called the VT mission the previous night. They found five dead and two wounded NVA. One of the wounded tried to escape, but the Marines shot him down. They carried the other soldier into their perimeter.

The other patrol carefully made its way to the half-buried enemy soldier. His wailing and moaning had finally subsided near dawn. And the Marines could see why. Not only had he suffered a number of shrapnel wounds from exploding ordnance, but the violent concussions had inflicted severe internal injuries. The Marines dug him out, rolled him onto a poncho, and carried him back to the perimeter.

The two enemy soldiers ended up near Bennett's CP. A corpsman gave them a quick exam and shook his head. The crowd of curious onlookers slowly drifted away. Both soldiers died a short time later.

Lieutenant Rogers was busy most of the morning calling fire missions on Hill 881S. The day started on a sour note for him. "I'd called for white phosphorus marking rounds before calling for the high-explosive shells," he said. "It was lucky I did because the first round whistled by real close and nearly hit a couple of Marines out in front of us."

Rogers quickly radioed back to the battery at the Khe Sanh Combat Base. It soon admitted it had made an error. The next rounds were right on target.

By the time Kilo 3/9 arrived at Mike 3/3's perimeter at 0800, two of Captain Bennett's platoons had already started toward Hill 881S. The third platoon had just cleared the perimeter. Bennett and his CP group stood nearby, waiting to move forward to the base of the hill.

Second Lieutenant Billy D. Crews's 1st Platoon of Mike 3/3 had the point that morning. A twenty-eight-year-old Floridian, Crews had been an enlisted Marine for nearly ten years. His transition to officer country was swift. "In November 1966 I was a buck sergeant on recruiting duty in St. Louis," he remembered. "Thirty days later I was in Vietnam wearing second lieutenant's bars and running a rifle platoon."

At Captain Bennett's briefing the night before, Crews learned that Hill 881S had two peaks, one at each end of the ridge. He was to advance to the military crest of the saddle between them and set up a 360-degree defensive perimeter. Lieutenant Mitchell's 2d Platoon would come up behind them, echelon left, and advance to the eastern knob. As soon as Mitchell's platoon was in position, the 3d Platoon, commanded by 2d Lt. Norman D. Houser, would move up and sweep the hilltop to the west. Crews's men would be available to assist either platoon.

As a final thirty-minute artillery barrage pounded the top of Hill 881S, the 1st Platoon started out at about 0800. Within an hour the entire company was strung out single file and moving up the hill. The normal starts and stops of a column of men slowed the movement, but by 0930 Crews had moved more than halfway to the top. From his position right behind the number-two, or slack, man, Crews spotted movement on the hilltop. He ordered a grenadier to fire his light antitank weapon (LAW), but the distance proved to be too great.

At first, Crews thought the NVA were showing themselves as bait to draw the Marines uphill. Later, he realized they were using the halt in artillery fire to move out of their protective positions and into their fighting holes.

Farther back in the column, Lance Corporal Hossack saw the NVA, too. Their boldness surprised him. He had seen NVA before in his five months in-country to be sure, but they were either at a distance or dead. Never had he seen them so close.

At the rear of Mitchell's platoon was a 60mm mortar squad commanded by Cpl. Douglas W. McKesson, one of the company's veterans. Just two weeks from his twenty-second birthday, he had joined Mike 3/3 the previous summer; he now had fewer than four months to go on his tour. McKesson had experienced a lot of combat in those nine months and had been decorated for his valor. On this day, he moved easily up the hill, enjoying the warm, sunny morning. For some reason he did not expect any action that day. "I don't remember why," he said, "but I just didn't think we were going to get hit."

McKesson's buddy, LCpl. Harold E. Kepner, was less assured. He had heard the NVA calling out their taunts the night before. "That scared me," he said. In his six months in the war zone he had never experienced anything like that. On days like this he wished he had listened to the Marine recruiter back in his hometown of Cleveland, Ohio. "You must be nuts," the sergeant had told Kepner after learning that his recruit was twenty-three and married and had just completed his junior year of college. But Kepner insisted, "I want to go fight commies." With a sly grin the recruiter had pushed the papers across the desk.

It did not take Kepner long to recognize he was not fighting Communist-influenced peasants. "The NVA were as good as they get," he claimed. "They were the equal of any Marine outfit in tactics and fighting spirit." Many Marines agreed.

At 0945 Crews radioed Bennett that his point man had reached the top of Hill 881S. Bennett acknowledged the call with a brisk, "Roger."

Crews ordered his squads into a large 360-degree circle. Lieutenant Mitchell's platoon lagged only a few minutes behind. Crews had to get settled in so he could provide support if Mitchell's platoon got hit.

Then the firing began. At first it was light, with only a few enemy soldiers shooting at them. Following standard operating procedure, Crews radioed a report of the contact to Bennett. "It's nothing we can't handle," he said. Bennett came back, "Carry on."

No sooner had Crews passed the handset back to his radioman, Pfc. Francis Palma, than the NVA opened up with an intensity that Crews had not previously experienced. "It seemed the NVA were everywhere," he said. "It was as if the entire hilltop was covered with enemy bunkers, spider holes, and firing positions. Some were less than a hundred meters away."

Crews's platoon frantically sought cover. Because the hilltop was thick with two- to four-foot-high sawgrass, small shrubs, and stands of trees, there was not much natural cover available. The grunts crawled to low spots or shell holes and returned fire.

When Lieutenant Mitchell's 2d Platoon crested the hill, it swung left and moved about a hundred meters clear of Crews's position. Mitchell intended to flank the NVA who had ambushed the 1st Platoon and relieve the pressure on Crews's unit. Then four Chicom grenades sailed out of the brush. The Marines dove to the ground. The point man, Pfc. Randall McPhee, hesitated a few seconds. He fell, riddled with shrapnel from the blasts.

Lance Corporal Hossack saw McPhee curled up in the thick grass. "Randy, you okay?" he asked.

McPhee looked up and smiled.

Hossack raced after Mitchell. "Just then we heard a tremendous amount of small-arms fire coming from Lieutenant Crews's position," Hossack recalled. "It was very heavy and very loud."

Mitchell urged his men forward. They made about fifty meters before firing broke out in front of them. Suddenly, six NVA charged out of a trench less than fifty feet away.

Rock-solid Corporal Wheeler, who had been with Mike since the previous August, quickly dropped to one knee, raised his M16, and calmly squeezed its trigger. Fortunately, his weapon worked. One, two, three, then four NVA fell. The last two turned and disappeared down the trench.

The 2d Platoon continued to advance as occasional small-arms fire snapped overhead. Thinking they were stray rounds from Crews's perimeter, Hossack radioed Palma and asked him to pass the word to stop shooting in the direction of the 2d Platoon. "That ain't us," Palma replied. "That's from the gomers."

Mitchell's men advanced another fifty meters before they were stopped by a barricade of fallen trees. Before the Marines could maneuver around the deadfall, the NVA opened fire. An incredible barrage of small-arms and automatic weapons fire poured out of the nearby woods. "Bullets were flying everywhere," recalled Hossack, "everywhere."

The fallen trees put the Marines right where the NVA wanted them, in the middle of an ambush. Sighting down cleared avenues of fire, the NVA unleashed vicious sheets of fire at the Marines. From bunkers and spider holes hidden in the elephant grass, the NVA opened up on Mitchell's men from all sides. There was no advance or retreat. The Marines were trapped.

Hossack hit the deck. To avoid being too prominent a target, he hastily folded down his radio's antenna. Just to his left, Mitchell knelt on one knee, his eyes sweeping the ground ahead for a target. An enemy round slammed into the officer's shotgun, shattering the stock. With splinters of wood sticking out of his face, Mitchell nonchalantly turned to Hossack. "Did you see that?" he asked.

"Yeah, you're drawing fire," Hossack shouted over the din. "Now get down."

Mitchell dropped to the ground.

Despite the heavy enemy fire, Marines all around Hossack bravely returned it. Lance Corporal Lester Calhoun repeatedly popped up to send grenades from his M79 flying into enemy bunkers. "He was deadly accurate with that weapon," Hossack said. "He took out at least four bunkers with his pinpoint fire."

Hossack watched an M60 gunner do a John Wayne. The man stood up, his weapon slung at the hip, and blazed away; a belt of ammunition disappeared as he swung the machine gun back and forth. When the gunner paused to reload, the enemy singled him out and he went down in a heap, his jaw torn off by a slug.

The gunner's squad leader, Cpl. William D. Early, crawled forward, patched the man up as best he could, and retrieved the weapon. It would not work. He snaked his way to a shell hole a short distance in front of Mitchell and Hossack. Distraught, he called out, "I can't fix it, sir. I can't." Then he slumped down in his hole.

Corporal Wheeler had been busy. Every time he spotted the muzzle flash of an enemy weapon, he squeezed off a burst from his M16 in that direction. Even when he did not have a specific target, he put out rounds. The nineteen-year-old Floridian must have caused considerable damage to the enemy, for they soon concentrated their fire on him.

"A round hit me in the left hip and came out my butt cheek," Wheeler recalled. "I couldn't walk, and every time I tried to crawl away the NVA shot at me. The firing was so heavy the doc couldn't get to me."

Then Cpl. James H. Whisenhut acted. He ignored the enemy rounds plunking into the ground all around him and made his way to Wheeler, patched him up, then pulled him to a safer position. Once assured that Wheeler was okay, Whisenhut returned to the fight. A short time later Wheeler saw him go down, hit several times by AK-47 rounds.

When Lance Corporal Hossack heard someone calling for help, he crawled through the grass to look for the man. He found Pfc. James A. Randall lying in the open, badly wounded. Hossack low-crawled to his side. He saw instantly that the twenty-one-year-old Somerville, Alabama, native was in death's arms. Frustrated and desperate, Hossack gazed skyward, seeking help that was not there. He crawled back to Mitchell.

Lieutenant Crews still had his hands full. The intense small-arms fire that had caught Lance Corporal Hossack's attention had not let up. In fact, although it did not seem possible, Crews thought it was getting heavier. The sharp crack of AK-47s continued in a near constant roar. Determined to break the enemy, Crews grabbed the handset off the PRC-25 radio carried by Palma. He radioed the fire direction center at Khe Sanh. He had just started to rattle off the coordinates for an artillery barrage when he heard a distinctive *thwack*. "I turned around and Palma was slumped over. I called for a corpsman and together we turned Palma over. A thin trickle of blood running out of the corner of his right eye told us he'd been shot in the eye. He never felt a thing."

There was no time for sympathy. Crews wrestled the radio off Palma's back and resumed his call for the fire mission. Soon he heard the satisfying blast of high-explosive shells dropping among the enemy.

A few minutes later the sight of several NVA running right through his lines startled Crews. He grabbed Palma's M16 and fired. The weapon jammed after just two rounds. Disgusted, he tossed the useless rifle away.

Around him Crews heard some of his men yelling that their rifles had jammed, too. Sometimes there was a flurry of AK-47 fire aimed at a defenseless Marine, followed by a horrible silence. The Marines' doubts about the new weapon were proving to be valid.

About an hour into the fight, Crews realized that, despite the artillery he had called in, NVA reinforcements were able to join the battle. They had to be stopped or his platoon would be overrun. He spotted M60 gunner Cpl. Robert J. Schley nearby and ordered the twenty-three-year-old Wisconsin native and his assistant gunner, LCpl. Michael R. Morgan, to move across the saddle and take up a position from which they could cover the reverse slope. The pair took off without hesitation. In a few minutes Crews heard the deep-throated bark of their automatic weapon. At least that flank was now covered, he assured himself.

When the firing started, the 60mm mortar crew took up positions in several bomb craters just below the top of the hill and waited for a fire mission. The volume of enemy fire amazed Lance Corporal Kepner. "It was just incredibly strong, very heavy," he said. Although they were defiladed from most of the enemy's fire, a constant buzz of rounds passed overhead. Kepner and a few others crept forward and fired a few magazines toward the enemy. They had no real targets but felt better doing something.

When Corporal McKesson received a radio request for a marking round, he hastily got it on its way. As he stepped to the forward lip of the crater in order to see where the round landed, he heard four distinctive *kathunks*. "I knew right away what it was," he said. "I turned and yelled at my crew, 'Run! Take cover!' Since most of them were fairly new and hadn't heard an enemy mortar before, they just kinda stared at me. I yelled again, 'Run! Get some cover!' But it was too late."

The first round landed nearly at McKesson's feet. "It blew me way up in the air and slammed me down on the other side of the crater,"

McKesson remembered. "By some miracle I wasn't wounded. But the blast and the landing sure rang my bell. It took me a while to gather my senses." When he did, he knew this was going to be a much bigger fight than had been expecting. Much bigger.

The NVA mortars did not spare the rifle platoons. One hit near Lieutenant Crews. "The blast shredded my flak jacket, ripped my helmet off, and threw me a good ten feet into a tree trunk," Crews said. "My flak jacket caught most of the shrapnel, but I still had some pieces of metal in my forearms and face. One piece went around my head under the skin and came out my neck. But the impact with the tree hurt me worse than the shrapnel.

"Crashing into the tree knocked my breath out, cracked a few ribs, and really stunned me. I don't know how long I was out, but I do remember one of my Marines crawling up to me. He asked me three times, 'Are you dead?' I couldn't answer but I sure thought it was funny."

Lance Corporal Hossack had been lying on his right side speaking to Lieutenant Mitchell when a mortar shell erupted about a meter behind him. The explosion blew the radio off his back, broke his right arm in two places between the elbow and shoulder, slammed a length of shrapnel through his helmet and into his head, and gouged a six-inch hole in his back just below his right armpit that deflated his lung. The blast got Lieutenant Mitchell, too. He lay face down, barely breathing. A piece of shrapnel had hit him in the right temple.

Stunned, and close to going into shock from his numerous wounds, Hossack rolled into a crater. He yanked his helmet off. The jagged length of shrapnel ran through the steel pot. So much for that protection, he thought. He lay back, his breath coming in rapid gasps. Then a sudden realization struck him.

"It came to me that my life hadn't passed before my eyes," he recalled. "As soon as I realized that, I knew I wasn't going to die. After that I was okay."

Buoyed by his newfound spirit, he crawled to Mitchell. He was dead. Then Hossack returned to his hole. He pulled his spare radio battery from his pack and peeled off the protective plastic. "Here," he said to the Marine next to him, "put this on my back."

No sooner had the man sealed off the sucking wound than an enemy grenade landed in the hole. Its blast tore a hunk of flesh off Hossack's left hip. The other Marine left the hole. Hossack felt very alone.

As soon as he learned of Lieutenant Mitchell's death, the platoon sergeant, SSgt. Terrance L. Meier, immediately assumed command of the 2d Platoon. Only twenty-two years old, Meier had already completed one four-year hitch before he joined Mike 3/3. Well liked, highly respected, and an outstanding Marine, the Portland, Oregon, native tried to reorganize the survivors of the 2d Platoon, but he could not. His new charges were too widely scattered and under such intense fire that they could not maneuver effectively.

In short order most of the Marines near Meier were hit. He found himself isolated from the rest of the platoon with six badly wounded men lying around him. Determined to save them, he kept up a steady fire that held the NVA at bay.

Not far away, Corporal Wheeler crawled into a shell hole filled with wounded men. Though in great pain from his wound, he picked up a discarded radio. He heard a call that help was on its way. He clicked the transmit button. "Put on your air panels," he advised the reinforcements. He hoped that by wearing the colored strips of cloth, the incoming Marines would not be confused for NVA by the desperate, pinned down Marines.

Soon after the fighting started, Lieutenant Houser's 3d Platoon was ordered into the fray. One of Mike 3/3's younger Marines moved with the point fire team. Private First Class Philip G. Curtis joined the Marines at age seventeen, just after graduating from high school in June 1965. A year and a half later, he arrived in South Vietnam and joined Mike 3/3 near the Rockpile. Although young, Curtis had a lot of savvy. He was one of the few Marines on Hill 881S armed with the M14. He had simply refused to turn his in when the new M16 was issued.

Now, two months shy of his nineteenth birthday, he hurried along toward the sound of the fight. No sooner had his squad crested the hilltop than his fire team leader came running back. "I'm hit! I'm hit," the leader yelled, then disappeared down the trail.

The crack of rifles and the bark of exploding mortar shells grew in intensity as Houser's platoon snaked forward through the tall grass. Curtis and four or five others crept into a shell hole. Before Curtis could fire a shot, an NVA round plowed into his back. The bullet slammed through his canteen and lodged next to his spine. "The pain was terrible but I could still move," Curtis said, "so I figured I'd be okay."

Moments later a corpsman appeared at his side. After putting dress-ings on Curtis's wound, the sailor crawled back into the brush looking for other wounded. "That guy was brave," Curtis commented.

Still determined to fight, Curtis and a few others in the crater turned their weapons outward. "We never did see any NVA but just fired where we thought they were," he said.

Closer to the front the 2d Platoon continued to take a pounding. Al-though the fight had been raging for almost two hours, the enemy rarely let up. "They just kept shooting and shooting," Hossack said.

He was hit yet again when a sniper's round tore into his back and went right through him. What the hell's gonna happen next? he asked him-self.

From somewhere he scrounged up a working radio. He called Cap-tain Bennett's radioman. "Lieutenant's a kangaroo," he got out, using the code word for killed in action. "You gotta get us help up here or we're not going to make it." Scully said there were two gunships on station, just waiting for targets. "That's no good," Hossack gasped. "The gooks are too close. We got too many dead to put out the panels."

As the battle raged on, those Marines still shooting back began to run low on ammunition. Some of the wounded stripped off their cartridge belts and threw them forward. Other Marines caught them and tossed them up to those who needed the rounds.

"Several times I heard Marines yelling that their M16s were jammed," Hossack said. "There were a lot of weapons around so we were able to pass them up front."

Wounded Marines began to drift rearward, seeking refuge. A machine gunner, blood gushing from a gaping hole in his shoulder, staggered into Corporal McKesson's mortar position. McKesson and Kepner sat him down and bandaged the wound. McKesson then helped the man down the hill. By the time he returned to the crater it was filled with other wounded. He selected another casualty and took him downhill. That was the way it went for the rest of the day for McKesson—up and down the hill, helping the wounded.

Lieutenant Crews slowly regained his senses. The battle still raged around him, but the firing from his Marines seemed to have slackened. He could only surmise that his platoon had suffered severely. Then a sudden sustained burst of M60 machine gun fire punctuated by the *pop-pop* of enemy AK-47s broke out to his right. That's where Schley was, he remembered. Crews crawled off in that direction.

When he neared Schley and Morgan's position he saw an enemy soldier, standing full upright, spraying them with rounds from an AK-47. Crews calmly aimed his M16, silently prayed it would not jam, and pulled the trigger. The NVA dropped. Crews crawled back to his platoon's shattered perimeter.

On the left flank the sight of two NCOs calmly walking toward him surprised Hossack. "All of a sudden here comes Sergeants Chutis and Bauer," Hossack recalled. "They were walking along, upright, totally oblivious to what was going on around them." As they approached Hossack's crater he called out, "Get down!" They both dropped to one knee but still seemed remarkably casual.

In response to Hossack's call for help, SSgt. John V. Chutis, platoon sergeant of Lieutenant Houser's platoon, and SSgt. Karl R. Bauer, the Weapons Platoon leader, came forward with a rifle squad to reinforce Mitchell's platoon. The situation was far more serious than they had expected. Hossack briefed them on what he knew and told them he had passed the same information to Captain Bennett. Bauer looked at him carefully, then said, "Hossack, you're a mess. Get outta here."

Hossack did not need to be told twice. He left them his radio and codebooks and moved rearward. He passed his buddy, Wheeler, who lay in his own crowded crater. Hossack found another crater filled with a dozen or so wounded and joined them.

Hossack did not know it, but he was probably the last man to see Chutis and Bauer alive.

Not far away from Hossack, Private First Class Curtis realized that of the dozen or so men in his shell hole only he and two or three others were still alive. The dead included his squad leader, Cpl. Larry M. Smith. A short-timer who did not have to go up Hill 881S, Smith had told his squad he wanted "to kill one more gook," so he stayed in the field. An exploding mortar fatally wounded Smith while he led his men forward. He never even had the chance to see another enemy soldier.

Most frustrating to Curtis was the complete lack of communication. After the corpsman left, he had had no contact with anyone else. The firing continued all around him for some time, but it eventually quieted down. Curtis thought his group might be the only survivors on the hill.

At his command post Lieutenant Colonel Wilder monitored Mike 3/3's radio net all morning. The intensity of the enemy fire, which he could hear in the background of open microphones, surprised him. "Up until then I hadn't really been certain there were NVA on the hill," Wilder said. "The vegetation was so thick up there we couldn't really tell how many bunkers were there. And in the past the enemy had always pulled out. I'd prepped the hill well the day before, pounding it with one thousand– and two thousand–pound bombs and all the artillery I could get my hands on. I knew I had to pull the infantry back."

Although his CP was crowded with the intimidating presence of Generals Walt and Kyle, as well as Colonel Lanigan, Wilder never hesitated in his decision. He had his S-3 contact Captain Bennett and ordered Mike 3/3 to pull back. "Get the wounded out," Wilder told him.

Wilder also ordered Captain Giles to move up and help get the wounded down. Captain Swigart would release two platoons for the rescue operation, too.

Chapter Eight

Kilo 3/9 had spent the morning of 30 April near Mike 3/3's night defensive perimeter. While it waited, artillery forward observer LCpl. Robert W. Stewart and his radioman, Pfc. John A. Krohn, watched a distant action involving a company of BLT 2/3.

Sometime before noon, word was passed to Stewart that Captain Giles wanted him to scan Hill 881S with his binoculars. Dutifully, Stewart and Krohn moved past their comrades to the top of the ridge finger. Stewart sat down, raised the binoculars to his eyes, and started focusing on Hill 881S. All of a sudden he felt a sharp, burning pain in his buttocks and he yelped.

Krohn turned. "What's the matter with you?" he asked.

Stewart did not know what to tell him. At first he thought a snake had bitten him. Then it dawned on him. With his binoculars to his eyes, he must have been taken for an officer by a distant sniper.

"I've been shot," Stewart blurted out.

In an instant, several Marines pulled Stewart back down the side of the finger. A corpsman appeared. "How're the family jewels?" Stewart demanded.

The doc assured him that everything important was intact. The sniper's round had torn into his right butt cheek and come out the left. In a few minutes Stewart was on his way to an LZ to await the arrival of a medevac.

Krohn shouldered his radio. Although he was alone and now the sole FO for the company, he was grateful that his buddy had made it out alive.

In the meantime, Giles moved his company to the base of Hill 881S. "I sent Lieutenant Woodall's platoon up on the far left, where they'd be able to flank the NVA on top. The Second Platoon, under Lieutenant Stephen Hepner, went up on Woodall's right, while I kept Staff Sergeant Stephen Cobb's Third Platoon in reserve," Giles recalled.

Woodall's platoon started uphill just after noon. Lance Corporal Flowers had the point. Fifth in line was Woodall, followed by his radioman, LCpl. John Rapp, a red-headed Hoosier. Lance Corporal Arthur V. Gennaro was the fourteenth man in the column. Just in front of Gennaro walked his buddy, LCpl. John B. Appleton, a native of Louisville, Kentucky. The platoon's other two squads were strung out behind Gennaro.

"The hill was covered with tall grass and thick brush, and very steep," Gennaro recalled. "Sometimes it was so steep we had to pull ourselves up by tree roots and branches. We were about two-thirds the way up the hill when the head of the column crossed over a slight rise. Just as I came up to it a sniper fired. Someone yelled, 'Corpsman up!' In front of me, a machine gunner fell. A second later another man's helmet flew off and he went down. Then it was like the whole world exploded in fire. Rockets, mortars, and small-arms fire were coming from a tree line to our left."

Gennaro hit the ground. Most of the Marines around him were firing at the tree line. Worried there might be NVA behind them, Gennaro rolled to his right and sprayed the surrounding foliage with a burst from his M16. Then grenades started sailing through the air at him.

"Appleton rose up off the ground to see if he could spot where the grenades were coming from. I yelled, 'Get down,'" Gennaro said. "But I was too late. A grenade went off right in front of Appleton. Shrapnel splattered his face and chest. I could tell he was dead as soon as he hit the ground."

Gennaro slipped another magazine into his weapon and pulled the trigger. He got off two or three rounds, then the rifle jammed. He fought off rising panic as he worked frantically to free the stuck cartridge. As he pried on the brass, two men behind him went down, hit by enemy rounds. Then Lance Corporal Rapp stumbled up to him, bleeding heavily from several wounds. Gennaro pulled him down and bandaged him. Because Rapp came back by himself, Gennaro understood that the others who had crossed the slight rise had been wiped out. Seconds later another grenade came in; it destroyed Rapp's radio and wounded him again.

Some distance behind Gennaro, LCpl. William Van Devander's M16 jammed, too. Try as he might, Van Devander, a twenty-year-old West Virginian who was still recovering from wounds he had received in September 1966, could not clear it. He picked up a discarded M60 and fired it at the enemy. He could not see them but he knew where they were by all the noise they made. He moved off the trail with a buddy and spotted an NVA bunker. A quick peek inside revealed two freshly killed enemy soldiers. Van Devander glanced down a trench leading away from the bunker. Movement caught his eye. Two NVA were fleeing. He fired the M60 from the hip but he missed; the enemy escaped without harm.

On the west flank Lieutenant Hepner's 2d Platoon had not fared any better. It had a hard time moving up the hill. The rugged terrain forced the troops to their hands and knees several times, and they often had to pull themselves along by grabbing tree roots and brush.

Private First Class Gordon Fenlon could hear heavy firing in the distance. It was Mike 3/3's fight. He knew instinctively it was going to be a bad day. The firing grew heavier as the 2d Platoon neared the top of Hill 881S. Enemy slugs passed overhead with alarming regularity. Fenlon joined a group of Marines hunkered down in a large crater. "It was crowded in there, and the only refuge I could find was behind a small mound of dirt toward the downhill side of the crater," Fenlon said. "Unfortunately, this exposed me to a sniper. Every time I tried to move, he fired. If it hadn't been for that little mound I'd have been killed. I was praying the sniper wouldn't move and get a better bead on me."

As Pfc. Harry J. O'Dell moved uphill with his squad of Kilo 3/9's 2d Platoon, the sound of enemy fire grew louder. One of the oldest members of the company, O'Dell had been snagged by the draft a year earlier, just before his twenty-sixth birthday. Although a father of two, a divorce had ended his marital exemption and the draft board sent him his notice before his birthday made him ineligible. He had joined Kilo in November and was considered one of the platoon's more stable veterans. Now enemy rounds chased after him as he dashed across a wide clearing. On the other side he noticed an NVA bunker. "I'd been in construction before I was drafted and I knew good construction when I saw it," O'Dell said. "And this bunker was well built. I couldn't imagine how they'd done it out there."

O'Dell did not have too long to ponder the quality of the enemy's work before Chicom grenades flew out of the bushes above him. The missiles erupted with sharp cracks that filled the air with dust and debris. Suddenly, one grenade came straight at O'Dell. "I rolled into the bunker," he said. "It went off. I came back out. I saw Bill Van Devander behind a skinny little tree about twenty feet away. The grenade had gotten him."

"A buddy'd been hit," Lance Corporal Van Devander remembered, "so I patched him up and took him to a crater full of other wounded Marines. We were pinned down there for a while. One sniper's round hit my helmet; it cut the cover, but it didn't get me.

"When the firing let up a little I crawled out, moving to my right. As I neared the bunker where O'Dell was, someone started shooting at me. The only cover I had was that skinny little tree. I moved behind it, but he got me in the thigh anyway. Then that grenade came and put a few more holes in my body."

When O'Dell popped back out of the bunker, a bullet snapped off a tree branch in front of his face. He searched for the sniper but could not spot him in the foliage. He heard other Marines yelling back and forth behind him. Then, without warning, a bright light flashed in front of him followed by a loud, dull roar. The next thing O'Dell knew, he was flat on his back in the bunker. He hurt all over. Then all went black.

Not far from O'Dell and Van Devander, Lieutenant Hepner's platoon sergeant, Stanley C. Butterworth, a twenty-two-year-old Rhode Islander with nearly four years in the Marine Corps, watched helplessly as one of his squad leaders died. Hit in the initial burst of fire, the man lay just ten meters away but no one could get to him. Anytime someone tried, the NVA unleashed a burst of fire. Finally, the Marines stopped trying; the firing was just too heavy. A short time later Butterworth realized that the man had bled to death.

Someone told Butterworth that a group of wounded Marines was trapped in a tree line about twenty-five meters away. Immediately Butterworth tapped Pfc. Charles B. Saltaformaggio and another man on the shoulder and headed toward the tree line. The trio made it to there unscathed. Saltaformaggio spotted a nearby bunker and flipped a grenade into it. The missile exploded in a storm of dust and debris. He had started to pull the pin on another grenade when an enemy soldier brandishing an AK-47 popped out of a spider hole just a few feet away.

"This guy points an AK at me and blazed away, spraying bullets everywhere," Saltaformaggio said. "I tossed my grenade at him and dove for cover. But I wasn't quite fast enough." The nineteen-year-old New Orleans native took rounds in the right knee and right chest. He did not know it then, but the ammo magazines strapped across his back stopped two other rounds. Bleeding but not out of the fight, the gutsy young Marine continued firing at the enemy.

In the meantime, Sergeant Butterworth spotted two NVA in a bunker. He triggered a burst from his M16. The enemy disappeared. Soon another NVA popped up. Butterworth fired again. That man fell. Then another NVA appeared. Butterworth realized then that the enemy probably had tunnels connecting their bunkers. He could kill them all day, but they would keep coming back.

Private First Class Fenlon remained pinned down with the others in their shell crater until the sniper finally turned his attention to a more promising target. Fenlon was able to scramble to a safer position. About that time, Lieutenant Hepner, who had also been pinned down, decided he had had enough. The stocky mustang told those around him he had spotted the pesky sniper and was going after him. He leaped out of the hole and made all of ten feet before he was cut down in a murderous hail of enemy fire.

It was apparent to Captain Giles that his beloved Kilo Company was in serious trouble. At his position at the base of the hill, he received word that both of his lieutenants had been killed. Casualties were heavy. His Marines could not do much to help Mike 3/3. Giles had no choice. He sent word for the company to withdraw with all the wounded. The dead had to be left behind.

When the orders reached Lance Corporal Gennaro, he and another Marine laid down a heavy base of fire so the wounded could be pulled back. The two walked backward and sprayed the tree line and nearby brush with hundreds of rounds to keep the enemy at bay. They eventually reached a defiladed position, where they paused to catch their breath while the casualties continued to move or be moved down the hill. They continued their trek after a few minutes. Once safely down, Gennaro collapsed; he was completely drained by the heat, humidity, and adrenaline-producing combat. All he could do was give thanks for being alive and unwounded.

Private First Class O'Dell came to and saw a dark figure kneeling over him, unfastening his gear. O'Dell did not know who the man was but assumed he was a corpsman. After he had been treated and the man left, O'Dell slowly got to his feet. Somehow he staggered out of the bunker and started down the hill. Still bleeding from wounds in the face and body, he made quite a sight as he stumbled his way to safety.

Although Lance Corporal Van Devander's leg wound had stopped bleeding, the limb throbbed with pain, and so did his numerous shrapnel wounds. He decided to pull back. "It was a problem because we didn't know exactly where we were," he said. "All the officers were dead and there were no NCOs around. None of us had any maps so we weren't sure which way to go. Finally, a couple of the less badly wounded guys got us organized and we headed downhill."

Van Devander soon found himself trailing just a few feet behind O'Dell. When they reached a flat spot protected from the enemy's fire, they both noticed one of the platoon's senior NCOs sitting on a log. The sergeant, a Korean War veteran, was intensely disliked by the troops for his near constant harassment of them. Regardless of how petty the offense, this NCO would berate, humiliate, and embarrass the Marine by yelling, screaming, and cursing. This sergeant would mete out punishment such as extra guard duty or filling sandbags for something as simple as having an unbuttoned pocket. He verbally berated the young Marines, repeatedly telling them they would never measure up to the Marines he had fought with in Korea. Now he was perched on the log sobbing uncontrollably. "Please, will someone help me down?" he begged between sobs. "Please. Please."

The sergeant was not wounded; he had just lost it. O'Dell and Van Devander said "No" and continued their downward trek.

Someone with a radio passed the word to Private First Class Fenlon that he could pull back. When the firing slowed, Fenlon crawled out of his shell hole as several of the wounded moved past him. The sight of his buddy, Harry O'Dell, going by startled him. About fifty meters downhill he came across the body of another good friend. Fenlon could not leave him there. He picked up the man's discarded M16 and slung it across his back, then grasped the dead man's feet and dragged him down the hill.

Enemy mortar shells dropped all around Fenlon and sent bits of hot metal into the back of his head, ears, neck, legs, and arms. The mortar blasts drove him to his knees several times, but he pressed on. After one particularly close explosion, Fenlon realized he had to leave his friend behind. "He was just getting too heavy and I was getting too weak," Fenlon recalled. "Plus, I could hear bullets passing by and I thought I'd get shot. It pained me to leave him there, but I had no choice. So I stopped, said an Our Father over his body, and headed down by myself. I've always felt bad I had to do that."

Fenlon was surprised by the complete lack of organization at the bottom of the hill. "Wounded were just standing or lying around. No one seemed in charge. There was no one to patch my wounds," he said. When a medevac came in, Fenlon simply staggered over to it and flopped aboard.

There were no corpsmen to treat Private First Class O'Dell, either. He also simply boarded a chopper when it came in. He ended up on the hospital ship *Repose*.

A corpsman did give Lance Corporal Van Devander a shot to dull his pain. Everything went black almost instantly. When he woke up and looked around, he was surrounded by dead bodies. When he sat up two people nearby screamed and nearly passed out from fright. Somehow Van Devander had been tagged as dead and flown to the morgue in Da Nang. Soon, though, he was on his way to the hospital.

At midafternoon a lot of Marines were still fighting on the hill. Private First Class Saltaformaggio heard some men talking about a sniper. He got directions from them and headed off to hunt him down. He crept through the thick grass to a clump of brush and peered through it. He spotted an enemy soldier just three meters away. He poked his M16 forward, squeezed the trigger, and put a full magazine of rounds into the NVA.

Saltaformaggio never did get the word to pull back. Instead, he kept moving up the hill. Finally he made contact with some Mike 3/3 survivors. Aided by several others from Kilo, he tended their wounds. "It was completely disorganized," he remembered. "No one was in charge. It was just get them patched up and move them down."

Sergeant Butterworth also spent the rest of the afternoon gathering up wounded. He shepherded them downhill in groups and returned to search for others. When he headed down for the last time, he did a quick head count. The numbers startled him. Half of his platoon, including Hepner, was dead or wounded.

At the base of the hill, Lance Corporal Gennaro received some bad news. The remnants of his 1st Platoon and the 2d Platoon, along with members of the 3d Platoon, were being sent back up the hill. They were to make a full search for any living Marines who might have been left behind. "I thought it was a suicide mission," he said. "There just wasn't any way to survive going back up there. I was scared, terrified." But he knew he had to go. The first eleven men in his platoon's line of march were missing. In a letter he sent to his parents a few days later, he said, "I felt like hiding some place but I knew I couldn't live with myself if I didn't go back with my platoon so up I went again."

On his way up the hill with the 3d Platoon, Private First Class Krohn was stunned at the number of casualties flowing past him. "They looked bad, real bad," he said. "A couple of them told me, 'Watch it up there, they're dinging for radio operators.'"

The enemy fire grew from a few sporadic rounds to a constant crescendo of small-arms fire as Krohn neared the top of Hill 881S. He dove behind a log. Sniper rounds smacked into the other side of it, sending wood chips flying through the air. Someone barked, "Get some fire in here!" Krohn called the coordinates into Khe Sanh. "Battery, fire for effect," he yelled, without wasting time with a marking round.

Nearly instantaneously, a cluster of shells impacted with a massive explosion less than fifty meters away. "That's too close!" Krohn called for a cease-fire before any errant shells dropped on him.

Lance Corporal Gennaro and his group turned left when they reached the top of the hill and moved toward where his platoon had been hit. "We had to crawl all the way," he said later. "Snipers were all around us. I tried to imagine myself as a snake so I could keep as low as possible. If there was a branch in front of me, I wanted to go under, not over, it."

In his letter home Gennaro noted, "There were bodies everywhere, like leaves off the trees in the fall. It was hot as hell. As we passed one crater I looked in and there was Flowers, his right side full of blood, top to bottom."

Gennaro crawled into the crater and helped revive the point man. When Flowers came to, he told how the NVA had run out of the nearby trees and tossed grenades into the crater, killing a number of the wounded. Then they had shot the bodies at point-blank range. Flowers had been shot at three times. Amazingly, all the rounds had missed him. He played dead and the NVA left.

During the rescue the NVA kept up a steady pace of fire at the Marines. Grenades flew at them from several directions. Then mortar shells dropped around them. "Every five minutes someone got shot or hit with a grenade or mortar," Gennaro wrote home.

A little while later, a group of Mike 3/9 Marines joined Gennaro and his small band in the crater. They were all pinned down, unable to advance or retreat. About 1830 when the fog started to roll in, they realized that if they did not get off the hill soon they might never be able to.

They hastily built a stretcher from ponchos, rolled Flowers into it, and stood up. A sniper zinged a few rounds past them and they dropped. They started out again a few minutes later. This time mortar shells crashed near them and they hit the deck again. The frustrated Marines agreed to just get up and go, no matter what the NVA threw at them. This they did. Disregarding the enemy fire, the small group hurried along as fast as they could. Finally, they reached a spot that was out of range. Without further enemy interference they got Flowers, and several other casualties they had picked up along the way, to safety.

Artillery FO Private First Class Krohn did not get to call in any more fire that afternoon. He was pinned down with several other Marines by such heavy enemy fire that he could not observe where any rounds hit anyway. After about an hour someone called out that they should pull back. The Marines crawled away when the enemy fire slackened. Krohn picked up a discarded M16 and a radio, slung them over his shoulder, and started down. The men around him were nearly running off the hill. He felt that some were on the verge of panic, but many were not. He passed a corpsman who was calmly performing a tracheotomy on a casualty. A machine gunner stood over them, protectively firing his M60 uphill.

The Marines from three rifle companies roamed across the face and top of Hill 881S. They all had one mission: recover the wounded and get them to safety. They reached Corporal Wheeler's crater in midafternoon. He and the other wounded who could not walk were laid on ponchos and carried downhill. At the medevac site Wheeler linked up with his buddy, Hossack, who had been helped down the hill earlier by a corporal who, according to Hossack, "quit the war. He just threw away his weapon and helmet, said he'd had enough, and started helping me. I wish I'd been able to do that." Hossack and Wheeler, and dozens of others, endured several pain-filled hours before medevacs arrived to carry them out.

Around 1300 a squad from Kilo 3/9 made it to Lieutenant Crews's little perimeter and told him of the order to pull back. Crews went down the hill to Captain Bennett's CP and Bennett confirmed the order. The gutsy Crews went right back up and spent the next five hours roaming the battleground in search of wounded. Whenever he found a man—and he found many—Crews gave him whatever medical aid he could and either sent the casualty downhill or helped him down. Crews made it all the way to his original perimeter, where he found that several of his men were still alive. He got them to safety, too.

Private First Class Curtis lay pinned down until late afternoon. During a lull in the enemy fire, he heard someone calling from a tree line below him. "Hey, come on down this way. Come on down." Curtis and a few of the others who could move crawled out of their shell hole and slid downward. "It hurt like hell, but I was able to walk," Curtis said. "Up until then I thought I was going to die up there so I was happy to be getting out. At the bottom a buddy saw me. He said I was as white as a ghost from losing so much blood."

During lulls in the fighting, Staff Sergeant Meier moved the six wounded men with him to the relative safety of an abandoned enemy bunker. When Meier realized that Mike 3/3 was pulling back, he braved sniper fire to move them one by one to a position from which other Marines could help them down the hill. To stymie the NVA, he radioed for white phosphorus (WP) artillery rounds to be laid on the top of the hill. Meier was able to get all his wounded charges headed to safety under the cover of this thick white smoke.

One of the WP rounds landed short. It hit between Mike 3/9's Hospitalman Michael A. House, a bespectacled nineteen year old from Barnett, Vermont, and a Marine. House was burned by the chemical, but the Marine was much worse; his leg was blown off and he suffered severe burns over most of his body. House ignored his own pain to help the man. After applying a tourniquet to the bloody stump and treating the burns with ointment, House pulled the man to cover. Some other Marines carried him away, and House turned his attention to other casualties. Several times he exposed himself to enemy fire in order to pull a Marine to safety.

Private First Class Ernest M. Murray was detailed with his fire team to provide rear security while the rest of the 1st Platoon of Mike 3/9 worked its way uphill. A native of Martinez, California, with nearly two years of service and a year in-country with Mike 3/9, Murray listened nervously to all the firing up ahead. They're really catching it, he thought. Then he heard a loud noise. He was right behind House when the WP round went off. "It sounded just like a freight train roaring past," Murray recalled. "Then there was a great deal of confusion. Wounded Marines were staggering past me, going downhill."

Murray saw one stateside buddy with a gaping hole in his throat. He helped him, then provided covering fire for those moving off the hill.

When he was convinced that no more wounded were coming, he moved downhill, too, walking backward and spraying the nearby shrubs with his M16. "I couldn't see any enemy but I could hear them in the brush nearby."

Murray had almost made it to safety when his platoon sergeant came up to him. "We need your help over here," the NCO said. Murray joined a group of Marines clustered around a wounded staff sergeant. He handed his M16 to a man who already had nearly a dozen weapons slung across his back, grabbed a corner of the poncho holding the casualty, and helped carry him down. Then Murray went looking for his weapon. "I found the guy who had taken my rifle, but he seemed in a daze and didn't remember what he'd done with it. I finally found a pile of discarded M16s. The first one I picked was jammed. So were the next three I looked at. Finally I found one that worked."

Lance Corporal Johnson followed Lieutenant Kresty up the hill, and they soon encountered a Marine carrying a corpse. It was obvious the man was struggling with the dead weight. He stumbled and fell in front of Johnson, and the corpse rolled a few feet. "I told the guy to leave the body, but he wouldn't have any of it," Johnson said. "He was crying and between sobs he told me, 'I can't leave him. He's my buddy. We went to high school together, we played basketball together, we went into the Marines together. I can't leave him. I can't leave him.'"

Johnson used a machete to cut down several saplings and made a stretcher with them and a poncho. Some men nearby helped him roll the body onto it. Three of them helped the sobbing Marine carry his buddy down the hill.

Among the last to come off the hill were Mike 3/3's Mortarmen McKesson and Kepner. They had spent the entire afternoon scouring the hillside for any overlooked casualties. Whenever they found a living Marine, they patched him up and started him downhill. At last they got the word to pull back. Kepner recalled, "We destroyed our mortars' sights but carried the tubes and base plates down with us. There was no one firing at us as we came down. I was very grateful to be out of there."

Lieutenant Dave Rogers spent the day alongside Captain Bennett, calling in artillery missions. As the day wore on and the extent of the casualties became apparent, the tragedy of the fight started to wear on the observers. To Rogers, Captain Bennett seemed particularly disheartened by what was happening. "Bennett was constantly on the radio with the two lead platoons," Rogers recalled. "It was all very confusing as the reports came back. Bennett appeared very frustrated."

As soon as the withdrawal order from Lieutenant Colonel Wilder reached Mike 3/3's CP, Rogers called in fire missions to cover the movement. "I called in artillery on the back side of the hill to stop any reinforcing NVA, but I had difficulty hearing the rounds explode due to all the noise from rifle and small-arms fire," Rogers said. "I could only adjust the rounds based on what the Marines up there told me. I fired a full six-gun battery, then waited for a radio call. I got a call to bring them in even closer, but I told the battalion CP that this would possibly result in the deaths of our own people, for I was calling rounds in on them. This situation hadn't been covered in any of my training and I never expected it to happen. The CP said to continue; we had to get the Marines off the hill at all cost. I radioed the battery to fire for effect."

The sight of so many horribly mangled Marines filing past Rogers had a profound and lasting effect on him. Not only did the hideousness of the wounds impress him, he noted the stoicism of the Marines. He remembered Staff Sergeant Meier, who came down carrying two rifles and a wounded man on his back. As Meier passed Rogers, he was cussing up a blue streak because he could not do more.

Marine combat artist Pfc. Austin Deuel also witnessed the carnage on Hill 881S. A twenty-seven-year-old reservist, Deuel had volunteered to go on active duty specifically to go to South Vietnam and paint what he saw. He had been in-country less than two weeks when news of the fighting at Khe Sanh reached his compound in Da Nang. He jumped aboard a plane headed north along with several other correspondents and photographers.

"I arrived after the wounded had started coming down the hill. It was bad. I'd never experienced combat before and it was far worse than anything I'd imagined," Deuel said. Although he had no specific role and was there as an observer, Deuel was first a Marine. He pitched right in, helping with the wounded, putting on dressings and escorting the men to the medevacs. When he could, Deuel scanned the hilltop with binoculars, mentally recording the images so he could later turn them into paintings.

By 1830 Captain Giles believed that all the living Marines were off the hill. To be certain, he ordered several of his men to move up the hill and call out to any survivors. When one of his men yelled, "Is anyone else up there?" a sharp response of "Yes" startled Giles. Seconds later, a helmetless black Marine came out of the darkness. Draped across his shoulder was the body of a white Marine.

When the man approached him, Giles asked, "What are you doing?"

"This is my squad leader," the Marine responded evenly. "I couldn't leave him up there." Then he continued on.

When no one else answered the calls, Giles pulled his Marines back. He then reported to Wilder's CP that Hill 881S was clear of living Marines. Kilo withdrew a few hundred meters and dug in for the night, its ranks badly depleted by the day's action. Fifteen members of Kilo 3/9 had been killed and thirty-five had been wounded and evacuated.

As the wounded moved down the hill, Mike 3/3's executive officer, Lieutenant Cialone, worked hard to keep track of his company's casualties. By the time the last medevac lifted off, he felt he had an accurate head count. The figures were shocking: Of the 161 Marines on its rolls at the start of the day, 26 were dead and 54 were wounded. Lieutenant Crews had begun with 50 men in his platoon; at the end of the day he had 19 left on their feet.

Mike 3/3's FO, Lieutenant Rogers, attended a debriefing that evening with Captain Bennett, the other surviving company officers, and several of the NCOs who had made it off the hill. The sergeants described what they had seen and experienced during the day. Their stories were upsetting. Particularly painful was confirmation of Lieutenant Mitchell's death. In the short time that Mitchell had been with Mike Company, Rogers had formed a strong friendship with the young Alabaman. His death did not seem real.

Rogers returned to his hole after the briefing. The events of the day deeply troubled him. The loss of so many fine young men for a worthless hill seemed a complete waste. Never one to express himself with the written word, Rogers nevertheless felt compelled to release his emotions by penning a poetic tribute to the fallen Marines. He scratched a few phrases on a scrap of paper, seeking the right combination of words to capture his feelings.

Just as he had completed his task, he received word to report to Bennett's CP. There he learned that, because the FO attached to Kilo 3/9 (Lance Corporal Stewart) had been evacuated, he and his radioman were being temporarily transferred to Kilo. "I thought we'd make the move the next morning," Rogers said, "but, no, they wanted us over there right now. Our positions were disjointed, so we had to walk across open ground in the dark to join up with the new company. Everyone was poised for a counterattack, and I was scared to death to make that hump. I made sure the other company knew we were coming. It was very spooky. I didn't want to be killed by some nervous, trigger-happy Marine. But we made it okay."

The night of 30 April–1 May passed uneventfully for the surviving members of 3/3. While they slept and stood watch, Lieutenant Colonel Wilder and his staff prepared for the next day. Mike 3/3 would be pulled out of the line because its casualty rate had rendered it ineffective. It would be sent back to the Rockpile via Dong Ha for an infusion of replacements, and Foxtrot BLT 2/3 would helicopter out in the morning to replace it.

Colonel Lanigan radioed Wilder with orders to take the hill the next day. Wilder refused; he wanted to proceed more slowly. He had had no intelligence information that there had been that many NVA on Hill 881S, and the severe mauling of his rifle companies deeply disturbed him. He did not want a repeat. Before he would send the infantry back up Hill 881S, he would blast it to pieces. He had his staff prepare the plans and orders for a daylong bombardment. Wilder wanted any remaining enemy soldiers to be corpses when his Marines went back up.

While the survivors of 3/3 settled in that night, few knew that less than two kilometers away their sister battalion, BLT 2/3, had also battled the NVA in a vicious series of clashes.

Part Three: Hill 881 North

Chapter Nine

Lieutenant Colonel Delong's BLT 2/3 had a dual mission on 30 April: Protect 3/3's flank as it went up Hill 881S, and seize several intermediate objectives for its own impending attack on Hill 881N. Echo Company, from its position on the southwestern side of Hill 861, was to move westward into the lowland between Hills 881S and 881N. Then it would swing north to seize its intermediate objective, a small knob about eight hundred meters southeast of Hill 881N's summit. At the same time, Hotel Company was to attack and hold the hillside from which the NVA had hit Mike 3/9's platoon the previous day. Golf Company would be the battalion reserve.

Hotel's Capt. Raymond C. Madonna had his troops up and under way soon after first light. A 1962 graduate of the Naval Academy, twenty-seven-year-old Madonna was one of the more experienced company commanders in BLT 2/3. He had arrived in South Vietnam in August 1966 as the S-2 (intelligence) officer of the 2d Battalion, 26th Marines. Upon his promotion to captain the following month, he was transferred to the captain-poor 2d Battalion, 3d Marines, where he took command of Foxtrot Company. He fought that company in the rice paddies around Da Nang and took it up north late that fall, earning a reputation as a solid, capable commander.

When 2/3 was ordered to Okinawa in late February 1967 for training to become part of the Special Landing Force, Madonna had been in charge of the battalion's advance party. Word of the destruction of his company and the loss of Lieutenant Colonel Ohanesian, the battalion CO, on 28 February reached Madonna while he was relaxing in the officers' club with other members of the advance party after they had put in a hard day's work preparing for the battalion's arrival.

"The news shocked us," Madonna recalled. "We, of course, had no idea the remnants of the battalion had been sent on a rescue mission. It was a very difficult night for all of us."

One of Pappy Delong's first objectives when the survivors of 2/3 reached Okinawa was to rebuild the battered companies, replacing weak commanders with strong. He shuffled his captains around, and Madonna ended up with Hotel Company.

Hotel had a good blend of veterans and newbies. Its executive officer, 1st Lt. David S. Hackett, a Princeton graduate, had four years in the Marine Corps and more than six months of combat experience. He would soon be ready for his own company. The 1st Platoon commander, 2d Lt. Ord Elliott, who had known Hackett when they attended Princeton together, joined Hotel in January. So had University of Southern California graduate 2d Lt. Thomas Givvin. Second Lieutenant Bruce E. Griesmer, a 1966 Naval Academy graduate, joined Hotel literally as it was boarding the ship to return to South Vietnam. The Weapons Platoon leader, 2d Lt. Thomas Mills, was even newer. He signed into Hotel two days before they settled in on Hill 861. Fortunately, an outstanding NCO, SSgt. Edward F. Crawford, had been running the Weapons Platoon and would break Mills in properly.

After the troops ate and policed up their perimeter that morning, they headed out with Lieutenant Givvin's 3d Platoon on point. It took them nearly an hour to reach the draw where Mike 3/9 had been hit the day before, but most of the troops did not know this. All Cpl. Gerald C. Pett, one of Givvin's fire team leaders, knew was that they were to descend into the draw before them and take the hillside opposite. It seemed like an easy mission to Pett, a combat-wise veteran who had been with Hotel since the previous summer and held the Bronze Star.

As Givvin's platoon started down the side of the ridge finger that formed the eastern wall of the draw, Lieutenant Griesmer's 2d Platoon paralleled it to the left. The going was fairly easy as the Marines worked their way downhill. The ground was steep but not difficult. Behind the two lead platoons, Lieutenant Elliott's men took up positions along the top of the draw where they could support the others if there was any action.

Staff Sergeant Crawford of the Weapons Platoon viewed the draw with a wary eye. He had witnessed Mike 3/9's action the day before. "I was concerned about going right back in there without any prep fire," Crawford said.

If there was one Marine moving down into that draw on 30 April 1967 who understood combat, it was Crawford. Born in Upper Darby, Pennsylvania, in 1928, he had changed his birth certificate and enlisted in the Marine Corps a few months before his seventeenth birthday. To his immense disappointment, World War II ended before he could see any action. But he did observe numerous clashes between the Communist and nationalist forces while serving on occupation duty in China.

Honorably discharged a few weeks before his twenty-first birthday, Crawford returned to Upper Darby, where he joined the county police force and the local Marine Corps reserve unit. The Korean War returned Crawford to active duty. In two years in the war zone he received three Purple Hearts. After he returned home he advanced steadily through the ranks of both the police department and the reserves. Life was good for Crawford, his wife, and their three children. Then in 1966 he was visited by a relative.

"My nephew, John Reid, a Marine, too, was on orders to Vietnam," Crawford recalled. "He came to see me because of my Korean War experience. He wanted some advice on how to survive. I told him, 'Listen to your NCOs. They've got the experience. Do what they tell you.'

"That night I talked to my wife. I told her I thought I could help these kids going to Vietnam. I could maybe keep some of them alive. She agreed. The next day I volunteered to go back on active duty."

Crawford tried for an assignment with his nephew's unit, but it had no slots open for a staff sergeant. Instead, he was assigned to Hotel 2/3, which he joined during its retraining cycle on Okinawa. Crawford quickly established himself as a noncommissioned officer who sincerely cared for the troops and who balked at the Marine Corps' petty rules. Rather than harass and bully the young enlisted men, as many NCOs did, Crawford went out of his way to befriend them. He shared his combat experience and knowledge in a positive way and wanted to do all he could to get as many of the kids home alive as possible.

Crawford had no time for nonsensical regulations. On one patrol soon after landing back in South Vietnam, a sniper fired at them. "Anyone see where that round came from?" he asked.

"Over there," one of his veterans said as he pointed at a thatched hut.

"Blow it up," Crawford ordered.

"I can't do that."

"What!"

The veteran explained that the rules of engagement prohibited them from returning fire unless they took automatic weapons fire.

"Bullshit," Crawford retorted. "I'll do it myself."

He loaded up a 3.5-inch rocket launcher and let it fly. The hut disintegrated in a cloud of dust and a flash of light.

Seconds later Crawford's radio crackled with a call from battalion. "What the hell was that?" they wanted to know. Crawford explained. He listened incredulously as the staff officer explained the rules.

"You give me a written order and I might comply," Crawford retorted. "I didn't come over here to fight a war that way."

The troops loved him for his attitude and respected him for his concern.

Now, as he walked toward the downslope, a young man whom Crawford had not previously seen appeared at his elbow. "Mind if I tag along with you?" the man asked.

Crawford eyed the newcomer. He was dressed in civilian safari-type attire, so Crawford pegged him as a reporter. "No, not at all," Crawford responded. The young man fell in at Crawford's side. "I'm Bob Handy," he said. Crawford nodded.

By now most of Hotel's two platoons had descended into the draw. They found the narrow bottom, not more than fifty feet wide, thick with two- to three-foot-tall elephant grass. Scattered bushes and thickets of shrubs dotted the area. Several hundred meters north, at the head of the draw, the foliage thickened with taller grass and stands of trees.

Captain Madonna's command group advanced along the top of the ridge finger. As the men moved, the finger gradually descended to join the bottom of the draw near its head. Just to Madonna's left front walked 1st Sgt. Kenneth R. Jones. Lance Corporal Clifford G. Davis, a pleasant young man from Amarillo, Texas, with more than ten months in-country, was a few feet to Madonna's right. The PRC-25 radio slung across his back was tuned to the battalion frequency. Lance Corporal Desmond T. Murray, who carried the PRC-25 tuned to the company net, kept a position about five feet to Madonna's left rear.

Twenty-three-year-old Murray, a naturalized citizen born in Ireland, had served with Hotel 2/3 since June 1966. With a year of college he could have sought a deferment or a commission, but he had not. "As a new citizen I felt I had a responsibility to serve in the military. The Marines were the best and I wanted to be the best," he said.

After a few months of toting a rifle, he took over as his squad's radioman. In November 1966 he was picked to carry a radio for the company commander. Although the PRC-25's long whip antenna made him an easy target, Murray enjoyed his new role. "I had a little better idea of what was going on than the average grunt," he said. "And, I didn't have to go out at night on listening posts."

By the time Murray and the command group started down the sloping finger, most of Lieutenant Givvin's platoon had reached the bottom of the draw, below and to Murray's left. To Givvin's left rear moved the members of Griesmer's platoon. Executive officer Hackett, the company gunny, and several others took up positions in a thicket of trees and bushes behind Captain Madonna; from there they could direct the fire of the company's M60s. The only sounds came from the clang of equipment or static erupting from a radio's speaker.

"All of a sudden, I heard a sharp crack," Murray remembered. "There was a spray of red and Davis dropped."

Murray yelled, "Grenade!" but realized as he hit the deck that a sniper's round had probably drilled Davis. From his prone position, Murray watched the bullets plow up the earth around him. The noise was deafening. Murray had been in dozens of firefights, but this was the most intense blast of enemy fire he had experienced. He swiveled his head in search of cover. There was none. Except for a few plugs of elephant grass here and there, the finger offered no cover whatsoever. "I never felt so exposed before," he said.

The heavy volume of enemy fire stunned Givvin and stopped his platoon in its tracks. "My point fire team was only ten or fifteen meters from the closest enemy bunker when the shooting started," Givvin said. "There was shooting and screaming everywhere. My men were firing back but I'm not sure what they were firing at. Screams for a corpsman seemed to be coming from everywhere."

The first blast of enemy small-arms and automatic weapons fire sliced through the Marines; they dropped left and right. From the head of the draw, the deep chug of a .50-caliber machine gun chilled the Marines' blood as its heavy slugs cracked overhead.

Corporal Pett dropped at the first sound of enemy fire. The direction and the volume of the fire surprised him. He had expected the NVA to be in place farther up the draw. Instead, they were dug in right along the facing slope. Most of their fire seemed to come from his left and left front.

"Bullets were hitting everywhere around me," Pett remembered. "They were popping through the air and smacking into the ground. I opened up at where I thought the NVA were. I got off about eight or ten rounds, then my rifle jammed."

Pett frantically pulled his cleaning rod from his weapon's stock. He forced the rod down the rifle's barrel. No good. No matter how hard he slammed the rod, it would not free the jammed cartridge. Disgusted, he tossed the weapon aside. He crawled through the grass until he came upon a casualty. He picked up that man's weapon and opened fire. It jammed after half a dozen rounds. Damn, he thought, we're going to die down here.

Lieutenant Givvin thought they were all going to die, too. The enemy fire kept up at an unbelievable rate. The rounds just kept coming and coming. Givvin tried to radio Madonna, but he could not get through. For all he knew he was the only company officer left alive. He switched to the battalion frequency, reported the contact, and requested artillery and air support. It was coming, he was told.

Givvin thought to mark his position with a smoke grenade. He pulled it free and tossed it to his front. No sooner had it left his hand than he realized that the arming spoon was still taped down.

Shit. We're done. We're finished, he told himself.

"Air would soon be coming in and I had no way of telling them where we were," Givvin said. "I didn't know my grid coordinates and I had no way of communicating with the air. I realized then that either the good guys were going to get me or the bad guys were. Either way I was dead and there wasn't anything I could do about it."

Most disappointing to him, though, was the realization that he had let his men down. He had vowed to send home alive as many of his Marines as he could. For the first time in his twenty-three years, he knew defeat.

Amazingly, that realization brought a sudden calmness to Givvin. He shrugged off his depression. Marine training took over; he started to bark out orders. He moved his machine guns into better positions to bring their fire to bear on the enemy. Only that way could they drive the NVA under cover, allowing his Marines to maneuver.

Lieutenant Griesmer was hit in the opening fusillade. A rifle slug ripped into his left buttocks and exited from his right thigh, carrying a big chunk of flesh with it. The blow spun him around to the ground.

Stunned, he lay there and watched in amazement as AK-47 rounds blew the radio right off the back of his radioman. The force of the rounds knocked the man out, but they never touched him.

Griesmer lay there for a few minutes, too stunned to move. Then a corpsman crawled up and dressed his wound. With no way to communicate his situation to Captain Madonna, Griesmer ignored the pain of his wound and started to direct the fire of his men. In a way, the action was thrilling. This is just like a war movie, he thought. This is what I've been training nearly five years for.

Then he heard the screams of the wounded and dying. This is real, he thought. This is no Hollywood flick. Though immobilized, Griesmer did what he could to keep his men's fire up.

After Lance Corporal Murray recovered from the shock of the initial blast of fire, he acted. He radioed back to Lieutenant Hackett's group for the senior corpsman to come forward to aid Davis. The doc crawled up, unmindful of the bullets that chewed up the earth around him. The corpsman took one look at Davis and shook his head. About the same time, Murray realized that his radio was not working. Without it he had no way of contacting battalion to ask for help.

Murray crawled forward right onto Madonna's back. Feeling incredibly exposed to the enemy's sharpshooters, he yelled for the doc to unscrew the longer antenna from Davis's PRC-25 and put it on his. Then he had the corpsman switch the frequency on his radio to the battalion net.

"We're getting hit! We're taking heavy fire!" Murray yelled into the handset. He then passed it to Madonna.

While the captain provided higher headquarters with a more detailed report of their situation, Murray signaled Hackett's radioman to come forward; he would have to take over the company net.

Captain Madonna took only a few minutes to tell battalion what had hit his company. "It's a buzz saw," he said, "a real buzz saw. We're gonna pull back so air and arty can come in."

Murray inched his way backward. When he got to where he felt he had a little protection from the firing, he arose and sprinted toward Hackett's group. Bullets snapped past his head. He dove for cover. Then he was up again. A few more feet and down again. Then up. Suddenly, he came upon another radioman, LCpl. Frank Correia. Blood coursed down Correia's face.

"You okay?" Murray asked between gasps.

"I'll make it."

Murray helped Correia to his feet, gave him a push in the right direction, and continued on. Murray spotted a break in the bushes and dove through it. A spray of bullets went right through his legs and hit Lieutenant Mills.

A short distance away, Lieutenant Hackett raised off the ground to peer into the draw. Murray heard a burst of fire and looked up just in time to see the XO throw up his hands and roll down the slope. Panting heavily from the heat and exertion, Murray thought it was the worst fifteen minutes of his tour. A few minutes later, Madonna and the rest of the command group burst into the clearing.

At the bottom of the draw, Staff Sergeant Crawford and his new friend, Bob Handy, had hit the deck at the first blast of enemy fire. As the bullets flew over them at an unbelievable rate, they stayed pinned down for some time. Most troublesome was the .50-caliber machine gun at the top of the draw. It fired off measured bursts of its half-inch-thick slugs whenever a Marine showed himself.

When the firing died down a little, Crawford looked around. Just behind him a corpsman crouched over the crumpled form of a Marine. Crawford wormed his way through the grass to the pair. One glance at the downed Marine told him all he needed to know.

"Move on, doc," he ordered. "You can't do anything for him."

As the enemy fire continued, Crawford realized he had to get the .50. Its firing down the draw had the Marines stymied. Crawford spotted an abandoned 3.5-inch rocket launcher; he could use that to knock out the .50. When he got to it, though, he found it had been shot up. He had one course of action remaining. He turned to Handy, still at his side.

"Let's move over to the left," Crawford said.

"Whatta we doing?" Handy wanted to know.

"We're gonna flank 'em and get that gun."

The two made their way forward along the western edge of the draw. They ran at a crouch, dodging between brush clumps. Suddenly, twenty feet to their front, the covers of two spider holes flipped open and an NVA soldier popped out of each one.

Without hesitation, Crawford and Handy each ripped off a quick burst from their rifles. Their slugs tore into the enemy soldiers, spilling them out of their holes.

Before Crawford could even register his kill, an AK-47 opened up on him. Its bullets tore the M16 out of his hands and sent it flying into the grass. The impact violently spun him around, so much so that he thought the pain he suddenly felt came from a strained muscle in his left leg.

"You're hit," he heard Handy say.

The wound did not hurt and Crawford could still move, so he shook it off. About then he heard Givvin yell to his men, "Pull back! Pull back!"

"I was afraid they'd move right back into the kill zone," Crawford remembered, "so I started yelling for them to sit tight. I didn't know Captain Madonna had given the order."

Now even more concerned that Hotel's Marines would be easy targets for the .50, Crawford rushed on. Handy sprayed the grass in front of them with his M16. Weaponless, Crawford pulled his entrenching tool from his web belt. It was better than nothing, he figured.

A few meters farther, while Handy fired into the thick grass to their left, Crawford spotted movement to the right. Not ten feet away another NVA emerged from his hole. Crawford sprang forward. He swung the shovel with all his might. The tool caught the enemy soldier full in the side of the head and killed him instantly. The determined pair continued their advance.

They finally saw the enemy position fifteen meters farther on. The deadly weapon sat in front of a bunker, behind a thick embankment of logs. Crawford did not see any NVA. He tossed two grenades into the pit and dove for cover. After the twin explosions Crawford looked up. A pall of dust and smoke hung over the emplacement. A dead NVA lay sprawled on top of the logs.

Satisfied with their work, the two started back. Halfway to their starting point they heard the scream of incoming artillery. They scrambled into a depression. As the shells exploded all around them, Handy asked Crawford if he would write to his parents if he did not make it out.

"Sure," Crawford responded.

Handy then wrote his name on the back of Crawford's flak jacket. When Handy finished, he rolled over and Crawford wrote his name on Handy's jacket so he could notify Crawford's wife if he did not make it.

Even as more shells crashed around them and tossed them around in their hole, the men exchanged information about themselves. After Crawford told Handy about volunteering to look after his nephew, Handy startled him by announcing he was not a reporter. "I'm with the CIA," he revealed.

Crawford did not know what to make of that.

When the artillery stopped a little later, Crawford heard jets circling overhead. "We gotta get outta here. We're gonna get cooked!"

The pair ran back down the draw as fast as they could. They finally spotted some other Marines. Crawford made it to the evacuation site, where a corpsman dressed his leg wound. A little later he boarded a medevac chopper. Crawford never saw Handy again.

The incoming artillery and air strikes allowed the Marines in the draw to gather up their casualties and move back to safety. "I didn't know who was directing the artillery, but it was right on target," Givvin said. He yelled orders to get the wounded taken care of.

When the firing died down, Corporal Pett helped the wounded. Some distance in front of him, hidden in the grass, he found his buddy, LCpl. Jerome Hanrahan, who, despite a huge hole in the left side of his back, was still alive.

A short-timer with less than ninety days left on his tour, Hanrahan, like Pett, was a native Chicagoan. The two had hit it off right away. Hanrahan took Pett under his wing and helped him learn the ropes of being a field Marine.

Hanrahan had been sitting outside his bunker the previous evening talking with Pett and some others. Out of the blue, one of the men said, "Wouldn't it be something if an artillery round landed right between us and blew us all up, just like that."

Several of the others agreed that that would be a good way to go. But not Hanrahan, who was a devout Catholic "Not me," he announced. "I'm gonna say my prayers before I die."

Now Pett, also a Catholic, knelt by Hanrahan's side, holding his hands, while Hanrahan recited an Act of Contrition. A corpsman threw a hasty bandage on the gaping hole in Hanrahan's back, then Pett and another friend, LCpl. John Radgoski, loaded Hanrahan on a poncho. The pair carried him uphill to the casualty collection station.

"Take care, Hans," Pett told his friend. "We gotta go for the others but we'll be back."

Pett and Radgoski spent the next several hours looking for casualties in the tall grass. Whenever they found a living Marine, they would call for a corpsman. When the doc was done, they would help the man back up the hill.

It seemed as if they found as many dead as wounded. Pett passed the bodies of Hackett and Davis. He also found the lifeless remains of another friend, Pfc. Julius Kessler. Kessler had been right behind Pett when the firing started. Why Kessler had been hit and not himself, Pett did not know.

Pett also found a number of jammed M16s. Several were broken open, and cleaning rods poked uselessly from the barrels. What kinda shit is this? he wondered.

By late morning Pett and Radgoski had carried the last casualty up the hill. Pett asked the senior corpsman if Hanrahan had made it out. The doc shook his head, then pointed to the row of poncho-covered corpses lining the sides of the LZ.

Lance Corporal Wayne Ithier of Lieutenant Elliott's platoon had followed the progress of the two advance platoons. The intensity and duration of the NVA's fire surprised him. No rounds were directed at him or the rest of Elliott's platoon, but a lot of them snapped overhead. Ithier watched helplessly as his buddies in the other platoons were cut down. All he could do was blaze away at where he thought the NVA were dug in and hope his fire was doing some good.

About fifteen minutes into the firefight, the platoon sergeant crawled over to Ithier's squad. "Lieutenant Elliott wants some of you to go down and help the wounded. Drop your packs and gear. And, there's a Bronze Star in it for you guys."

Possessed of a tremendous sense of responsibility instilled in him by his career-Navy father, Ithier never hesitated. Although he was still dizzy and light-headed from the concussion he had suffered four days earlier, the eighteen year old shucked off his pack and went down the steep hillside into the draw with his fire team. Enemy rounds tore into the dirt all around them and zinged past the volunteers, but they never sought cover; they were focused on aiding the wounded.

Ithier turned right at the bottom of the draw. He moved only a few steps before he found his first casualty—a gut-shot Marine on his back, writhing in pain. Ithier and a buddy, Lance Corporal Hughes, knelt by the man's side and offered words of encouragement as they poured water on his exposed insides. It was obvious they could not do more or move him without a stretcher or a poncho. Ithier debated what to do, then the wounded man solved the dilemma. "Get some of the others; they're worse off than me."

As Ithier crawled forward, he realized the firing had stopped. "I figured the NVA had stopped shooting because they'd achieved their objective of stopping us," Ithier said.

Slowly he stood up. In the grass all around him he could see the crumbled forms of Marines. We're gonna need a lot more help down here, he thought.

He and Hughes found a Marine who had been shot in the legs. They formed a saddle with their hands to support him and started uphill. It was a difficult climb, and they jostled and bumped the casualty. He, in turn, moaned and complained about his intense pain. Sniper rounds snapped past them several times, but they finally reached the casualty collection station. The intrepid pair returned to the bottom of the draw four more times and brought back a wounded man each time.

As the artillery hit the enemy-occupied hillside, Lieutenant Givvin began to pull back. Marines he did not recognize appeared to pick up his dead and wounded. The damage to his platoon was devastating; of thirty-three men who had started down into the draw with the 3d Platoon, four were dead and twenty-six were wounded.

"I felt very bad about the losses," Givvin said. "I hadn't fulfilled my promise to protect them. All that training I'd gone through, and I'd failed in my mission. It took me several days before I got over it. Then all I wanted to do was get even and avenge the deaths of my men."

From his prone position Lieutenant Griesmer saw Givvin's platoon withdrawing. He radioed Madonna, who told him to pull back, too. As Griesmer passed the orders, he heard someone ask, "Who's gonna carry the lieutenant?"

"I didn't think I was that badly wounded, and I didn't want to be carried out. So I stood up," Griesmer said. "I passed out immediately."

The next thing Griesmer knew, he was being roughly carried up the hillside. His rear end constantly bounced off the ground, sending spasms of pain through his body. At the LZ someone gave him a morphine shot and he floated away.

As soon as the casualties were tended to, the remnants of Hotel Company pulled back to Lieutenant Colonel Delong's CP. There, the difficult task of reconciling the company roster began. The results showed that Hotel had lost nearly half its strength. Nine Marines were dead and forty-three were wounded. Madonna had only one intact platoon, Elliott's. It was an inauspicious start to BLT 2/3's drive on Hill 881N.

The airplane that brought combat artist Austin Deuel to Khe Sanh on the afternoon of 30 April carried a number of other correspondents. Among them was the fiery French photojournalist Catherine Leroy, a freelancer who had been covering the war for more than a year. In that time she had established herself as a feisty, outspoken critic of the American effort in South Vietnam. She frequently debated staff officers at press briefings and often challenged their reports of events she had witnessed. In fact, III MAF had banned her for six months for doing just that. Her credentials had just been reinstated when the Hill Fights began.

Upon arrival at Khe Sanh, Leroy and the other reporters received an up-to-the-minute brief from a member of the Combat Information Bureau located at the airstrip. The correspondents then split up to travel to the various field units. Leroy hitched a ride on a resupply helicopter going out to Hill 861.

"I was wearing a white head band when I left the helicopter," she remembered. "Soon a sniper fired at me. A Marine yelled for me to take off the head band. I did."

An escort took Leroy to Pappy Delong's CP. Delong briefed her on BLT 2/3's action so far that day, including the beating that Hotel Company had taken. He then took her with him to Golf Company. Delong told its CO, Capt. James P. Sheehan, "You've got the honor of taking that hill." As soon as the fast movers and the artillery finished blasting the slope, he continued, Golf would go in. The enemy-held hillside had to be taken before the advance up Hill 881N could proceed. "And," Delong told Sheehan, "Cathy's going with you."

Sheehan, a thirty-year-old Philadelphian with eight years in the Marine Corps, was not too pleased. He did not need a correspondent, particularly a female one, hanging around. To discourage Leroy, he told her it was primitive where they were headed.

"I can take care of myself," she retorted.

"I can't spare anyone to protect you."

"I don't need protection," she snapped back.

There was no time to argue with Leroy, and Sheehan had too many things to do to prepare for the attack, so he turned Leroy over to his gunny, William H. Janzen.

Janzen took Leroy to the ravine where the company waited. She proved an instant hit when she passed out cigarettes to the troops. They enjoyed having a "round-eye" female in their presence. One of the troops had torn trousers that allowed his privates to hang in plain view. "Turn around for Chrissakes," Janzen barked at him.

"That's okay, gunny. I'm married," the Marine responded, bringing laughter to the assembled troops.

Sheehan and Janzen watched Hotel's futile advance from the vicinity of the battalion CP. The fight developed right in front of them; they had a grandstand seat. But it seemed to be a distant fight—until a sniper's round whistled between them. They both dropped. When Janzen saw Hotel pulling back a little later, he knew that the enemy would still have to be routed. And he knew who would be doing the routing: Golf Company.

Another Golf Company Marine, nineteen-year-old Oklahoman Pfc. Robert J. Maras, had watched Hotel's action with some apprehension. Not only was this Maras's first exposure to combat—he had joined Golf on Okinawa—he feared for his new friend, Staff Sergeant Crawford. Maras was one of the newbies whom Crawford had taken under his wing while the replacements waited for the battalion to reach the island. Despite the difference in their age and rank, the two had hit it off immediately and become good friends.

Now, as Maras watched the action unfold below him, he recognized Crawford. He followed the plucky NCO's progress up the draw and winced when he saw Crawford get hit. When his friend continued his attack, Maras realized he was witnessing an incredible act of bravery. Then he lost sight of Crawford in the thickening brush. He said a silent prayer that his friend would survive.

At his CP, Captain Sheehan briefed his platoon leaders on his attack plan. The 1st Platoon would go up the NVA-held hillside while the 2d Platoon secured its right flank. The 3d Platoon would lay down a base of fire for the 1st Platoon.

The artillery fire did not cease until late in the day. Sheehan used the time to move his company forward. The troops spent a tiring ninety minutes hacking their way through the thick foliage that clogged the draw on the east side of the sloping ridge finger.

The 1st Platoon moved into position. Its leader, 2d Lt. Peter M. Hesser, had been in command for only a few weeks. A June 1966 graduate of the Naval Academy, Hesser had joined BLT 2/3 just three days before it sailed from Okinawa. This would be his first major combat action. He was nervous and he did not want to let his troops down. He would be dependent on his rock-solid platoon sergeant, SSgt. Ruben Santos, to keep the attack moving.

Finally, with darkness nearly on them, Sheehan ordered Hesser to go.

Santos took the lead on the left flank while Hesser led on the right. They raced across the intervening gully and started up the enemy-held slope. Behind them the 3d Platoon unleashed a fury of M16 and M60 fire, which pinned down the defenders. Off on the far right, the 2d Platoon kept up a steady stream of fire, too.

"Most of the trees had been blown down by the barrage so there was very little cover," Hesser recalled, "but we were moving. Then the enemy opened fire and we went down."

Determined to get some action pictures, Cathy Leroy told Gunny Janzen she wanted to go with Hesser's platoon. He knew there was no way to change her mind, so he took her to Lieutenant Hesser just before the platoon jumped off. As she advanced near the rear of the platoon, Leroy found the terrain so torn up by the artillery and aerial bombs that she could hardly keep her footing. The intensity of the fighting startled her. "There was so much noise it was unbelievable," she said. "The explosions of the M16s, the yelling of the Marines. I was scared to death."

A few feet in front of Leroy, Lieutenant Hesser told each of the men around him to get out a grenade. "When they had them ready, I had them throw them uphill at the same time. As soon as they went off we attacked again. It was just like a training film."

Not far from Hesser, Hospitalman Vernon Wike stopped to catch his breath. The climb up the steep hill through the soft earth had tired the husky nineteen year old. A former football player, the Phoenix, Arizona, resident still carried close to two hundred pounds on his six-foot frame. Even though he had arrived in South Vietnam in December, during the intervening weeks on Okinawa his body had grown unaccustomed to the country's brutal climate.

Above Wike, on the hillside, the platoon's forward elements closed on some enemy bunkers, which forced the 2d Platoon to hold its fire. For the first time, Wike could hear the crack of NVA AK-47s. Just then, not twenty-five feet in front of him, LCpl. William Roldan's M16 jammed. Instead of seeking cover to clear the weapon, Roldan turned to his right and bent over as he pulled the cocking lever back. From higher up the hill, an NVA shot Roldan. The twenty-year-old New Yorker collapsed in a heap.

Lieutenant Hesser reached forward and pulled Roldan toward him. Someone nearby started screaming, "Corpsman! Corpsman!"

From her position a little behind Hesser, Leroy saw Wike bound forward. She brought her camera up as he bent over Roldan. Branches from a tree stump blocked her view. She broke them off. Then she pressed the shutter. In the next few seconds she captured Wike in a series of images that would become some of the most famous of the Vietnam War.

"As soon as I reached him I saw it was 'Rock,'" Wike remembered. "We'd just met that morning. He told me he had less than sixty days left in-country. I put my hand on his chest. It slipped in all the blood. Then I found the entrance wound on his left side. I put a bandage on it. I was talking to Rock, but he was unconscious. I then put my head on his chest. I could hear his heart, but it was getting fainter. Then I found the exit wound and knew he'd been hit in the lungs. Then Rock died."

Though Wike had seen dead Marines before, this was his first combat death. The sense of loss overwhelmed him.

"I stared uphill, trying to find the sniper. I felt so frustrated. Then rage filled me and all I wanted to do was get revenge."

Wike vaulted over Roldan's body, grabbed the dead man's M16, cleared the jam, and dashed up the hillside. He passed within feet of Leroy, who had stopped taking pictures because of the fading light. As Wike passed her, he muttered, "I'm gonna kill 'em all!"

Before he got too far, a voice reached him. "Don't do it, doc. J. K's been hit and needs your help." That stopped Wike. He turned. Twenty feet away, LCpl. J. K. Johnson lay sprawled on his back. Wike hurried over.

Gunny Janzen watched the whole drama unfold in front of him. He spotted the muzzle blast from the sniper who had shot Roldan. From his position on the facing slope, he ripped a burst of M16 rounds at the enemy bunker. He did not know if he had done any good, but he sure felt better.

Wike had no more finished treating Johnson than another cry for a corpsman came from higher on the slope. Wike ran up to a crater, where he found a Marine with a bullet hole in his thigh. As Wike wrapped a bandage around the wound, Cathy Leroy and another correspondent flopped down beside him. They lay there panting from the exertion and excitement.

Most of the firing had died down. Then an outbreak of shots erupted from Sergeant Santos's sector. One of Santos's men, Cpl. Richard T. Schmitz, had spotted movement in a bunker. Perhaps thinking he could capture a prisoner and take advantage of Delong's standing offer of an in-country R and R as the reward for a POW, Schmitz dropped his weapon and crawled into the trench fronting the bunker.

From his position across the draw, Captain Sheehan realized what Schmitz was trying to do. Certain of the outcome, he yelled "No!" but Schmitz never heard him.

The NVA inside the bunker shot Schmitz, then pulled his body in with them. Corporal David M. Coleman saw Schmitz's body disappear into the bunker. Disregarding the danger, Coleman dropped into the narrow trench and grabbed Schmitz's feet. He tried to pull his friend free in a deadly game of tug-of-war, but the NVA had other ideas. They fired through Schmitz's body and hit Coleman five times. Although Coleman was thrown to the ground and was bleeding heavily from his legs, he returned to his task.

Staff Sergeant Santos rushed over. He quickly sized up the situation, pulled Coleman from the trench, and turned him over to a corpsman. Then he tied a rope to Schmitz's legs and tried to pull him free.

The NVA inside fired again. Santos was so close he suffered flash burns from the muzzle blast on his face and hands. With Schmitz clearly dead, Santos had no option. "Gimme a grenade," he called to those gathered around him.

Private First Class Maras freed one from his belt and tossed it to Santos. The gutsy sergeant pulled the pin.

"Fire in the hole," he yelled.

He pitched the grenade over Schmitz's body into the bunker. Seconds later it exploded with a muffled *karumph*. Santos ordered some men to block the entrance with logs and dirt.

By this time it was nearly dark. No more firing came from the enemy positions. The entire action had lasted less than ten minutes. Sheehan ordered the rest of Golf Company up the steep slope. The darkness made the climb even more difficult. Gunny Janzen got tired halfway up. He paused and watched with jealousy as the young Marines scooted right past him. Until then he had not thought that thirty-six was old.

Sheehan put his platoons into a hasty night defensive perimeter at the top of the hill. He wanted to be ready in case the NVA came back. A medevac was called to get the casualties out. Two Marines had been killed and nine wounded in the skirmish. It could have been much worse. Obviously, most of the NVA had pulled out earlier and left only a squad-sized unit behind to slow the Marines.

The night passed without an enemy attack, but Hospitalman Wike heard some NVA on a nearby hill calling to them. "Some of the Marines on the line returned the taunts," he said, "and we thought we'd get hit but weren't. It was a very long and nervous night."

At first light Santos sent a fire team to recover Schmitz's body. Amazingly, at least one NVA inside the bunker remained alive. The Marines retrieved Schmitz, tossed several grenades into the bunker, then sealed it up, entombing whoever remained inside.

The company radioman called for a medevac to remove Schmitz's remains. When it arrived, Cathy Leroy hopped aboard. She wanted to get back to Saigon as fast as possible to get her film developed. She hoped she had some shots she could sell to an American magazine.

Captain Sheehan received orders to pull back soon after Leroy departed. Two intermediate objectives north and west of his position were scheduled to be shelled. After they were, Golf would assault them in a movement aimed at positioning the company northeast of Hill 881N. Sheehan passed the orders to his platoon leaders. Within minutes the troops were saddled up and ready to move out. No one regretted leaving the killing ground.

Chapter Ten

When he led Echo BLT 2/3 off Hill 861 on the morning of 30 April 1967, twenty-seven-year-old Capt. Al Lyon might have been the most contented Marine at Khe Sanh. Contented because he was doing what he wanted most to do: command a rifle company. A Marine since 1958 when he dropped out of Ohio State University to enlist, Lyon had worn officer's bars since 1963 when he completed a program that sent promising young enlisted men to college for their degree and a commission in return for a four-year service commitment. Lyon had arrived in South Vietnam in August 1966 with 2/26. As soon as he received the double bars of a captain, he, along with his good friend Ray Madonna, went to 2/3. But unlike Madonna, Lyon did not get a rifle company.

Lyon spent six frustrating months in rear staff positions, all the while longing for his own company. As the first months of 1967 passed, he could not help but feel that his training and experience were being wasted and his career was over. Fortunately, Lieutenant Colonel Delong recognized Lyon's potential. During the retraining rotation to Okinawa, Delong named Lyon the new commander of Echo. Lyon could barely contain his elation. He had worked hard for eight years for this chance and now, at last, command was his. He vowed to be the best company commander the Marine Corps ever had.

To help him achieve that goal, Lyon depended on his platoon leaders. Key among them was 2d Lt. James R. Cannon, as hard-core a Marine as ever wore the uniform. He was born in Fredericksburg, Virginia, in 1936 and grew up with solid values and a high level of patriotism. Four months before his seventeenth birthday, Cannon finagled his way into

171

the Marines. He knew instantly he had found a home. The tough physical demands, the strong discipline, and the single-minded focus on mission attainment satisfied him completely.

Cannon went to South Vietnam in August 1965. Five months later he
returned to the States to attend warrant officers' school. No sooner had
he pinned on those bars than he received a temporary commission as a
second lieutenant and orders back to the war zone. In October 1966, after four months with Golf 2/26, he transferred to Echo 2/3.

Cannon quickly established himself as the toughest, meanest, and
most aggressive platoon leader in the battalion. He was so aggressive, in
fact, that some of the men in his platoon considered him too eager to
close with the enemy, too willing to risk the lives of his troops. Rumors
floated through the battalion during its retraining on Okinawa of a plot
to take Cannon out during an exercise in the Philippines. No one will
ever know if the rumor was true, because the battalion never went to the
Philippines. From Okinawa it headed straight back to South Vietnam,
and Echo's Marines soon had other targets for their frustrations.

Echo Company's objective for 30 April was a small knoll guarding the
southern approaches to Hill 881N. Once that position was taken, the battalion's left flank would be secure and it could continue its attack on Hill
881N.

"The low area between the two big hills was my major concern," Captain Lyon said. "There was a lot of brush and some dense woods that
could hide a lot of NVA. I expected them to be there, so, throughout the
day, I kept an eye on that area."

As his company neared its objective a little before noon, Lyon received
word that groups of enemy soldiers had been spotted on a ridgeline on
his right, or east, flank. He did not realize that these NVA were probably
fleeing Hotel Company's ambush site; he thought they were maneuvering
to attack him. He promptly ordered air strikes and gunships. While the
aircraft blasted the enemy, Lyon briefed his platoon commanders on his
plan of attack. The 1st Platoon, commanded by 1st Lt. Frank Izenour, and
Cannon's 2d Platoon received the mission of attacking the intermediate
objective. The 3d Platoon, under another mustang, 2d Lt. John Eller,
would secure the high ground on the right flank, actually a ridge finger
just west of where the NVA were under attack by the air support.

The 1st and 2d Platoons approached their jumping-off positions
through dense vegetation. Cannon recalled, "The undergrowth was

much thicker than it had appeared from a distance. The grass was waist high. The bamboo thickets were well over our heads."

Before the two platoons could actually begin their attack, heavy firing suddenly broke out along the right flank. The 3d Platoon was in trouble.

Second Lieutenant Clifton Canter, a twenty-three-year-old Floridian commanding the Weapons Platoon, had voluntarily accompanied the 3d Platoon on its foray to the right. With all his troops parceled out to the rifle platoons, he had no one left to command. A hard charger who had previously led the 1st Platoon and served a short stint as the company exec, Canter was not content to remain behind with the CP group, so he tagged along with Eller's platoon.

The 3d Platoon easily ascended the ridge finger and turned left, preparing to follow the finger to where it joined the intermediate objective. A burst of M16 fire punctured the morning quiet. Eller's point fire team had spotted NVA on the high ground to the right. Answering bursts of enemy fire splattered across the finger and sent the Marines sprawling.

Canter hugged the dirt, fervently wishing that he had something more than grass stalks to hide behind. When he learned that several wounded from the lead squad needed immediate medical attention, Canter looked around for Eller, but he could not see him. Although it was not his platoon, Canter knew that something had to be done. He pulled his lanky six-foot-four frame off the ground and dashed forward.

He found several wounded sprawled in the dirt and, under fire, quickly organized their evacuation. Then he gathered a handful of Marines and attacked a brush line in which he thought the enemy was hiding. Fortunately, they were not.

When he spotted another wounded Marine, Canter ran over and knelt beside him. The man had taken a round through both ankles. Canter turned him over to check for other wounds. A split second later, two enemy rounds hit the dirt where the casualty's chest had lain. The NVA were not giving up.

In rolling over, the man's canteen had gotten underneath him and slightly raised him off the ground. "I'm too high," he screamed. "Let me down. Let me down."

"Four inches higher didn't seem like it would make much difference," Canter recalled, "but then two more rounds passed right between us and one took off the front pocket button of his utilities. I pulled his web belt off and got the canteen out from under him. He calmed down."

A corpsman appeared and treated the Marine.

Because of the number of casualties that Eller's platoon had taken so quickly, Lyon dispatched Sgt. James J. Marden's 3d Squad from Izenour's platoon to help. Although he had been a Marine for more than three years, twenty-one-year-old Marden had been in South Vietnam less than two weeks. He had spent the previous two and a half years as part of the Marine detachment aboard the USS *Boston,* a cruiser based in his hometown of Boston. "It was the worst duty possible," Marden said. "The petty harassment made life aboard that ship absolutely miserable. I kept requesting transfer to Vietnam. It took two years, but I finally got out of there."

Marden arrived on Okinawa in early April as a senior corporal with no combat experience. Regardless, he received an immediate promotion to sergeant and took over a squad filled with veterans. That irritated the men. "I knew I was resented, but I tried to learn as fast as I could by asking a lot of questions and listening to the veterans," Marden said.

Now, as he rushed through a shallow gully and up the side of the finger toward his first combat, Marden tried to remember everything he had learned in boot camp and in the Marine Corps Institute correspondence courses he had been forced to take aboard the *Boston.* It all started to come back. He put his men on line across the finger and maneuvered his fire teams uphill. Before they had moved very far, Marden received a radio message that ordered him to halt and mark his position with a smoke grenade. He did so. More gunships came in to strafe the enemy.

In the meantime, Lieutenant Canter picked up a casualty's M16. He squeezed off several bursts before an AK-47 round slammed into his right arm just above the wrist. The bullet traveled up his arm, tearing away a huge chunk of flesh as it exited his forearm in a spray of blood.

A corpsman appeared as if by magic and put a field dressing on the shattered limb. Canter moved back down the finger. He did not get far. The NVA had him in their sights and shot him again. This slug shattered a Japanese camera he carried in his utility shirt's front pocket, then slammed into his right hand. The impact spun him around and knocked him down.

The same corpsman came upon him again and treated Canter a second time. While he did, an NVA took aim at him. The NVA missed the sailor but hit Canter.

"The round meant for the doc hit dead center in my right butt cheek," Canter remembered. "It smashed my hip, traveled through the inside of my leg down to the knee, but didn't exit. It damaged my sciatic nerve and paralyzed my right leg. It hurt like hell. The corpsman ripped open my utilities, checked the entrance wound, then bandaged my hand. I guess he didn't know how bad my leg was.

"After he left I lay there thinking I was the last one left alive on the hill. I had no weapon. I figured if the enemy came I'd use my last grenade to blow us all up."

While he lay there finalizing his death plans, two young Marines suddenly appeared at his side. They had been looking for him and were elated to find him. Because of Canter's size, the two had a hard time getting him to the LZ, but they managed. Someone gave him a shot of morphine. It did not dull all the pain, but at least he knew he would live. Soon a CH-46 came in; he was loaded aboard and was gone, entering the pipeline that carried the wounded from the battlefield to the hospital.

While Lieutenant Cannon waited to jump off, he had spotted several enemy bunkers firing on the 3d Platoon. Anxious to join the fight and take the pressure off Eller's platoon, Cannon radioed Lyon for permission to attack. Lyon said yes. Cannon and Izenour signaled their platoons forward.

"The going was tough and control was difficult, but we managed to stay abreast by coordinating via our radios," Cannon said. "I got about halfway up when several shots rang out. The next thing I knew I was flat on my back several meters downhill with my radioman tearing at my clothes. A spent AK round had hit me just above my heart. By some miracle it hadn't penetrated the skin. Another round had creased my left forearm and gone into my pack, shattering a ration can. A third round hit the M79 grenade launcher I carried and destroyed it."

Cannon shook off the wounds and rejoined the attack. Minutes later the two platoons broke out of the tall grass. The military crest of the little knoll lay but a few meters ahead. In short order the Marines swept over the hill. The tactic worked. No more enemy fire came. The NVA facing Eller's platoon fled, and that allowed medevacs to come in to extract the wounded. Then the 3d Platoon moved out, picked up Marden's squad, and joined the rest of the company.

By the time Captain Lyon and his command group arrived on the knob, Cannon and Izenour had swept the area. It was obvious the NVA had recently occupied the position: Numerous fighting holes and dozens of well-constructed bunkers covered the ground. Even the rawest recruit could tell that the NVA had been there in strength.

Lyon ordered patrols sent out in several directions. Squads were detailed to clear avenues of fire through the thick grass. Other Marines deepened some of the fighting holes. No one doubted that the enemy would be coming back. The listening posts went out at dusk. Fifty percent watches were the norm throughout the night.

Echo Company experienced no enemy probes that night. When the sun peeked over the horizon on the morning of 1 May, everyone breathed a sigh of relief. The men began their morning routine. Plans were made for area patrols, the LPs returned to the perimeter, hungry fingers clawed through packs in search of something good for breakfast, and those who had heat tabs ignited them for their morning coffee. A few men shaved. The forward air controller, on his first ground mission, propped a mirror in the crook of a tree, lathered up, and ran a razor across his stubble.

The veterans heard it first—the distant but distinct *kathunk* of a mortar round leaving its tube. Several more followed in quick succession.

"Incoming! Incoming!" The desperate cry echoed across the knob.

The Marines scrambled for their holes. Asses and elbows dove for cover. Most made it. Some did not.

Private First Class Donald E. Hinman, one of Cannon's men, had been a Marine nearly three years but had joined Echo on Okinawa only a month earlier. The sound of an incoming mortar shell was foreign to him, but he quickly got the message when he saw everyone running around. He raced back toward his hole with two other newbies. He almost made it.

A shell landed between him and his two buddies. Splinters of red-hot shrapnel peppered the twenty year old's left chest and arm. He crumpled in a heap a few feet from his hole. His squad leader, Sgt. Billy J. Like, popped out of his hole, grabbed the collar of Hinman's shirt, and pulled him in.

Shards of shrapnel also tore into Captain Lyon's chest and left arm. He stayed upright, though, and made it to his hole.

For some reason the FAC seemed oblivious to the threat. Perhaps because he was new, he did not understand what was happening. Perhaps he was so intent on his shave that he had blocked out his surroundings. Whatever the reason, he remained blissfully unaware as a round landed close behind him. A jagged hunk of shrapnel slammed into the back of his head, tearing a huge hole in his skull. He crumpled in a heap.

Nearly two dozen mortar rounds walked across the perimeter with uncanny accuracy. Bits of metal riddled everything aboveground. When the mortars stopped, rapid bursts of small-arms fire ripped across the perimeter. Then, slowly, quiet fell along the perimeter.

Marines and corpsmen cautiously emerged from their holes. They set about treating the several casualties. Three Marines were killed outright and sixteen were wounded. How many of them might have escaped injury if they had had their flak jackets will never be known.

Corporal Fred Monahan, the S-2 scout attached to Echo, remembered the FAC. "I can still see his blood mixed with the shaving cream. It stood out because only officers had shaving cream; the troops shaved dry."

Captain Lyon did not think the FAC would make it. "He was so severely injured I was sure he'd die before the medevacs got in." (Thirty-three years later, Lyon was pleasantly surprised to meet the man at a 2/3 reunion.)

The casualties were carried to an LZ to await the helicopters. Hinman lay on a poncho and talked to a group of Marines. "All of a sudden someone yells 'Incoming!' again," he recalled. "Before you know it everyone's gone, leaving all us wounded untended and uncovered."

Much to Hinman's relief, the incoming rounds landed some distance away. Finally the medevacs arrived. Hinman and the others were loaded aboard and flown out.

One of the corpsmen tagged Captain Lyon for evacuation, but he tore the tag off and threw it away. "There was no way I was leaving that easy," Lyon said. "I'd worked too damn hard to get that company and I knew I'd probably never have another chance."

In the first twenty-four hours of its mission, Echo had lost more than twenty men, more than 10 percent of its strength. Because of that, the movement by Echo toward Hill 881N was delayed. Instead, the company was to remain in its position and send out patrols to probe for any lingering enemy.

Sergeant Marden took his squad out to sweep up a neighboring ridge finger. "What really stuck in my mind was the order to recon by fire. We never did that," Marden said.

Marden led his squad in a northeasterly direction. When they reached the base of the objective, Marden ordered his men to fire their M16s uphill. To his immense shock every M16 jammed within a few rounds. "That really spooked us," he said. "This was the first time we'd really fired these new weapons since getting them on Okinawa. To have them all jam was scary. I had the M60 and M79 prep the area while my men cleared their weapons."

Another patrol found the site from which the NVA had fired their mortars. Wooden firing platforms were built on the reverse slope of a nearby hill. In addition, the entire area was dotted with enemy-dug spider holes and bunkers. Any doubt anyone had about the NVA being in the area immediately evaporated. They were there in strength, and they were watching the Marines.

Convinced there were more NVA in the hills than anyone suspected, Lieutenant Colonel Delong opted to make maximum use of his supporting arms. With his three maneuver companies held in check, he ordered a full-scale, daylong aerial and artillery bombardment of Hill 881N.

BLT 2/3's strongest company, Golf, waited patiently on the eastern slopes of Hill 881N for its first objective to be prepped. When the artillery fire lifted about 1000, Captain Sheehan moved his company forward. After the troops occupied the hillock, they settled in to wait while the artillery blasted the next objective.

One of the Khe Sanh–based batteries made a mistake. Because of the position of Hill 881N from the combat base, Golf Company was right on the gun-target line. With all the ordnance flying overhead, no one heard the inbound rush of the errant shells. The first 105mm shell slammed down at the base of Golf's hill. A split second later the next two hit with an incredible roar, one near the CP, the other a little higher up the hill.

Forward observer 2d Lt. Brian R. Jackson's radiomen grabbed his handset. "Check fire! Check fire!" he screamed into the mike.

No more rounds came in.

The misfire killed three Marines and wounded several more. One of the dead was a married rear-echelon sergeant who had just joined the company in the field that morning so he could see a little action.

While waiting for the medevacs to arrive, Jackson noticed some of the Marines glaring at him. "Obviously, they thought I was responsible for the fire mission," he said. "They didn't know I'd had nothing to do with it. Those missions were laid on by the battalion."

The twenty-two-year-old Rhode Islander felt terrible about the incident. He had just joined Golf after being assigned to Bravo 1/12 on Okinawa. "I'd been an artillery officer for over a year, but I'd never really seen the awesome destruction of an artillery shell," he said. "It had a chilling effect on me."

An hour after the choppers flew off, Golf Company stood atop its second objective of the day. The little hill showed evidence of recent occupation by the enemy. The probing Marines uncovered an extensive bunker complex. A search of the bunkers revealed a quantity of enemy equipment and a handful of ammo. Everyone felt that the enemy still lingered nearby. Golf set in for the night, taking advantage of the enemy's bunkers. Captain Sheehan sent out extra LPs and cautioned them to remain alert. The possibility of a night counterattack loomed large.

The bombardments ordered by Lieutenant Colonels Wilder and Delong for their individual objectives on 1 May were nearly unprecedented in the Vietnam War for their intensity and duration. Nearly fifteen hundred 105mm and 155mm artillery shells pummeled Hills 881S and 881N. One hundred sixty-six air strikes dropped 650,000 pounds of ordnance, including 130 one-ton bombs. In the morning hours, Hill 881N received the bulk of the bombs and shells. In the afternoon the focus shifted to Hill 881S.

Despite the daylong pounding, the NVA replaced its battered forces with fresh troops. Sometime on 1 May the enemy commander withdrew the shattered 18th NVA Regiment from the battlefield. The 95th Regiment of the NVA 325C Division slipped through the Khe Sanh hills to take up positions on Hill 881N. The fresh troops were eager to tangle with the United States Marines.

Lieutenant Colonel Wilder used the cover of the bombardment to regroup and reorganize 3/3. On the morning of 1 May, he ordered Captain Bennett and the survivors of Mike 3/3 back to the battalion CP.

Lieutenant Cialone recalled that when they reached the CP, "It was on top of a rather steeply sided plateau, so the climb up it was hard. Captain Griggs had returned from R and R a couple of days earlier. In fact, he had watched the attack from the battalion CP. He was reaching out to help pull the men up the last few steps, offering them words of encouragement." Captain Griggs later said, "Captain Bennett and the Mike Company Marines performed valiantly during that battle and I have always been proud of them."

Choppers flew in just before noon. The weary members of Mike 3/3 climbed aboard for the short flight to Khe Sanh. The same helicopters then ferried Foxtrot BLT 2/3 out to 3/3's CP. They assumed the role of battalion reserve for 3/3.

Because it was the last 2/3 unit to arrive at the Khe Sanh Combat Base, Foxtrot had stayed there as the reserve force. Foxtrot's troops spent most of their time manning the base's perimeter bunkers and conducting short patrols. But that did not mean they escaped the horrors of the fighting in the hills.

Private First Class William Ryan recalled: "We went out almost every day, patrolling the area south of the base. We never made any contact or saw any sign of the enemy. Though we could hear the artillery and jets bombing the hills, the war seemed far away. Then I took a walk over to the airstrip."

What he saw stunned him. "Lined up neatly along the runway was a long row of body bags. I couldn't believe there were that many. All I could think was, What the hell is going on out there?"

Staff Sergeant Bob French could have told him. He had helped unload the casualties from the helicopters. Lieutenant Colonel Delong had been true to his word. He had sent the logistical support unit, complete with French's provisional rifle platoon, to Khe Sanh. There, French's ersatz combat Marines contributed by manning perimeter bunkers and filling work details around the base. But when they were not so occupied, Staff Sergeant French and his Marines willingly pitched right in to help unload the medevacs. "The wounded would be on top of the body bags, which were sometimes two deep. It was horrible work, but it had to be done. Several of the rear echelon gunnys chewed me out for helping, saying that NCOs were above that. One even threatened to put me on report. I told him to shove it and stay out of our way."

Colonel Lanigan tapped Echo 2/9 to replace Foxtrot 2/3 as the reserve. It arrived at Khe Sanh around noon on 1 May. Captain William Terrill placed his men in the all-too-familiar positions around the base. He sent Sgt. Spencer Olsen and his platoon to garrison Hill 861 and prevent any return by the NVA. Olsen had never expected to see that deadly hill again after his 16 March fight there, but he was back, and he would spend two weeks on Hill 861 before being relieved.

The pounding of Hill 881S with high-explosive aerial bombs and artillery shells began anew at first light on 2 May. From their positions near the base of Hill 881S, the Marines of Kilo and Mike 3/9 could not see the actual hits on top of the hill, but they could definitely hear the explosions and watch the jets screaming in on their bombing runs. "That was very comforting," said Pfc. Charles Saltaformaggio of Kilo 3/9.

But being that close to the bombardment had its dangers. Mike 3/9's Pfc. Ernest Murray remembered that pieces of shrapnel thudded into the ground all around the Marines. A few found flesh.

As he crouched in a hole during one aerial strike, Mike 3/9's Lt. Edward Kresty scooted over to make room for another man. At that instant a sharp explosion erupted nearby. "Whether it was a short round or an enemy mortar shell I never knew," Kresty said. "But shrapnel from it hit my right forearm and hand as I moved. The whole arm swelled up pretty bad."

Kresty had just earned his third Purple Heart in two wars.

At precisely 1100 every howitzer at Khe Sanh let loose at Hill 881S. For fifteen minutes they hurled shells across the sky, one after another, until they melded into a continuous roar. When they stopped, Wilder gave the signal: Kilo and Mike 3/9 started forward.

Captain Giles, Kilo 3/9, followed Lieutenant Woodall's earlier route up the hill. He found the silence eerie. "All I could hear were the grunts of my Marines and the clang of their equipment. We could have been the only people out there for all I knew." Two-thirds of the way up the hill, Giles saw his first NVA bunker. Even a quick glance revealed how well built it was.

As he followed Mike 3/3's route, Lieutenant Kresty could not believe the steepness of the slope. Several times he had to pull himself up by exposed tree roots. How could anyone fight in this? he wondered.

Many of the Marines working their way up the hill eagerly anticipated a revenge-filled tangling with the NVA. But not everyone shared the blood lust. Private First Class Saltaformaggio felt apprehensive about going back up. He had no feeling of revenge or pending victory. As far as he was concerned, it was just another day at war.

The two companies reached the top of Hill 881S ninety minutes after starting out. What they found both surprised and disappointed them. Two days of near-constant bombardment had completely denuded the hilltop. The destruction amazed Private First Class Murray. "There was barely a tree standing. There were burn marks everywhere from napalm, craters all over the place, and dirt thrown up everywhere."

Kilo 3/9's LCpl. Arthur Gennaro did not even recognize the hill. "Almost all the vegetation was gone and it looked different," he later wrote his parents.

And there would not be any revenge. Within minutes of topping the hill, the Marines realized that the NVA had departed. How and where they had gone was a mystery, but there was almost no evidence they had even been there. Nothing. (Not until sometime later did the Marines learn that the Khe Sanh hills were honeycombed with caves and tunnels that provided the enemy with easy escape routes.) Captain Giles found the scene hard to believe. "Sometime between the time we pulled off that hill and when the artillery started, the North Vietnamese had thoroughly policed it. And I mean thoroughly. We didn't even find expended brass. It was just incredible they could have done this."

What the Marines did find were the remains of the comrades they had left behind. Most of the bodies had been horribly mangled by the hundreds of tons of explosives that had fallen on the hilltop. But before the NVA had left, they had taken the time to put two or three corpses on display. The bodies lay spread-eagle on top of bunkers, their penises pulled out of their pants.

The NCOs formed details to collect the remains. Gunnery Sergeant John Hatfield sauntered over to forward observer Pfc. John Krohn and a group of men. "Okay, Krohn, let's do it," he said. The Marines used entrenching tools to scoop the remains onto ponchos. It was nearly impossible to identify individual bodies. Only dog tags allowed that.

Mike 3/9's corpsman, Doc Hoffman, helped police up the dead with a detail of other Marines from his company. "We dug one Marine out of a crater," he said. "Only his arm had been sticking out." When Hoffman had volunteered six months earlier to leave a cushy assignment at a naval hospital in Japan to become a field medic with the Marines, he never expected to see anything as bad as this. "We spent the entire afternoon picking up body pieces and tagging and bagging the dead."

A Marine approached Captain Giles during the cleanup. He had found the bodies of Lieutenants Woodall and Hepner. Did the captain want to see them? "No," Giles said emphatically. He wanted to remember them as the vibrant young men they had been.

Lance Corporal Gennaro remembered the overpowering stench. "It was nauseating. None of us could eat. It took us two days to find everyone. Even after that the smell of death hung over the hill for a long time."

Lance Corporal Ira Johnson of Mike 3/9 found the body of his boot camp buddy, Robert Schley. "We thought we'd found all our guys, so we were searching the bunkers. Way down the back side of the hill we came across Schley. It was almost by accident we found him." It would be years before Johnson learned of Schley's gallant actions on Hill 881S.

Not until the next day were all the remains recovered. Helicopters flew the bodies to Khe Sanh, where Staff Sergeant French and his men had the unpleasant task of off-loading the ponchos. From Khe Sanh the bodies and body parts went to various morgues for positive identification and processing before being returned to families in the United States.

Several of the corpses ended up at the morgue on the USS *Princeton*, a World War II aircraft carrier converted to a helicopter ship and home to a portion of BLT 2/3. Hotel 2/3's SSgt. Edward Crawford occupied a bed in its hospital ward recovering from his wounds when a Navy captain approached him.

"Do you know anything about booby traps?"

"Yes, sir, a little. What's up?"

The medical officer explained that one of the corpses in the ship's morgue had been booby-trapped; the NVA had placed a grenade in its skull cavity. No one knew what to do.

Without hesitation Crawford said he would take care of it. At the urging of some other patients, he draped himself with several flak jackets, although he joked, "If that thing goes off, these won't do me any good."

Once all nearby personnel had been evacuated, Crawford entered the morgue. A short time later he emerged with an American grenade cradled in his bloody hands. He walked gingerly down several passageways, reached an open hatch, stepped outside, and dropped the missile into the sea.

On his way back to the ward, one of the witnesses noticed that Crawford was not wearing the flak jackets. Crawford had removed them in the morgue because they were too cumbersome.

Back on Hill 881S, Lieutenant Colonel Wilder found himself besieged by members of the press. Helicopters had ferried in more than forty correspondents. They roamed the hilltop for more than an hour taking pictures and interviewing Marines. When they finished, they returned to Wilder to arrange helicopters for their return to the airstrip so they could file their stories.

"Sorry," Wilder told them. "No one leaves until all Marine casualties are taken off. Then you can go."

The reporters flew into a rage. They did not want to be anywhere near the danger; they only wanted to record the aftermath. Wilder held his ground. Finally, as dusk neared, Wilder let them leave. Some correspondents filed formal complaints with III MAF, but Wilder did not care.

Late that afternoon a severe thunderstorm erupted over the Khe Sanh hills. Dark clouds boiled over the mountaintops, the temperature dropped drastically, and a heavy rain with strong winds and lightning lashed the area. Combat artist Pfc. Austin Deuel hunkered down in a bunker atop Hill 881S. Several Marines pulled the ponchos off some corpses that had not been evacuated. Wilder yelled a threat to court-martial the next man to do so.

The entire scene seemed unreal to Deuel. The thunder and lightning reminded him of the artillery barrages that had pounded the hill just hours earlier. As he watched, a lightning bolt struck several nearby Marines. The man in the next hole muttered, "Even God's mad at us."

Deuel decided that was an apt assessment.

On the slopes of Hill 881N, Echo and Golf BLT 2/3 spent the morning of 2 May in preparation for their attack on the hill. Barrage after barrage of artillery shells blasted the top and sides of the hill. Some hit so close that shrapnel struck several of the waiting Marines. A piece embedded itself in the left arm of Golf Company's Pfc. Robert Maras. One of the company's corpsmen, Lloyd Heath, put a dressing on it. "You can get on a chopper and get out of here," Heath told Maras. Maras did not think the injury that bad, so he declined. He did not want to leave his buddies.

At 1015 Captain Sheehan received the order for Golf to move out. The first objective for the day was a small knoll on the northeast slope of Hill 881N. From there the company would be in a good position to continue to the top of the hill. Golf's 3d Platoon, led by 2d Lt. Andrew "Mac" McFarlane, had the point that morning.

At thirty-seven, McFarlane humorously referred to himself as the "oldest second lieutenant in the Marine Corps." He had joined the Marines at age eighteen in 1948 from his home of Teaneck, New Jersey. Two years later he was battling Chinese in the frozen mountains of the Chosin Reservoir area of North Korea. A stellar career followed until one day in the spring of 1966, while stationed at the Marine Barracks, Bermuda, Mac received his well-deserved promotion to first sergeant. A few hours later he returned to the commander's office, where, as he put it, "I was demoted to second lieutenant."

McFarlane went to South Vietnam in September 1966 and joined Foxtrot 2/3 near Da Nang. When the battalion was selected for the SLF, he went with Captain Madonna and the advance party to Okinawa. It was there he received word of the 28 February destruction of his company.

During the retraining on Okinawa, McFarlane took over Golf Company's 3d Platoon. To the men of the "Third Herd," McFarlane represented all that was right about the Corps. Far above the petty harassment that defined many senior NCOs, McFarlane treated his men with respect and gave them the benefit of his nearly two decades of service and his combat experience. He knew and understood war as few men did. As far as he was concerned, the better he prepared his young Marines for the horrors of war, the better were their chances of surviving.

Golf Company moved easily up a narrow ridge that ran along the eastern slope of Hill 881N. To the right the ground fell away steeply. On the left the ground rose sharply to the top of the hill. The company entered an area of thick woods and dense brush about 1430. After the point man, LCpl. James Boda, forced his way through it, he entered a clearing about twenty-five meters deep. On the other side rose a small, wooded knob.

Boda paused. He scanned back and forth intently for any sign of the enemy. Satisfied, he stepped into the clearing. Behind him, the rest of his 1st Squad, followed by Lieutenant McFarlane and his radioman, LCpl. William Vlasek, moved out, too. By the time they were halfway across the clearing, the 2d Squad had emerged from the woods. When it reached the midpoint of the clearing, the 1st Squad entered the wooded knob. To the rear, the 3d Squad had just reached the edge of the wooded area.

A violent blast of AK-47 fire erupted from the wooded knob without warning. Several Marines dropped, riddled with bullets. Others hit the ground and frantically scurried for cover.

McFarlane huddled behind a tree at the front edge of the wooded knob. Vlasek lay nearby, a bullet in his temple. Mac grabbed the handset to report the contact to Sheehan.

Captain Sheehan, all action, had already moved to the forward edge of the woods that protected the rest of his company. Crouched nearby, Pfc. Tom Huckaba, a member of McFarlane's 3d Squad, heard the lieutenant tell Sheehan that his radioman was down and he had several other wounded.

"Don't worry, Mac," Sheehan replied. "We'll get you out. I'll call up the sixty-mike-mikes [60mm mortars]."

While the mortar teams set up, Corpsman Heath tried to reach one of the wounded. He barely made it to the knoll before a fusillade of fire cut him down.

Recovery of the wounded remained a priority. With two others from his squad, Private First Class Huckaba got the nod to attempt the rescue. Huckaba, a nineteen-year-old mailman from Lockport, Illinois, swallowed hard. He had just joined Golf on Okinawa. The fight on 30 April was his first, and it had been scary. He had not wanted to fail his new buddies, or himself. He did not. And he would not now.

"The three of us moved into the clearing and headed toward the knob," Huckaba recalled. "We used our instincts and our training to jump, crawl, and zigzag through the open area to avoid being targets. I couldn't see the NVA, but they could see me. Their bullets were passing so close to my head that I not only heard them snap past my ears, I could feel their heat, too."

The first man they came to, James Golden, had taken a round in the spine. Huckaba and the others picked him up, then, oblivious to the danger, ran back across the clearing. Once in the safety of the woods, they turned Golden over to the corpsmen.

The three returned to the clearing without hesitation. They found another Marine. They loaded him on a poncho and raced rearward. Then it was back again into the clearing. This time intense enemy fire pinned them down. Determined to save more lives, Huckaba and his companions again ran, rolled, and zigzagged across the clearing. This time they made it all the way to Vlasek. "He was still alive, but barely breathing," Huckaba remembered. "As we gathered him up, Lieutenant Mac gave me a nod, as if to say we'd be okay."

They got Vlasek to the aid station. Then they headed back once more. Unfortunately, despite their valiant effort, Vlasek died a short time later.

Captain Sheehan decided to pull back. It was too dangerous to risk an attack across the clearing; he did not want any more casualties. He radioed McFarlane to withdraw. McFarlane agreed. He told Sheehan that all the other casualties were dead. Under a heavy cover fire, McFarlane and the survivors made it back.

Carrying its recovered casualties, the battered company moved toward a clearing several hundred meters to the rear. Before they reached it, a severe squall, from the same storm line that had engulfed 3/3 on Hill 881S, barreled down on them. Rain, whipped by forty-mile-per-hour winds, fell in torrents. Thunder crashed and lightning bolts flashed out of the sky.

Private First Class Huckaba's buddy, Pfc. Dennis Johnson, who held the other end of the poncho carrying Vlasek, remarked, "I think this is God's way of crying. He's just as sick of this as we are."

During the trek in the blinding rainstorm, the CP group somehow became separated from the rest of the company. As they tried to find their way, artillery FO Lt. Brian Jackson grew so apprehensive about their chances for survival that he pulled his .45-caliber pistol from its holster. If the NVA are coming after us, he thought, I'm gonna be ready.

But before he had to use his weapon, the CP group found the rest of the company. When they reached the clearing they called for medevacs. A CH-46 made it in despite the rainsquall. The most severely wounded were loaded on board and flown to safety.

Golf Company dug in for the night. The rain continued unabated, bringing with it colder temperatures. The Marines spent a miserable night in their holes. Huckaba recalled it as one of the worst nights of his life. "We had little food, little water, and hardly any cigarettes. Three of us split one cigarette. That was our luxury for the night."

Gunnery Sergeant William Janzen wrapped himself in a poncho and crawled into a shell hole. Despite the wet and cold he soon fell into a deep sleep. The next morning he awoke in water up to his neck.

Lieutenant Jackson spent such a cold, wet night that he did not care if the NVA came. "If they came and got me, at least I'd be out of my misery," he rationalized.

After the mortar attack early on 1 May, Captain Lyon's Echo BLT 2/3 spent the rest of the day patrolling the area and strengthening its positions in anticipation of an enemy ground attack. If Echo's Marines were not on patrol or detailed to unload resupply helicopters, they worked to enlarge the positions originally dug by the NVA. Digging in hard soil with entrenching tools was backbreaking work, but by nightfall Echo was as ready as it could be. Around the perimeter Lieutenant Cannon's 2d Platoon held the sector from ten o'clock to two; Lieutenant Eller's 3d Platoon covered from two to six; and Lieutenant Izenour's held from six to ten. In that sector Sgt. James Marden's squad held the middle position. Just after his men settled in, Izenour radioed Marden to move his squad downhill about twenty meters. "I argued with the lieutenant about this because the First Squad, on my right, never moved down to tie in with us. As a result we had a big hole on our right. He ordered me to move anyway. I had to dig a one-man hole in the center of that gap and put a man out there all night to make sure no one came through. Fortunately, they didn't."

Although all hands were eager to tangle with the enemy, Echo had to hold in position the next morning, 2 May, for preparatory fire and to coordinate its attack on Hill 881N with 3/3's movement on Hill 881S. As Captain Lyon moved around the perimeter without his helmet, he caught a piece of shrapnel from a friendly artillery round in his head. "I felt stupid because I was always after the troops to keep their helmets on. Once again the doc thought I should go to the rear, but I wouldn't. I wasn't hit that bad and I still wasn't going to give up my company."

At about the time Golf Company was given its orders, Captain Lyon received his. Echo was to head for the top of Hill 881N in conjunction with Golf's movement on its flank. "Saddle up and move 'em out," Lyon ordered his platoon leaders.

It took the company nearly an hour of hard uphill humping to reach its jump-off position. During that move an aerial observer radioed to ask if Echo had left any men at its old position. No, he was told. "Well, I see a bunch of people moving over it," he said.

Corporal Fred Monahan, the S-2 scout, was ordered to retrace the company's route. All was quiet at the old perimeter, so he returned to the company.

By then Echo had started its attack on Hill 881N. The company moved easily up the hill, encountering only token resistance. For Captain Lyon, his years of training and waiting were finally paying off. "I had Cannon's platoon in the middle, Izenour's on the left, and Eller's on the right," Lyon said. "The rifle platoons moved just as they should have. One leapfrogged forward while the other two provided covering fire.

"I was so proud of the platoon leaders and their men. They were like a well-oiled machine working their way up that hill."

Stopping only to call in artillery fire, Echo Company steadily closed on the top of Hill 881N. It had nearly reached the summit by 1530. Resistance was light, almost too light. Only a few sniper rounds harassed the Marines during the assault. One stray round ricocheted into Sergeant Marden's calf. It was not anything serious, so he kept moving.

Echo reached the top just before 1600. "I felt like an eagle as I looked down into the valleys below us," Lyon recalled.

Echo still had not encountered any enemy, but Lyon could not shake the gnawing feeling that the NVA were waiting on the north side of the hill to pounce on his single company after it set in for the night. He just knew they were there.

As Lyon briefed Lieutenant Colonel Delong via the radio about his situation, the same heavy squall line that had washed over Golf Company and 3/3 erupted right on top of Echo. "It had been a sunny, hot day,"

Lyon said. "All of a sudden the temperature dropped dramatically. Within minutes it started to hail. The wind built until it felt like a gale. I discussed my options with Pappy. I believed I was very vulnerable on that hilltop, without any support. I still thought the NVA were lying in wait for us just on the other side of the top. I told Pappy I thought it was best for us to return to our old positions and set in for the night. The next morning, with the storm gone and Golf in a better position to support us, we'd go back up."

Delong concurred. Within minutes Captain Lyon had ordered Echo Company to move back down the hill. Not everyone agreed with the retreat. Lieutenant Cannon, in particular, disagreed. "How strange, I remember thinking. Nothing stops the assault except the enemy and we hadn't even made contact with them." In his opinion, Echo should have dug in where it was regardless of any threats.

Nonetheless, orders were orders. Echo turned around and started back to the plateau on which it had spent the last two nights. The Marines, who moved cautiously down the slippery slope, did not reach the familiar site until after dusk. Once there the troops were told to find their old positions and reoccupy them.

Sergeant Marden had his men make a quick check for booby traps. They found none. He still had great concern about the gap on his right. Lieutenant Izenour never had moved the 1st Squad down. To fill the dangerous gap, Marden put his twelve men in six two-man holes. They would be on 50 percent watch all night.

As Echo's Marines settled in, the rain changed to intermittent showers. Then a thick ground fog formed. It promised to be a long, cold, wet night.

Chapter Eleven

Sleep eluded Echo BLT 2/3's Capt. Al Lyon. The adrenaline rush from the day's action on Hill 881N and the throbbing pain from his two wounds kept him from getting more than a few minutes of sleep at a time. Finally, around 0400 he crawled out of his bunker. Layers of fog blanketed the plateau. A light rain fell from the dark sky. Lyon urinated, then returned to his bunker. Centrally located, the bunker put him about thirty yards behind his platoons' positions.

A few minutes later he heard someone to his front, in Cannon's sector of the perimeter, issue the classic military challenge, "Halt, who goes there?"

In response, an incredible blast of small-arms fire lashed the still night.

Lyon immediately radioed news of the attack to battalion, then ordered up illumination rounds from the 81mm mortars. Then he radioed Cannon.

Lieutenant Cannon had moved into his old bunker, where he was joined by his platoon sergeant, SSgt. Robert Morningstar, and his radioman, Lance Corporal Hovietz. Cannon had had a busy night as he oversaw the setting up of his platoon's defenses. His young Marines were good, but they had a tendency to slack off if he did not stay on them. The rain and cold further dulled their enthusiasm. Cannon and Morningstar made sure the Claymore mines and trip flares were set up to guard the likely avenues of approach. Cannon ordered a 50 percent watch. Only when he was assured that all preparations had been handled did he return to his bunker. He removed his boots and socks. After he wrung out his socks, he turned his boots upside down to drain out the water. Then he turned in.

"At 0415 I heard my Third Squad leader, Sergeant Billy Joe Like, an excellent Marine, issue his challenge," Cannon recalled. "The volume of fire that followed stunned me. The whole northern side of the perimeter just exploded with fire. I could hear a fifty-caliber machine gun off to my right front firing in long bursts."

Cannon barked out orders. He yelled for Morningstar and Hovietz to follow him outside. As he stepped into the open, a mortar blast blew a Marine in on him. Cannon freed himself from the casualty and told his platoon sergeant, "Take care of him." Then he grabbed Hovietz and went back outside.

He found a nightmare. Mortar shells were erupting all along his platoon's front. Bursts of AK-47 fire seemed to be coming from everywhere. Shouts from the NVA and screams from wounded Marines filled the night. Fleeting forms of infiltrating enemy soldiers darting through his lines told Cannon that this was more than a probe.

"My First Squad radioman, Private First Class John R. Meuse, radioed me that he'd been hit and needed a corpsman. I didn't have one to send, so I just told him to hang on and I'd get help to him as soon as I could. Then he briefed me on his squad's status. Their machine gun had been knocked out and they had a lot of casualties. The squad leader wanted to fire his Claymores. Permission granted, I told him. Seconds later the mines erupted. This time the screams came from the NVA."

A wounded Marine staggered up out of the darkness. Cannon directed Hovietz to leave his radio and take the man to Morningstar's bunker. Cannon radioed Lyon, "I need artillery and a flare ship!" he demanded. Lyon's response angered him.

"I had to tell Cannon that I couldn't give him artillery. Because the mortar flares weren't bright enough, I'd called up the flare ship, Puff the Magic Dragon. I couldn't bring in artillery while Puff flew overhead," Lyon remembered. "It was a difficult decision, but it also allowed me to use Puff's Gatling guns just in front of Second Platoon's position."

Soon the neon-like red tracers from Puff's machine guns streaked earthward, plowing up the earth in great chunks and putting a protective wall of hot lead in front of the 2d Platoon's line.

The opening blasts of fire shocked S-2 scout Cpl. Fred Monahan out of his sleep. He had taken refuge in a bunker near the right end of the

2d Platoon's sector. The rocky ground fell away steeply in front of him, so he had felt secure. He had been asleep less than four hours when the explosions woke him. He could hear Vietnamese voices shouting what he took to be orders. "I decided to fight it out from my hole," he said.

"Then I heard one of our corpsmen call to me, 'Who's in there?' When I responded he told me he had a casualty whose hand had been blown off. I gave them my bunker."

Outside, in a flare's glow, Monahan could see NVA attacking the bunkers on the perimeter. He heard one Marine scream hysterically, "They're taking me away!" as he was pulled out of his hole.

Monahan linked up with two Marines from his former rifle squad. Together they took up a position above the steep drop-off. The three of them fired their M16s downhill at voices they heard below them. After just a few rounds, Monahan's weapon jammed. He crawled back to his bunker and swapped weapons with the wounded Marine. "Clear mine, will ya?" he asked the corpsman.

Back on the line, Monahan continued his stand against the NVA invaders. His weapon jammed several more times. Each time he crawled back to his old bunker and exchanged rifles with the corpsman.

After nearly half an hour of steady fighting, Monahan decided to check on the Marines in the holes to his left. Alone, he headed down a barely discernible trail. After just a few meters, he spotted a crouching figure. In an explosive flash he saw that it was an enemy soldier. Monahan pulled the trigger on his M16, but the rifle jammed. Cursing, he retraced his steps in search of a bayonet. He found one, but on his way back a grenade went off near him; it blew the bayonet off his rifle, wounded him in the hand, and covered his face with mud. He wiped the mud from his glasses and continued down the trail.

Unable to find the enemy soldier again, Monahan climbed into a hole occupied by two dead Marines. While he searched them for ammunition, a figure suddenly rushed out of the night at him. Monahan instinctively jabbed upward with his useless weapon. He felt the barrel slide into the man's eye socket before a horrible scream erupted from the enemy soldier's mouth. The intruder fell at the edge of the hole, writhing for a few minutes before going limp.

Monahan could not find any living Marines along that portion of the perimeter, so he returned to his original position. Alone—the other two Marines had disappeared—and convinced that death was only minutes away, he swore to take as many NVA with him as he could. "Come on, you bastards. Come and get me," he yelled defiantly. Maybe, he thought, the NVA would come for him instead of attacking the wounded. He held his position through the night, throwing grenades whenever he heard movement below him.

The chaos and carnage that engulfed the northern portion of Echo's perimeter quickly spilled over to the rest of the company. On the southwest sector held by Lieutenant Izenour's 1st Platoon, Sgt. Jim Marden had wrapped himself in a poncho and fallen asleep behind his hole. The sudden blast of a mortar shell ten meters to his right brought him instantly awake.

"I rolled into my hole thinking the NVA would be coming up the hill at us. I couldn't see much due to the fog. Then firing started coming in from behind us," Marden said.

Thinking it was some of the new guys mistakenly shooting at them, Marden yelled up the hill for them to stop.

So did Pfc. James R. Mason from a few holes to Marden's left. "Hey, you pogues, stop shooting!" he yelled. Several nearby Marines barked out stronger commands. Then Mason's bunker mate moaned, "I've been shot. Get down."

Mason, a St. Paul, Minnesota, native who had been with Echo since December, patched up his buddy, then turned his attention to his front. The fog bank limited his visibility, so he could not be sure whether anyone lurked out there. Rather than risk it, he flipped a grenade in front of his hole from time to time. He wanted to keep the NVA at bay so he could celebrate his nineteenth birthday in two days.

When the rifle fire from his rear continued, Sergeant Marden radioed Izenour. "Who the hell's shooting at us up there?" Marden asked.

Izenour's response chilled Marden. "Quiet," the lieutenant said. "I got a gook right on top of my bunker."

Jesus, they're everywhere, Marden said to himself. After he dispatched a couple of men to take care of the sniper, he saw shadowy figures flitting through the fog below him. Had they already slipped through the gap on his right? he wondered. If so, he would personally see to it that no more NVA got through. From then on, whenever he saw something move below him, he pegged a grenade at it.

Nineteen-year-old Pfc. George Sternisha, of Eller's 3d Platoon, scrunched down in his fighting hole at the six o'clock position, just about

the same spot where Lieutenant Cannon had come through two days earlier. The crackle of small-arms fire along the northern sector alerted him
to the enemy attack. Then mortar rounds dropped in front of him. When
the barrage stopped, several rifle shots came at him from behind. Sternisha, who had played in the Little League with Golf Company's Private
First Class Huckaba back in Crest Hill, Illinois, turned and yelled at the
shooter to knock it off. The firing slowed down, but it did not stop. About
ten minutes later, after several more rounds snapped past his head, Sternisha turned around again. He froze. "Not five feet away knelt a gook
with an RPG, all ready to fire," he remembered. "All I could think of was,
Wow! Before I could bring my weapon up, another guy shot him."

The situation along the 2d Platoon's sector had gone from bad to
worse. NVA roamed the area at will, killing wounded Marines and toss-
ing grenades into bunkers. The sharp crack of AK-47s and the blast of
grenades filled the night. The screams and sobs of the wounded and dying reverberated off the layers of fog and turned the sector into a night-
marish place. Within the first thirty minutes, nearly every Marine position in that sector had been overrun.

Somehow, Private First Class Meuse hung on and kept Cannon informed of the situation in his squad's area. Despite his painful wounds
and Cannon's urging, Meuse refused to crawl to the rear for treatment.
A few minutes before dawn, his radio fell silent.

Cannon radioed Captain Lyon to say he had to have help if he was to
hold. Lyon ordered Izenour to send a squad forward to fill the gaps in
the 2d Platoon's line. "The lieutenant radioed me to bring my squad up
to him so we could sweep over toward Second Platoon," Marden said.
"However, when we got up to Izenour's bunker, he told us to return to
our positions. He was going to send Sergeant Powell's Second Squad instead."

Marden continued, "That pissed me and the rest of the guys off. Obviously, Izenour had no confidence in us because I was new. We went back
downhill and spread out, taking over Powell's position, too. We were
spread awfully thin."

Although initially upset, Marden was later grateful for the change. As
Sgt. Robert Powell led his squad forward, he was hit almost immediately.
He received treatment and returned to the fray, but an enemy rifleman
killed him a short time later. Most of his squad died, too, before they
reached Cannon.

Particularly deadly to Cannon's platoon was the .50-caliber machine gun set up in front of its lines. It fired at will and cut down Marines wherever its heavy slugs flew. Determined to eliminate this serious threat, Cannon radioed Lyon to send up a rocket team.

When they returned to the plateau the previous evening, LCpl. Thomas Rice and his rocket team had settled into a bunker near the junction of 2d and 3d Platoons. The opening rounds immediately brought Rice out of his sleep. The intensity of the enemy fire startled him. In his six months in-country, he had never heard anything to equal this. The enemy seemed to be everywhere. Not twenty meters in front of him he saw Sergeant Powell's squad from the 1st Platoon working its way forward. A burst of deadly accurate machine gun fire cut through the squad, killing or wounding most of them. God, this is really bad, Rice thought.

A little later an airborne flare lit the night. In an instant, NVA snipers hidden in trees around the perimeter opened fire on the helpless Marines. "They're in the trees," someone yelled. "They're in the fuckin' trees. Cut the flares. Cut the flares."

Rice spent a hectic hour hunting down the snipers. They were hard to spot, so Rice and his buddies sprayed rounds into all the treetops. "Then my M16 jammed, so we tossed grenades wherever we thought the gooks were," Rice recalled. "Our wounded were moving back through the grass at the same time, screaming for help. We crawled around to get them, calling out, 'Marine coming,' so our own guys wouldn't shoot us. It was very, very confusing.

"Somewhere in there I got word to join up with Cannon. He wanted us to fire a marking round at an NVA machine gun sitting across a ravine. My gunner, Private First Class Phillip G. Skinner, and I would have to move into the open to get a good shot at the gun."

Rice looked at Cannon. "I'll do it if you cover us."

Cannon nodded.

Rice carried the launcher and Skinner carried the rockets and Rice's M16 as they crawled into an open area. They barely made five meters before another NVA machine gun spat lead in their direction. It missed. Rice thought he spotted the weapon. "I asked Skinner for my rifle," Rice recalled. "He raised up just a little to pass it over to me and was shot and killed."

Rice aimed his M16 and fired. It jammed after one round. He cleared it and fired another round. It jammed again. Disgusted, Rice picked up his rocket launcher and ran back up the hill. He dove into the safety of a nearby bunker. How can we fight with weapons like this? he wanted to know.

Still determined to bolster 2d Platoon's front, Captain Lyon commandeered a detachment of engineers. Armed with the reliable M14, the engineers worked their way forward and took up positions behind Cannon's line. Their steady fire helped plug the gap, but more help was needed. Lyon did not have many men left to send; only a few of the headquarters personnel remained. The captain turned to his battalion radioman. "I told him to link up with Cannon. He looked at me with real sad eyes," Lyon remembered, "then headed down the trail. He was hit almost immediately by the fifty. He just dropped; no sound. He was dead."

Around the perimeter in complete disregard of the danger, other Marines also responded without hesitation to requests for help. Private First Class Sternisha recalled that the 1st Platoon's platoon sergeant suddenly appeared behind his hole. "He had a big bandage on his shoulder. He told me he needed help in getting his wounded to the aid station. I crawled out of my hole thinking my two buddies were coming with me. After we crawled a little distance, I looked back. No one was there. Then I looked back toward the sergeant. Now he was gone, too."

Undaunted and determined to help, Sternisha crawled on. By the time he neared 2d Platoon's lines, he had entered a world of unimaginable horrors. There seemed to be dead or wounded Marines everywhere he looked. One Marine he found just lay there, shaking; the enemy attack had been too much for him. He passed a Marine sergeant with the top of his head neatly cleaved off. The gruesome scene stunned Sternisha and stopped him in his tracks. Finally, he gathered his wits and all his courage and helped wounded men back to the casualty collection area. Whenever he spotted an NVA moving around, he tossed a grenade or fired his pistol in that direction. Sometime that morning Sternisha caught a load of shrapnel in his hands from an exploding mortar round. He shook off the sharp pain, had a corpsman bandage the wounds, and returned to his self-appointed task.

The roar of battle on Echo's plateau resounded throughout Khe Sanh's hills. Across the wide valley to the south, the fight made quite a light show for the Marines on Hill 881S. The flash of grenades and exploding mortar rounds reflected vividly off the low clouds. The stream of rounds from Puff the Magic Dragon appeared like a bright red neon stream of light. The visual effect was so striking, it was easy to forget that the red light represented thousands of tracer rounds, which were only every fifth round fired. The light of the aerial flares exposed the attacking NVA to the 3/3 Marines.

"We could see the NVA swarming around the base of the knoll where Echo was dug in," Lieutenant Colonel Wilder recalled. "They looked like ants going up the hill. I radioed Pappy for permission to fire my heavy weapons. Within minutes my howtars [4.2-inch wheeled mortars] were pumping shells out. They'd wipe out entire squads when they hit."

Private First Class John Krohn, Kilo 3/9's artillery FO, had been sound asleep behind a 106mm recoilless rifle when someone yelled for him to get out of the way. After he crawled out of the back-blast area, the weapon's crew opened fire. The shells hit all around the base of Echo's knoll and sent the NVA flying.

The sounds of Echo's battle also carried across the small ridge separating it from Golf Company. Soon after the noise awoke Captain Sheehan, he received a radio message from the battalion S-3. Be alert, it said; you might be next on the NVA's hit list. Sheehan alerted his platoons.

Private First Class Tom Huckaba had completed his watch and dozed off despite the rain and cold. Then someone shook him. "Wake up. The gooks're hitting Echo. We're on full alert." Huckaba and the others spent the rest of that miserable night wide-awake, waiting for marauding NVA to hit them, too.

At the 2/3 CP, Lieutenant Colonel Delong and his operations staff immediately prepared a plan to seal the gaps in Echo's lines and kill the intruders. One of Pappy's first acts was to request from Colonel Lanigan the operational control of his own Foxtrot Company, the only undamaged company at Khe Sanh. Lanigan immediately agreed.

"Have one of your platoons ready to go at first light," Foxtrot's executive officer, 1st Lt. Richard D. Koehler, remembered Delong saying when the call came.

"Aye, aye, sir," Koehler responded, then awoke the CO, Capt. Merle G. Sorensen, and relayed the message. "We heard Echo's fight as soon as it started," Koehler recalled. "They were less than a kilometer north of us. But we couldn't see them because of the terrain. It sounded like a hell of a fight."

Koehler, nicknamed "Rock" by his basic school buddies for his inability to swim, knew all about night combat with the NVA. A twenty-three-year-old native of Pittsburgh, he had had his baptism of fire on 28 February. In fact, as the senior functioning officer that hellish night, Koehler had been in command of 2/3 from the time Ohanesian died until Pappy Delong arrived the next morning. Koehler's coolness under fire had impressed Delong.

"When we got the orders to send one platoon to Echo, Captain Sorensen immediately turned to the First Platoon," Koehler said. "Its commander, Lieutenant John R. Schworm, was one of the most experienced platoon leaders in the whole battalion. He'd been around so long that he had less than a month in-country when we went to Khe Sanh." Sorensen briefed Schworm with what little information he had.

After contacting Foxtrot, Delong sent for Hotel Company's CO, Capt. Ray Madonna. Following its brutal fight and heavy losses two days earlier, Hotel was relegated to duty as the battalion CP's guard. Now, it represented Delong's only chance to squeeze the NVA from the outside while Foxtrot's platoon applied pressure from the inside.

Delong laid out his plan to Madonna: He wanted Hotel's strongest platoon, Lt. Ord Elliott's, to make a wide swing to the north, around Echo's position, and hit the enemy from the rear. The rest of Hotel would follow in echelon. The enemy would not have a chance. Madonna left to prepare his company for its mission.

The first CH-46 touched down at Foxtrot's position about 0700. Schworm's men quickly loaded up. In minutes they were on their way to Echo.

In the rear of the lead chopper, twenty-year-old Pfc. Clarence S. Powell nervously fingered his 3.5-inch rocket launcher. Though he had been a member of Foxtrot since January, the Burlington, Iowa, native had missed the big fight on 28 February, so he was now facing his first combat. Before he could dwell on that too much, he felt the helicopter touch down.

"As soon as I reached the door someone outside was yelling 'Break left' or 'Break right' to each Marine. I got a break right, turned that way, and headed for cover," Powell remembered. "No sooner had I started to crawl than we got pinned down by heavy fire. Then my squad leader came over and got me. 'Keep your head down,' he warned."

Powell could not use his rocket launcher; the NVA were much too close. Instead, he used an M16 he picked up somewhere and a pistol. "I was scared, but my training took over. We just fired whenever we spotted the enemy."

Schworm's 1st Squad leader, Cpl. Jerry K. Fite, proved instrumental in pushing the enemy back. He boldly led his men in attacks that knocked out enemy-held bunkers. It was slow, methodical, and dangerous work. One of Fite's fire team leaders, LCpl. Larry H. Weaver, disregarded heavy fire from two mutually supporting bunkers and single-handedly launched an assault against one of them. Weaver ignored a flurry of enemy rounds zinging by just inches overhead and crawled up to the closest bunker. He dropped two grenades in quick succession through an opening. As he turned and ran for cover, he raised up a little too high. Enemy rounds slammed into his shoulder, cut a furrow across his head, and knocked him to the ground. As he lay there grimacing in pain, two enemy grenades plopped down alongside him. He curled up as small as possible. Though stung by the twin blasts, Weaver ignored the pain and went right back to the bunker. A couple more grenades and a few blasts from his M16, and the enemy inside were dead.

It went that way all morning as Schworm's Marines slugged their way through the enemy.

About 1030 Lieutenant Cannon met Lieutenant Schworm near Cannon's old position. "I briefed Schworm on the situation and cautioned him that my platoon sergeant, radioman, and two casualties were still in my bunker," Cannon said. "We had to be careful."

Cannon cautiously inched his way forward. He knelt down next to a machine gunner and pointed out targets, but after a few rounds the machine gun stopped firing. "Damn jam, I thought," Cannon said. "Then I turned. I saw why the firing had stopped."

A trickle of blood ran down the gunner's face. Cannon rolled the man over so a corpsman could treat him. Then the assistant gunner crawled up and took over the M60. The close-quarters fight to clear out the enemy continued.

Just before noon, Lieutenant Cannon finally reached his old bunker. "The look on Sergeant Morningstar's face when he crawled out of that bunker was one of disbelief. He hadn't expected to survive his seven-hour ordeal."

On the right flank of Cannon's lines, Cpl. Fred Monahan was munching crackers when elements of Schworm's platoon reached him. "I told them not to get too close to the edge 'cause there were still gooks down there. One guy didn't listen to me and stood near the edge. The NVA shot him in the face."

About an hour after Lieutenant Schworm's platoon entered Echo's perimeter, a flurry of activity suddenly erupted in front of the junction between 1st and 3d Platoons. To the surprise of those who watched, a small force of NVA suddenly swarmed out of a tree line. Captain Lyon said, "I'd been expecting a secondary assault to come from that area. I was ready. The NVA didn't seem too organized. It was more like they were milling around leaderless. It didn't take long for Eller's men to take care of them."

No one could understand why these NVA attacked when they did. The most likely explanation is that the lack of effective communications kept this group of North Vietnamese soldiers from learning that the main attack had been over for several hours. Whatever the reason, the NVA were easily mowed down. They never posed a serious threat to Echo's southern flank.

Not long after this attack was beaten off, Sgt. Jim Marden noticed movement in front of his position. Certain it was an enemy soldier trying to sneak up on the perimeter, he alerted his squad members. Soon others spotted an individual moving steadily toward their lines. As the figure closed on the perimeter, Marden realized it was a red-haired male. What the hell is this? he wondered. A few minutes later Marden barked out, "Halt!"

Startled, the man stopped. With his weapon at the ready, Marden advanced to the man. "Who the hell are you?"

The stranger explained that he was a reporter. He said he had spent the night at battalion headquarters and watched Echo's fight from across the valley. "I wanted to see what was happening," he told Marden.

When he mentioned he had simply walked over from the battalion CP, Marden could not believe it. The entire area had just been swarming with NVA and this guy strolled right through them. It was so unbelievable, it had to be true. Marden turned the reporter over to the first sergeant.

Someone told Echo's Captain Lyon about the reporter, but he had no time to spare. Despite Cannon's and Schworm's best efforts, the NVA still manned the .50-caliber machine gun outside the perimeter. From there it fired down a corridor into the center of Echo's perimeter and cut down a number of Marines. It had to be taken out before the perimeter could be considered secure.

With no one else to take on the mission, Lyon decided to handle it himself. He rounded up two nearby Marines, one of whom was the air liaison officer's radioman. Using that man's radio, Lyon reached an orbiting Huey gunship. "I told the pilot we'd sneak up close enough to mark the bunker with smoke grenades. He could then make his run from south to north—my left to right—and take out the gun with his rockets."

Lyon and his two companions crawled forward. Somehow they made it undetected to within grenade range of the enemy weapon. Lyon tossed a smoke grenade in front of the machine gun bunker. Then he radioed for the pilot to make his run.

"As soon as I heard him coming in from my right I knew we were in trouble."

Lyon yelled a warning. The three men hunkered down, but it was too late. The brace of rockets flashed in with a mighty roar.

"The rockets might have gotten the bunker—I don't know—but they sure got us," Lyon said. "The radioman died instantly. The blast threw me up in the air and tore me up pretty bad. The other Marine was messed up, too."

The next thing Lyon knew, someone was carrying him back to his old bunker. Then he blacked out. When he came to, he heard his executive officer, 1st Lt. John P. Adinolfi, and the first sergeant talking to him. Over the battalion net on a nearby radio he heard his best friend in the battalion, Captain Madonna, saying, "He's been hit three times. He's gotta be evacuated."

Despite his pain, and in the haze of semiconsciousness, Lyon protested. "I still didn't want to give up Echo. I felt guilty about leaving. It was my company. I didn't want to go."

But go he did. When the next medevac landed, LCpl. Tom Rice, who had spent most of the morning helping wounded back to the LZ, picked up one end of Lyon's stretcher and carried it into the aircraft's hold. A few minutes later Lyon was on his way to the airstrip at Khe Sanh.

Hotel Company's trek toward Echo began tragically. Soon after Hotel headed out, a friendly artillery round landed short amid Lieutenant Elliott's platoon, killing two and wounding six. The company set up in defensive positions while medevacs flew in and evacuated the casualties. Then the hump resumed.

The long column worked its way through the trailless elephant grass. By midmorning the hot sun added its heat to the misery of the fast-moving Marines. Although some felt exposed without their flak jackets, most of the men were glad they did not have the extra weight to deal with.

At least one Marine, though, considered it a good day regardless of the circumstances. Lance Corporal Wayne Ithier woke up wet and cold but very pleased. It was his nineteenth birthday. A few days earlier he had not been sure he would be alive to celebrate this event. Now his new goal was to live through the day.

The march continued without any sign of the enemy. By late morning Hotel had completed its movement. "As we neared Echo's position I saw there was a deep gully between us and Echo," Elliott recalled. "That's where the NVA were dug in. They were right there, so close I could see the surprise in their eyes as they turned around and saw us."

Elliott sent Ithier's squad into the gully. Ithier remembered, "We fixed bayonets and went into this ravine. There were bunkers and spider holes everywhere. We were killing NVA left and right as we swept down the hillside. We used rifle fire and grenades to clear out each bunker. It was obvious they were surprised to find us coming in from behind them."

Elliott watched with admiration as his men cleared out one position after another. "I watched one kid jump into a hole with an NVA and kill him with his pistol."

That was Pfc. Roy W. DeMille. The gutsy youngster repeatedly used his .45 with deadly efficiency and crawled into bunkers with the North Vietnamese and blew them away.

The squad of Hotel Company Marines steadily fought its way through the bunker complex. The last enemy positions sat right up against Echo's lines. Lance Corporal Ithier helped clean them out, then advanced into Echo's lines. "Echo, we're coming in. We're coming in!" he and others called out.

Ithier's squad moved forward slowly, alert for any enemy presence, but there did not seem to be anyone alive. A few meters into Echo's lines, they finally found one of that company's Marines crouched in a bunker. Dead NVA littered the ground in front of his position. By 1230 the linkup had been completed.

Lieutenant Elliott and the rest of his platoon moved into Echo's lines. "The first thing I saw was a bunch of dead Marines," Elliott said. "The entire perimeter had been chewed up bad. When we started to find live Marines they looked pretty scared."

Elliott made his way to Echo's CP, where he reported in to Lieutenant Adinolfi. The rest of Hotel streamed into Echo's perimeter behind him.

As soon as the linkup with Hotel occurred, Lieutenant Cannon and what remained of his 3d Squad surveyed his platoon's former positions. Cannon hoped they would find some of the members of his 1st and 2d Squads alive. But it was not to be. They found dead NVA and dead Marines everywhere they looked, some locked together in death's embrace as testament to the close-quarters fighting. In one bunker Cannon found Private First Class Meuse, his radio's handset still gripped in his cold hand, and five dead NVA clumped at the entrance. Meuse probably could have made it back to the aid station, but he had elected to remain behind to relay information about the enemy attack to Cannon.

"There were bodies everywhere, mostly NVA," Cannon remembered. "About eighty enemy dead littered the ground in front of the First and Second Squad's positions. No doubt others had been dragged away by their comrades. Dead Marines lay there, too. I couldn't tell a black from a white Marine. Four hours in the sun had already badly decomposed the bodies.

"I should have cried, but I didn't. I didn't have time. But the memory of those dead Marines will stay with me forever."

The enemy attack was costly. Twenty-seven Echo Marines were killed and eighty-four were wounded. Foxtrot suffered two dead and more than a half dozen wounded. Hotel lost the same.

The Marines counted 137 dead NVA in Echo's perimeter. No one would ever know how many more had been carried away or wounded.

Once all of Hotel Company had entered Echo's perimeter, its Marines went to work checking out bunkers for any remaining NVA. They set about their task with a ruthless efficiency. Working together, a team of men would flip a grenade into a bunker, then spray the inside with a burst of M16 fire. That took care of any enemy soldiers. Then word spread that Lieutenant Colonel Delong promised a five-day in-country R and R to anyone who captured an enemy soldier. In short order, three POWs were sitting at the LZ.

In response to their interrogator's questions, the prisoners readily revealed they were members of the NVA 325C Division. They had crossed into South Vietnam on 13 March and arrived near Khe Sanh a week later. They also revealed that their division had planned another attack for that night. The news set off a flurry of activity.

Teams of Marines searched the battlefield once more for any overlooked casualties. Dead Marines were wrapped in ponchos and stacked around the LZ to await the choppers that would carry them to Staff Sergeant French at Khe Sanh. The enemy dead were unceremoniously dumped into empty bunkers. Helicopters rushed in ammunition, Claymores, grenades, and defensive materials. The Marines spent most of the afternoon stringing concertina wire, improving bunkers, clearing fields of fire, and setting out Claymores. Foxtrot Company's two other platoons were choppered in. That put three rifle companies at Echo's position. If the NVA came again, the Marines would be ready.

While the Marines worked at strengthening their position, the inevitable horde of correspondents descended on the battlefield. They swarmed over the area, eager to interview the combatants. A CBS news crew approached Private First Class Sternisha. He was not sure what he would say, but he knew what not to say. A little earlier an officer had come by telling the troops, "Don't say a word about the M16. Not a word. That's an order."

Sternisha told the reporter, "It was like a nightmare. They were all over the hill. I never saw anything like it." (Back in Illinois, Sternisha's parents saw the broadcast the next day. They could scarcely contain their pride, and their joy at knowing that their son was alive.)

Someone spotted the red-haired reporter as he photographed the rows of Marine dead. A senior NCO accosted the man and ripped the camera from his hands. "You can't do that!" the reporter screamed as the NCO pulled the film from his camera. "Oh, yes he can," retorted one of the watching Marines. "He's the first sergeant and he can do whatever he wants." No more pictures of the dead were taken.

Just as the POWs had revealed, the North Vietnamese hit 2/3 that night, but not in any strength. Two probes by small, marauding bands of NVA brought down a flurry of hand grenades from the Marines. Everyone spent the rest of the night wide-awake, but the three companies were not bothered again. At first light a patrol found five fresh enemy bodies where one of the probes had occurred.

The NVA did not hit 2/3 with any strength because they had another target. At 0330 on 4 May, a series of sharp explosions rocked the U.S. Army Special Forces camp at Lang Vei, a short distance down Route 9 from Khe Sanh village. The American commanders of the indigent troops thought they were on the receiving end of a mortar attack. They realized too late that the blasts were the result of enemy sappers clearing lanes through their barbed wire perimeter fence.

Once through the barricade, the NVA, aided by comrades who had recently infiltrated the ranks as recruits, swarmed all over the camp. The traitors pointed out key installations, which were quickly blown up. In the opening minutes both the American commander and his executive officer were killed.

The first word the Marines had of the attack came when a frantic radio message crackled over the artillery battery's radio at the airstrip. It was the Special Forces communications sergeant. He asked in a desperate voice for a concentration to be fired west and south of the camp. Unfortunately, the Marines could not comply. The sergeant had no map and no knowledge of any preplanned artillery concentrations. Also, the sergeant had the only working radio in the camp, and he kept changing frequencies to talk to two patrols in the field.

In response to the sergeant's repeated pleas, the Marine artillerymen did fire several rounds into the grids south of the camp, but the sergeant, deep in a bunker, could not make any corrections. Instead, the Khe Sanh–based tubes fired several preplanned concentrations well to the west of the camp. They kept sending shells flying through the night until two gunships arrived over the camp at 0430.

At first light the district advisor, Army captain James Whitenack, and four others raced out of the Khe Sanh Combat Base in a jeep; close behind them followed a relief force. In minutes Whitenack arrived at the Lang Vei camp. He found it all but destroyed.

The NVA had blown up nearly every structure in the little camp. Besides the two Army officers killed, two other U.S. soldiers had been wounded. Twenty of the indigent troops had been killed and another thirty-four were missing. The bodies of seven NVA lay amid the ruins.

After overseeing the evacuation of the casualties, Captain Whitenack reorganized the survivors. He also set into motion plans to move the camp to a more defensible site, farther west on Route 9.

Rather than launch a final attack on Hill 881N, Pappy Delong used 4 May to reorganize and reorient his rifle companies. Although greatly weakened by its losses on 3 May, Echo was one of the two companies designated to attack Hill 881N from the south; the relatively unbloodied Foxtrot would launch the main attack. Hotel Company would remain in reserve at the battalion CP, and Golf Company would maneuver into a position from which it could attack Hill 881N from the northeast.

Golf's Capt. James Sheehan had been eager to resume his advance. He thought the two-day delay allowed the NVA to reinforce their positions. And he still had the bodies of four of his men to recover. Sheehan even went so far as to vent his frustration to the BLT's S-3, Capt. Douglas Lemon, who told him to sit tight. Golf was out there alone with no protection on its flanks, Lemon said. Sheehan would have to be patient.

When Sheehan finally received orders on 4 May to reposition Golf, he set out knowing he would first have the gruesome task of recovering his dead. Lieutenant McFarlane's platoon had the point; they were his people left out there and McFarlane wanted to be the one to get their bodies. The NVA were long gone when McFarlane approached the wooded knoll. He had not really expected any resistance. As far as he was concerned, the enemy had simply launched a well-executed delaying ambush. Their tactic had worked.

The three Marines—LCpl. James Boda, Pfc. Anderson Carter, and Pfc. James Hill—and Navy hospitalman Lloyd Heath were found in a little cluster where they had been hit. Private First Class Tom Huckaba helped police up the bodies. "All three of their M16s had jammed. One guy had a cleaning rod sticking out of his weapon," Huckaba remembered. Hospitalman Wike stared at the remains of his buddy, Doc Heath. Nearby, an officer whom Wike did not recognize examined the body of a Marine who had tried to pry his jammed cartridge free with a pocket knife. The officer handed the knife to Wike. "Here, doc. Remember this day." Private First Class Robert Maras saw that his friend, Hill, had tried to free his jammed cartridge with the tip of the Bowie knife he always carried. "One of the other Marines took the Bowie knife and stuck it in his belt. He was hit later on. We threw the knife away after that, figuring it was a jinx," Maras said.

Blame for the jammed weapons was immediately placed on the Marines' failure to keep their rifles clean. Some of the senior NCOs went around warning the troops, "Ya gotta keep it clean. Don't let this happen to you. Clean your weapon."

One squad leader scoffed at the admonition. He pointed to one of the dead men. "He always cleaned his rifle. Always. Something else is wrong."

It was the first time anyone thought the failures could be the weapon's fault. But no one paid any attention to the squad leader.

Helicopters were called in. Huckaba, Maras, and several others wrapped the four bodies in ponchos and carried them aboard the choppers. The rest of Golf dug in. The company would remain overnight at this spot, then go up against Hill 881N the next day.

On the other side of the intervening ridgeline, Echo and Foxtrot Companies had moved forward, too. They advanced several hundred meters before halting and digging in for the night. They would launch their final attack the next morning.

While Pappy Delong's rifle companies maneuvered into position, yet another fresh company arrived at Khe Sanh. Charlie Company, 1st Battalion, 26th Marines, was flown in from Phu Bai. It would not only provide assistance to Echo 2/9 for security of the airstrip, it would be available to help if BLT 2/3 got chewed up on Hill 881N.

Chapter Twelve

The 105mm howitzers of Foxtrot 2/12 at Khe Sanh fired their rounds as soon as the rising sun on 5 May burned off the patchy fog that had drifted across Hill 881N. The high-explosive shells slammed into the hilltop for more than an hour and sent columns of dirt and smoke into the sky. When a flight of jets reported overhead, the artillery ceased firing. The high-pitched scream of the diving jets preceded the deep boom of their 250- and 500-pound bombs, which tore up more NVA-held ground.

Based on the NVA's actions over the previous two days, Pappy Delong decided to make maximum use of his supporting arms before sending his Marines up the hill. He did not want a repeat of the carnage on Hill 881S.

On the south slope of Hill 881N, the waiting grunts of Echo and Foxtrot BLT 2/3 took comfort in the bombardment. Each NVA killed by the bombs and artillery was one less for the grunts to fight and kill. And, as the members of the rifle companies tasked with making the main assault on Hill 881N, they wanted as many dead NVA as possible before they went up.

Because his company would lead the attack, Capt. Merle G. Sorensen used the time to carefully brief his officers. Although Foxtrot BLT 2/3 was his first command in South Vietnam, it was not his first combat command. Sorensen had taken Alpha 1/6 ashore during the 1965 insurrection in the Dominican Republic and led it through the following weeks until the rebels surrendered. Now thirty-one, the Kansan was a senior captain who did not expect to spend much time at the helm of Foxtrot before being promoted to major and a staff slot in the rear. Nonetheless, he planned to make the most of his limited time in the field so he could do a better job on the staff.

The taciturn Sorensen laid out his plan to his platoon leaders at his briefing early on 5 May. The steep, rugged terrain allowed only limited maneuvering room, so one platoon would lead the attack. The other two would remain in support. Because Sorensen showed no favorites and regularly rotated the point among his three platoons each day, the honor of leading the attack fell to the 2d Platoon.

Its commander, twenty-eight-year-old 2d Lt. Charles P. Chritton, had left his home in New Ulm, Minnesota, in 1957 to enlist in the Marine Corps. Following his discharge four years later, Chritton enrolled at Wisconsin's La Crosse State University, where he also joined the campus naval ROTC unit. After graduation he received his commission as a Marine second lieutenant. He joined Foxtrot Company upon his arrival in-country in January 1967. The brutal fight on 28 February north of Camp Carroll indoctrinated Chritton to the horrors of the war in South Vietnam. But since flying into Khe Sanh, his platoon had missed all the action. That was about to change.

In Sorensen's briefing, Chritton learned that his objective was the knob dominating the western end of Hill 881N. Echo Company would be on Chritton's right flank, guarding it and attacking its own objective. Foxtrot would go when the air and artillery fire ceased. There was not anything else Chritton needed to know, so he returned to his platoon area to brief his squad leaders. The supporting fire halted at 0850. Chritton signaled his platoon to move out.

Chritton's Marines advanced slowly but steadily up the hill. Only the occasional crack of a distant AK-47 and the snap of the round zinging overhead revealed the presence of any enemy. By the time the 2d Platoon reached the crest, Chritton was feeling optimistic. Maybe they're gone, he thought. Maybe the bombs and artillery got them all.

With all his people on top of the hill, Chritton turned his platoon west and started toward the knob, which rose several hundred meters away. A few steps later the enemy fire increased significantly. Within seconds it grew again, dramatically. Marines dropped, screaming in pain as enemy rounds tore their flesh. Some men dove for cover in the thick underbrush. Others returned fire. The crack of AK-47s and the quick bark of machine guns quickly melded into a steady beat with the return fire of M16s.

When he realized that most of the enemy fire was directed against his 3d Squad on the left flank, Chritton unhesitatingly raced through the enemy fire to join them. He steadied his men in a calm, reassuring voice. "Pick your targets," he told them. "Keep up the fire. Maneuver forward." But it was not easy. The NVA were in well-concealed bunkers and spider holes amid the brush covering the approach to the knob. Only an occasional muzzle flash revealed their positions.

Under Chritton's watchful eye, the squad gained some ground. But as it inched forward, more Marines cried out. Several crumpled without a sound. "About then I realized I had more than I could handle," Chritton said.

He radioed Sorensen. "I'm pulling back," he told the captain. He already had several dead and a half dozen wounded. He wanted more air and artillery.

Chritton passed the word, and the 2d Platoon started working its way backward. Private First Class Stephen W. Amodt found it harder to go downhill than up. The nineteen-year-old son of a career Air Force officer, Amodt humped a bulky backboard loaded with nine rockets for a 3.5-inch rocket launcher, plus all his normal equipment. Because the Marines used the rocket launcher primarily to mark targets for jets, Amodt had not even had the satisfaction of seeing any of his rounds fired.

"That backboard weighed a lot," Amodt recalled. "Whenever I hit the ground the damned thing rode up and slammed into the back of my helmet. The front edge of that would then bang into my nose. That happened a lot as we made our way back down the hill."

Chritton remained on the hilltop to make sure all his men had made it off. Just as he started down, he noticed one of his men hobbling painfully along. "The corporal had been hit in the legs and couldn't walk very fast, so he'd fallen behind the others. I got him in a fireman's carry on my back. He was a big fellow and carrying him was hard work."

As he staggered downward under his load, Chritton suddenly realized he was all alone. That worried him, until he heard the click of a camera shutter. There on the trail in front of him stood a civilian magazine photographer. He had been calmly snapping photos all the time Chritton had been struggling downhill.

Chritton blew up. "Put that fuckin' camera down and help me with this guy," he barked in his strongest Marine officer's voice. The civilian seemed shocked at the command but he responded. He slung his camera around his neck and helped Chritton. Together they got the wounded man back to the casualty collection point.

As soon as the medevacs had carried out the casualties, Chritton's men regrouped while artillery and napalm tore into the western half of Hill 881N's crest. During that time Lieutenant Adinolfi brought Echo Company up on Foxtrot Company's right flank, where it could deliver supporting fire.

As his men assembled for the renewed assault, Chritton learned that one of his Marines did not want to go back up. Although it was a very serious matter that could lead to a court-martial, Chritton opted to treat it as a minor annoyance. "I told my platoon sergeant, 'That's your mission for the day. See that that guy gets up the hill.' The sergeant immediately went back to the guy, grabbed him by the nape of the neck and threw him up the hill. That's all it took. The Marine, a veteran, did his job that day. Nothing more was ever said about it."

At 1300 Sorensen ordered Chritton to go again. This time Chritton's men knew where to find the enemy. Not only had the earlier attack pinpointed their bunkers and spider holes, the napalm had burned off most of the vegetation. The Marines went after the NVA with a vengeance, methodically taking out one bunker after another.

The assault passed in a blur for Private First Class Amodt. He did not get rid of any of his awkward, heavy rockets, but he did burn up a number of M16 magazines. "I can't remember any specific targets, just that I was putting out rounds," he said. "Wherever we thought there was an NVA, we blasted him outta there. Just putting out rounds."

On the right flank, Pfc. William Ryan's squad pushed through a patch of heavy foliage unscarred by the napalm. "Suddenly a gook popped out of a hole right in front of us," Ryan, a twenty year old from Charleston, Massachusetts, remembered. "My squad leader fired his M79. The gook was so close, the round didn't have time to arm, but the impact killed him."

Lieutenant Chritton joined his men in clearing the bunkers. While the troops laid down covering fire, the platoon leader crept forward, threw open the hatch of a spider hole, and tossed in a grenade. *KABOOM!* One more bunker cleared. Then they went after the next one.

Chritton spotted one enemy soldier in a hole near the edge of the ridge. The man popped up several times, ripped off a couple of rounds, then disappeared. He never stayed up long enough for Chritton to draw a bead on him. Chritton signaled his radioman to move forward with him. "We'd just started out when I heard this heavy thump on the ground between us," Chritton remembers. "I heard this sputtering and looked down. A Chicom grenade was right there. Instinctively, I jumped and rolled one way while my radioman went the other."

Blam!

Miraculously, both men escaped injury. Undaunted, Chritton picked himself up and crept closer to the enemy bunker. He was ready the next time the NVA popped up. He squeezed his pistol's trigger. The thick round hit the North Vietnamese squarely in the head, cleaving it open as if an axe had struck him. Chritton continued on.

A few minutes later he found Pfc. T. J. Brown frantically trying to clear his M16. The weapon had jammed as Brown snuck up on a spider hole. "Here," Chritton said, thrusting his pistol toward Brown. The young Marine took the weapon, crawled forward while he squeezed off several rounds, dropped a grenade in on the unsuspecting NVA, and crawled back, grinning broadly.

Private First Class Ryan spotted an enemy soldier in a hole, too. He armed a grenade, crept close, and flipped the missile in. It came flying back out! Ryan curled into a tight ball, his muscles tense for the shrapnel he knew was coming. But it did not. The grenade rolled down the hill and exploded harmlessly.

Determined to get the enemy soldier, Ryan readied another grenade. This time he held it for a few seconds, then reached over the lip of the bunker to set the grenade down. Before he could withdraw his hand, the missile exploded. "The concussion blew my hand back, but didn't hurt me," Ryan said.

The fearlessness of his young Marines impressed Chritton. In the face of sustained enemy fire, the young men kept moving forward, wiping out one enemy position after another. Firing their M16s and M60s at point-blank range, the Marines fought their way through the enemy positions just as their older brothers had in Korea and their fathers had on a dozen South Pacific islands. It was war at its most personal and brutal level.

To those who fought there, the battle seemed to have taken longer, but by 1445 it was over. Hill 881N at last belonged to the Marines. There was no sense of triumph, no feeling of great victory. It was just over. Chritton radioed the news to Sorensen. A short time later the captain brought the rest of Foxtrot forward. While the men dug in, Chritton took a quick head count. His casualties were surprisingly light. In the final assaults, fewer than six Marines had been wounded and none were killed.

With Hill 881N securely in Marine hands, Lieutenant Colonel Delong ordered the rest of his companies to the crest. Captain Sheehan brought Golf Company up, and it settled in along the hill's northeast edge. Most of its day had been spent maneuvering along the finger that led up to Hill 881N. Fortunately, there was no resistance. Lieutenant Peter Hesser, whose 1st Platoon had the point that day, remembered his arrival on Hill 881N as anticlimactic. "It definitely was not a Mount Surabachi affair. In fact, we never really made it to the top of the hill. We were always on the north and northeast slopes."

Lieutenant Adinolfi set in Echo Company to the east of Foxtrot, along the hilltop's southern edge. Though Echo had supported Foxtrot throughout the day, it had taken no casualties. But it knew the enemy had. Twenty-three-year-old Adinolfi remembered, "It stunk up there. The smell of death was everywhere. Those one thousand– and two thousand–pound bombs took a terrible toll on them. We found shreds of clothing, bits and pieces of bodies, but nothing you could put together."

Lieutenant Colonel Delong established his CP near the middle of the hilltop with Hotel Company as security. His staff prepared orders for patrol activity by the companies. Delong did not believe that the enemy would so easily relinquish the area and wanted to keep them off balance.

In the meantime, Lieutenant Chritton, who was utterly exhausted from the day's fighting, collapsed on his air mattress. As the sun dropped below the horizon and his eyes started to close, he suddenly realized he had not walked the perimeter to make sure the troops were properly set in. Though he barely had enough energy to roll off his mattress, Chritton knew he had to get up. If he did not do his duty, he could not expect his men to do theirs. He arose and moved toward the line. He made all of four steps when he heard the distinctive whistle of an incoming mortar round. He hit the deck. The round landed on his air mattress and destroyed it. Reenergized, Chritton hurriedly rolled into a nearby hole. More rounds came in and crashed across the perimeter.

"I think the troops, including myself, were a little lackadaisical that night, thinking the fighting was all over," Private First Class Ryan remembered. "I was asleep on a poncho outside my hole when someone screamed, 'Incoming!' I stood up and dove headfirst into my hole. My back hurt like hell, but I was safe."

On a listening post (LP) in front of the line, the enemy mortar rounds startled Private First Class Amodt and his two foxhole buddies. They thought the NVA were long gone. Convinced that a ground attack was imminent, they raced back up the hill. "LP coming in!" they screamed for all they were worth.

Before they reached cover, a round landed between Amodt's two buddies. The explosion drove a huge hunk of shrapnel into LCpl. John Stone's head. The ghastly wound caused Amodt to think Stone would not survive long. He helped carry him to cover, then found refuge in a hole along the perimeter. With the position's two other occupants, Amodt fired downhill. If the NVA were coming, they would find a wall of hot lead waiting for them.

Amodt and his foxhole comrades soon ran out of ammunition. Amodt said he would go to get more. Swallowing his fear, he jumped out of the hole and stayed low as he ran toward the far side of Foxtrot's perimeter. As he leaped over one hole, the flash of an exploding mortar round revealed the body of a buddy; a mortar round had landed squarely in the hole. Near the company CP, Amodt found a Marine who gave him a bandolier full of M16 magazines. Amodt made the dangerous trip back across the perimeter and returned unscathed to his hole. After he passed out the rounds, he hunkered down to wait for the enemy infantry.

A few minutes later Amodt heard the desperate screams of a badly wounded Marine. The youngster had been blown out of his hole and could not get back into it. The casualty cried repeatedly for someone to help him. But the enemy 82mm rounds came too fast. No one went to the man's aid. His screams for help continued for a few more minutes, grew fainter, then stopped.

During the barrage, the 4.2-inch mortar observer spotted the enemy muzzle flashes. He quickly calculated the coordinates and ordered counterbattery fire. By watching the explosive flashes, he was able to walk his rounds into the enemy position. The incoming fire finally ceased. In all, ninety-two enemy mortar rounds had dropped from the night sky.

The battered Marines slowly emerged from their holes. A casualty count showed that Foxtrot Company had lost one killed and half a dozen wounded.

Although some of the enemy mortar rounds landed within Echo's perimeter, none of its Marines was hit. But they clearly heard the agony of Foxtrot's wounded; their wails filled the night. "It was awful," Pfc. George Sternisha remembered.

Medevacs were called for a dangerous night extraction mission because several of the wounded, including Stone, would not survive without immediate care. Private First Class Amodt helped to move the wounded to the LZ. He spent some time there comforting Stone, knowing that no one could survive such a serious wound. When the chopper finally came in about midnight, Amodt loaded Stone aboard. Then he returned to his hole, sad that he had lost another friend in these god-forsaken hills. (Amodt would learn more than thirty years later that Stone had survived his injury.)

All the Marines on Foxtrot's side of the hill fully expected a ground attack. But none came.

At a company commander's meeting the next morning, 6 May 1967, Lieutenant Colonel Delong briefed the officers on his patrol plan. Pappy believed that the enemy still lurked in the area, so he wanted each company to send out a two-platoon patrol every day, starting that day. The S-3 would give each company its patrol route and checkpoint grid coordinates. The patrols were to exercise every precaution and make generous use of the available artillery and air support. Then Delong dismissed the officers.

The daily patrols, which extended mostly west and northwest of Hill 881N, were grueling affairs. The troops were up and ready to go before dawn. They headed out soon after first light, humped between twelve and fifteen kilometers out and back over rugged, steep terrain, and returned to their perimeter on Hill 881N at dusk. Because one of the two platoons had to go out again the next morning, there was precious little time for chow, cleaning gear, or completing other chores before nightfall. To add to the misery, observation posts (OPs) and listening posts still had to be manned, as did perimeter watches. After several days of this schedule in the enervating sun, the troops were beat. But to the great relief of the Marines, few enemy were spotted, and contact proved to be even more limited. But no one doubted that the NVA were still there.

Lance Corporal Desmond Murray remembered a company-sized patrol that took Hotel Company west from Hill 881N. "We came to a wide, long valley that stretched toward Laos," he said. "About seven hundred meters out we could see a huge hole. It didn't look like a bomb crater. We sent one platoon to investigate."

Murray recalled the intense quiet that followed. "It felt eerie. We knew the enemy was out there, just watching us, just waiting for the right moment to strike. You could feel it."

The lone platoon had covered about half the distance to the mysterious hole when Captain Madonna suddenly recalled it. Everyone felt great relief at this order.

On 8 May Lieutenant Chritton led his platoon on a westerly heading from Hill 881N. The point man discovered an abandoned NVA field hospital near the bottom of the hill. Based on the condition of the camp and the many blood-soaked bandages lying around, Chritton estimated that the enemy had been gone only a few days. "I understood then why they had fought so hard on top of the hill," Chritton observed. "They were buying time to evacuate their casualties."

After radioing his find to Captain Sorensen, Chritton signaled his platoon forward. "As we moved beyond the hospital, the smell of death increased to a nauseating level. It just poured out of the ground. There had to be a lot of dead buried around there.

"Everyone of us knew we were being watched. You could literally feel it. They were there, but we just couldn't see them. My Marines didn't make a sound as they walked. There was no noise, no equipment rattle. Everyone used hand signals. I was very proud of my troops for their discipline."

The patrol moved west another five kilometers, reached its checkpoint, then circled wide to return to Hill 881N. It was a relieved platoon of Foxtrot Marines that topped the hill that afternoon.

While Chritton's platoon silently worked its way through the hills that day, Foxtrot's 3d Platoon commander received a frightening order. Late on the morning of 8 May, Lieutenant Colonel Delong summoned 2d Lt. Patrick G. Carroll, a twenty-four-year-old native of Elgin, Oregon, to his CP. Delong ordered Carroll to take his platoon on a recon patrol to the bottom of a nearby deep ravine. Carroll looked at the map and gulped. If he found NVA in the ravine, there was no way he could get any help. The mission was just too dangerous. His four months of combat experience, including the bitter 28 February battle, had convinced him that the NVA were tenacious foes who rarely passed up an opportunity to kill Marines. This recon mission would give them that opportunity. He looked at Delong. "Aye, aye, sir," he said.

Back at his CP, Carroll outlined the mission to his platoon sergeant. "He instantly recognized the patrol's imminent danger. He asked me what I was going to do. I told him I didn't know."

For the rest of the morning and into the afternoon, Carroll wrestled with his dilemma while he waited for the command to saddle up. As a graduate of the Naval Academy, he fully appreciated the seriousness of refusing a direct order, but he also recognized the foolishness of the mission. Nevertheless, as the hours passed, Carroll began to relax. Finally, late in the afternoon, Delong canceled the mission. "I didn't have to make the decision, but to this day I believe I would have refused," Carroll stated.

One day, while not on patrol, Hospitalman Vernon Wike Golf BLT 2/3 looked up from where he lounged by his hole to see photojournalist Cathy Leroy striding determinedly toward him. "Thank God you're alive," she announced. "I thought you'd be dead by now."

Nice greeting, thought Wike as Leroy shoved a copy of *Stars and Stripes* under his nose. The photo of Wike huddled over the dying Lance Corporal Roldan filled the front page.

"You're famous. I need your name," Leroy said to Wike.

"I didn't think too much about the pictures after I sent them off," Leroy recalled. "Then they ran in the States. AP [Associated Press] received many inquiries from family members wanting to know if the dead Marine was their relative. They told me they wanted to identify the two men."

As soon as she could, Leroy had hopped a flight that took her back up north. She eventually arrived at Khe Sanh, and a resupply chopper carried her to Hill 881N.

Wike and Leroy visited for a few minutes. He told her what he could about Roldan, which was not much, because the two had just met earlier on the day that Roldan had died.

Leroy left after a few more minutes. Wike put the clipping in his wallet. The photo impressed him, but he had no idea that it would become one of the most famous of the entire Vietnam War.

Keeping to his strict duty roster, Captain Sorensen scheduled Lt. Jack Schworm's 1st Platoon and Lt. Pat Carroll's 3d Platoon for the 9 May patrol. As usual, Sorensen planned to accompany the force. "Captain Sorensen always went with the majority of the company," Lieutenant Koehler noted. "As a result he'd been out on patrol for three days straight. He looked beat. I offered to go in his place. That way he could have a full day of rest."

Sorensen declined. "I couldn't do that," he said. "I was the CO and belonged with my troops."

After an early morning briefing where he laid out the route, the checkpoints, and the day's final objective, Sorensen, his CP group, and the two platoons—about seventy Marines in all—headed northwest off Hill 881N. Their objective was the abandoned village of Lang Xoa. In a straight line, it was just three thousand meters away, but the intervening hills and ravines more than doubled the distance.

At the same time that Foxtrot headed out, Lieutenant Adinolfi readied two platoons from Echo for their daily patrol. Their route would parallel Foxtrot's to the southwest. Echo's final objective was Hill 803, just to the south of Lang Xoa. Adinolfi had Lieutenant Izenour's 1st Platoon and Lieutenant Cannon's 2d Platoon with him. To bolster Cannon's weakened platoon, Sgt. James Marden's squad was assigned to work with him that day. That did not sit well with either Marden or Pfc. James Mason. "Cannon was too gung-ho," Mason commented.

The two patrols cleared the battalion perimeter soon after first light. Foxtrot had an aggressive patrol schedule. The distance to its objective, combined with the rugged terrain, slowed them down. It arrived late at its checkpoints, which prompted the battalion operations center to urge Sorensen to move faster.

By the time the Foxtrot Marines neared Hill 778, about three klicks northwest of Hill 881N, it was after noon. Steep terrain and dense underbrush hindered their movement. If they were going to reach Lang Xoa on time, they would have to move faster.

Carroll's point man came upon a trail that led down the steep southwestern side of Hill 778 toward Lang Xoa. "Everyone knew we shouldn't go down the trail but we had no choice," Carroll recalled. "We had to take it to get to our objective on time."

After descending the hillside, Carroll's platoon entered a wide, flat ravine. A major ridge finger that ran northwest off Hill 778 paralleled their right flank. High terrain leading up to Hill 803 rose off to their left.

Carroll halted in the center of the ravine to look at some footprints that one of his men had discovered. Another Marine pointed to a pile of fresh feces. At the same time, the point squad reported it had come to another ravine that intersected its own from the right about a hundred meters from Carroll's position.

"As I stood there I suddenly had this overwhelming feeling we were getting into trouble," Carroll remembered. "The intense feeling affected my entire body with a sense of impending doom. I knew I had to get those Marines out of that spot immediately."

Carroll whirled around. He pointed up the ridge finger running down from Hill 778. "Up there," he ordered his platoon. "Get up there."

The Marines raced across the ravine at double time and started up the side of the finger. When the first squad reached the top, it ran into a force of NVA. "We got gooks right here!" someone radioed to Carroll.

Carroll realized that enemy soldiers had climbed the opposite side of the finger to come in behind his platoon as it worked its way along the ravine. Only his premonition had saved them from being cut off.

"Shoot 'em!" Carroll radioed back.

The second squad reached the ridge top and they, too, found themselves face to face with NVA soldiers. By the time Carroll closed up behind this squad, it was heavily engaged with the enemy at point-blank range. When Carroll looked up the ridge finger to his right, he spotted a squad of NVA moving up the slope to maneuver above him. If they made it, Carroll and his men would not have a chance.

Carroll ordered 3d Squad, just now coming up behind him, "Get up that finger." He pointed out the enemy squad. "Whatever you do, don't let them get on the ridge!"

Carroll grabbed the handset from his radioman and called Sorensen. "I got five of 'em on the hill," he said.

Captain Sorensen's radioman, twenty-year-old Cpl. Joseph P. O'Connor, an eight-month veteran of Foxtrot, remembered the call: "Lieutenant Carroll radioed he'd spotted five NVA. I passed the message to Captain Sorensen, who immediately said, 'Don't go after them.' He saw it for the classic ambush tactic that it was."

But the order did not matter. Carroll's two squads were already heavily engaged with the NVA. "Every man had a problem directly in front of him," Carroll said. "The enemy was within fifteen meters of us. They were attacking us from everywhere. They were throwing grenades and firing their rifles."

The Marines fought back valiantly. Corporal Albert W. Potts, a Fort Wayne, Indiana, native who had celebrated his twentieth birthday just a few weeks earlier, aggressively moved his M60 team forward. His gunner, LCpl. Terrence White, blazed away at enemy soldiers clearly visible as they flitted through the nearby trees. Potts and White could see the enemy fall, so they kept putting out rounds as fast as the assistant gunner could place a fresh belt into the gun's feedway.

In the meantime, nineteen-year-old Pfc. Lance M. Campbell, who had been a member of Foxtrot's 3d Squad since his arrival in South Vietnam the previous November, rushed up the ridge finger with his squad mates. "We made it about two-thirds of the way up before a buddy got hit in the back," Campbell said. "At the same time all kinds of firing broke out from below. Those guys down there were hit hard."

The squad continued up the finger, enemy rounds zinging past and chewing up the dirt. Campbell and another Marine ducked behind a tree just as a burst of enemy machine gun fire tore great hunks of wood from its trunk. Across the ravine to the front of their position, Campbell saw NVA. He turned his M16 toward them and squeezed the trigger. At one point Campbell spotted six NVA moving down the ravine. He wriggled from behind his tree to get a better shot. Almost instantly a savage blast of enemy machine gun fire passed overhead. He quickly scooted back behind the tree.

Marines around Campbell were cursing their jammed M16s. Livid with frustration, they frantically tried to clear their weapons. Most succeeded, only to have the rifles malfunction a few rounds later. Campbell saw a corpsman hand his pistol to a Marine. "Here," the doc said, "I got too much to do to worry about this," then turned back to his casualties. The Marine fired the pistol across the ravine. Though he did not think the Marine could hit anything with the .45, Campbell thought the man looked satisfied that he at least had a working weapon.

Though not in communication with Carroll, Lieutenant Schworm moved his platoon forward as soon as the firing broke out. The lead squad made it about halfway down the ravine when NVA hidden in a tree line opened up with a vicious blast of small-arms and automatic weapons fire. "It was as if every tree had a gook behind it," Pfc. Clarence Powell remembered. "It was just a tremendous blast of fire."

When Powell hit the ground, his bulky 3.5-inch rocket launcher tumbled from his grasp. He reached out to pull it closer to him, but suddenly his hand flew backward. "I didn't know what was happening. It took me a few seconds to realize I'd been hit."

Unable to use the launcher with his shattered hand, Powell unholstered his .45. He caught a glimpse of an NVA soldier about twenty meters away darting from tree to tree. Powell waited, carefully sighted on his target, and squeezed the trigger. The man dropped.

A little later, Powell's assistant gunner wrapped a dressing around Powell's damaged hand. About then the squad's radioman, lying just in front of Powell, suddenly rose to his knees. Turning around he yelled, "Pull back. Pull back."

A split second later, a burst of enemy fire shattered the man's radio and blew out his chest in a spray of blood and tissue. He said in a clear voice, "I'm a dead man," and fell over. Powell hugged the earth as he wondered if he would survive the fight.

Not more than fifteen minutes had passed since Lieutenant Carroll sent his men racing up the side of the finger. During that time the two squads with him had suffered several casualties. "My First Squad radioed they needed a corpsman," Carroll said. "The doc nearest me jumped up without hesitation and headed down to the left to help. I doubt he made it there."

The corpsman had barely disappeared into the grass when Carroll felt a sharp pain in his right leg. "It was like someone stabbed a knife into it," Carroll said. "Fortunately, the slug had either passed through someone else or had hit the ground before it ricocheted up into my leg, because it hit the bone and stopped."

Carroll frantically radioed Sorensen: "I'm hit in the leg. I need help up here."

Unsure of the exact tactical situation because of the confusion of the close-quarters fight, Sorensen radioed Carroll and Schworm to meet him near the top of the finger. Sorensen and his CP group went straight up the side of the finger toward Carroll. About twenty-five yards behind the 3d Platoon's line, as rounds steadily cracked overhead, Sorensen huddled with his two platoon leaders. He pointed up the finger. "We're pulling back up there and setting up a three-sixty," Sorensen yelled over the din.

"I've already sent a squad up there," Carroll told him. "If you try to go up there, you'll get your ass shot off."

Before Sorensen could respond, a flurry of heavy fire broke out farther down the finger. "I gotta get back to my men," Carroll said and crawled back up the hillside. Schworm headed back to his men, too.

Sorensen told the artillery FO and the FAC to call in supporting fire, but the high terrain blocked their transmissions. Sorensen then ordered them to move up the hill by different routes. Maybe, he thought, if one of them could get high enough, the signals could get out.

As the enemy fire roared all around, Sorensen ordered his command group to move up the finger. They made only a few steps when a .30-caliber round slammed into the captain's right hip. He dropped in a heap, unable to move.

At first, his radioman, Corporal O'Connor, who was a few feet ahead of Sorensen, did not realize his CO had been hit. When he did, O'Connor unslung his radio and darted into the open. While rounds popped all around him, O'Connor reached Sorensen and pulled him toward a clump of trees. Somehow they made it to safety without either getting hit.

While a corpsman treated Sorensen, O'Connor tried to reach Carroll or Schworm. Neither answered the radio calls. But O'Connor did raise an F-8 flying nearby and described Foxtrot's plight. Unfortunately, the pilot had already expended his armament on another target. He offered to make some dummy runs. O'Connor accepted; it was better than nothing. The jet made two low, threatening passes over the enemy positions but could do no more.

Over the next hour O'Connor repeatedly tried to raise Carroll or Schworm, but he had no luck. He did not know where they were or how they were doing. As wounded Marines staggered into his little perimeter, O'Connor patched them with the small amount of medical supplies he could gather. Several times, when a wounded man could not make it to safety, O'Connor fearlessly exposed himself to enemy fire to carry the man in.

Back down the finger, the fighting grew more desperate. Enemy grenades landed all around Carroll and erupted with sharp flashes. He would roll first left, then right, then back left, then right again. The lethal missiles seemed to come endlessly.

"The fighting had been so intense for so long, my men were running out of ammo," Carroll remembered. "Everyone was yelling for more. I ran out of magazines for my forty-five. Sure enough, a gook popped up and started running toward me. I crawled around, picked up a discarded M16, and fired. Fortunately, it worked. The gook fell dead just feet from me."

The ammunition shortage, the close-quarters fighting, and the failed M16s spelled disaster for Carroll's men. "The two squads down from me on my left, just past a tree that grew up from the enemy's side of the ridge finger, were overrun. The NVA just swarmed over the hill. They were killing my men, shooting the wounded point-blank."

Carroll continued. "I grabbed my wounded radioman by his web gear and tried to pull him uphill to some cover. I was looking down at my hands when my left thumb just exploded in a spray of red. One second my thumb was there, the next it was gone."

Despite his two wounds, Carroll pulled his radioman to safety. Then, before he could take any further action, a tremendous blow shook his left leg. Stunned, he lay there for several minutes before he recovered enough to look at the wound. What he saw sickened him. "My boot was laying at ninety degrees to my leg. I tried to straighten it, but it flopped over the other way.

"You shot my goddamn leg off, you bastards!" he screamed across the battlefield. "What more do you want? Goddamn, isn't this enough?"

Realizing there was no more he could do, Carroll crawled uphill. He dug his elbows in and crept forward a few inches at a time. Oblivious to the pain, unaware of the damage done to his elbows by the sharp rocks, Carroll pulled himself along. Foot by painful foot, he struggled uphill. Ten feet, then twenty. Finally, he moved out of the killing zone. A few more feet and he rolled into a shallow depression. Four or five other wounded men already lay there. They all huddled together, waiting for the end.

Instinctively, reacting to their training, other surviving Marines moved toward the high ground. In the ravine below him, Pfc. Clarence Powell saw NVA just meters away. They were methodically shooting the wounded lying in the grass. Powell spotted a cluster of Marines up on the hillside. He ran toward them. He slipped a few steps later and sprawled headlong in the dirt. He got up and started running again. Behind him he heard AK rounds splattering the ground where he had lain. Powell made it up the hill and to the others. Weaponless, he took a wounded man's M16 and pointed it uphill. "The enemy was all around us and I wanted to make sure they didn't get us from the rear."

From his position a hundred meters higher on the ridge finger, Pfc. Lance Campbell witnessed the final minutes of the action. As he watched, the NVA fought hand to hand with his fellow Marines at the bottom of the slope. Unable to do anything, he felt completely helpless.

Unknown to Campbell and the other patrol survivors, however, there were more witnesses to the carnage. And they *could* do something.

The two-platoon patrol from Echo Company proceeded along its route that day without incident. It approached each objective in a combat-assault formation, but fortunately no enemy troops were encountered. Their final objective, Hill 803, loomed over them as Cannon and Izenour maneuvered their platoons forward.

"About this time we picked up Foxtrot's transmissions to battalion," Cannon recalled. "At first we heard something like, 'Pygmalion Six, this is Foxtrot Six. We've got one kangaroo and three wolves.' In no time we heard, 'We've got five kangaroos and nine wolves.' They were in deep shit."

The two Echo platoons deployed for the assault on Hill 803, then up they went. The sounds of heavy rifle fire grew louder as they climbed. When the Marines reached a flat area a few hundred meters from the summit, they hastily formed a perimeter. Cannon dropped to his belly and crawled to the edge of the little plateau. He uncased his field glasses and swept the terrain below him to determine what was happening to Foxtrot.

"What I saw horrified me," Cannon said. "The North Vietnamese were all over the men of Foxtrot. They were stabbing and shooting what appeared to be wounded Marines. I saw several NVA attempting to drag away a wounded man."

Cannon sprang into action. He grabbed a machine gun from a nearby M60 crew. "I could see a treetop that seemed to mark the closest the NVA had gotten to Foxtrot. That would be my reference point. Everything to the left was either dead Marines or NVA."

Cannon loosed a long burst of heavy slugs. He raked the ridge finger from the treetop to its base. Although the range was more than a thousand meters, the tracers testified to Cannon's accuracy. He paused and turned to the Weapons Platoon sergeant. "Take the other gun. Watch my tracers. Hit everything to the left of that tree," he barked as he pointed at the ridge finger.

Together the two men blazed away. Their fire cut a swath through the NVA and drove them to cover.

Lieutenant Adinolfi came up behind Cannon. Unaware of the unfolding events, he screamed, "Cease fire! Get off that damn gun!"

"Go to hell," Cannon retorted. He knew that the CO had not seen what he had.

After he fired a full belt of ammunition, Cannon turned the weapon over to the gunner. "Keep the enemy off that finger," Cannon ordered. The gunner opened fire.

Lieutenant Adinolfi informed Cannon that he had learned Foxtrot 6 had been hit. And the company had suffered so many casualties it could not move. He told Cannon to take his platoon down to Foxtrot, clear out the enemy, and evacuate Foxtrot's casualties. In the meantime, Lieutenant Colonel Delong was on his way with a platoon from Hotel, some mortars, and a 106mm recoilless rifle.

"I asked Lieutenant Izenour to guide me to the base of the finger where the tree I'd used as a reference point was located," Cannon said. "I had a supply of pencil flares. I'd pop one every few minutes and Izenour could adjust my route."

Within minutes 2d Platoon was on its way down Hill 803's eastern slope. The route was thick with brush but passable. The platoon members carefully picked their way downhill until they reached the ravine where Lieutenant Carroll had examined the footprints.

Halfway across the ravine, two rifle shots rang out, startling Cannon. He halted the column and cautiously moved forward. He soon came upon his point man. The young Marine had two AK-47s slung over his shoulder and a big grin on his face. He explained that he had spotted two NVA slinking through the brush. Before Cannon could respond, the point man directed his attention to the head of the ravine. What Cannon saw surprised him and answered a lot of questions.

"Stretching up the little valley were freshly dug graves. A lot of graves. Bloody NVA web gear lay in several piles." Cannon now understood what had happened to Foxtrot. "Their patrol route must have taken them very near to this burial site. No doubt the North Vietnamese didn't want it discovered. That's why they'd ambushed Foxtrot. It also told me there had to be a lot of them in the area," Cannon observed.

"I decided it was too dangerous to move right up to Foxtrot's position. The NVA might get us or the Marine survivors might shoot us," Cannon said. He radioed Adinolfi his change of plans. "I'll take the high ground and sweep down the ridge finger," Cannon told his CO. After detailing S-2 scout Cpl. Fred Monahan and another man to remain there and count the graves, Cannon headed out.

Helicopters carrying Delong, his S-3, Lieutenant Elliott's platoon of Hotel Company, and the heavy weapons arrived at Adinolfi's position. While the weapons were being set up, Delong raised Captain Sorensen on the radio. "I want to fire some 106 rounds," he told Sorensen. "Give me some targets."

"No, sir," Sorensen told him. "The NVA are too close and I don't know where my men are."

That angered Delong.

Back in the ravine, Corporal Monahan finished his count. He radioed Adinolfi that the burial site contained 203 graves. Adinolfi ordered Monahan to remain in position, protect Cannon's rear, and wait for the Hotel platoon to reach him. Monahan would then guide them to Cannon.

Cannon's platoon soon crested the high end of the ridge finger. The troops turned left and swept downhill, with Sergeant Marden's squad on the point. Marden placed a fire team on each side of the finger and one in the center. He was not comfortable, though. Danger hung heavily in the air. He fully expected the NVA to open fire at any minute. But they did not. What Marden's squad found instead were dead and wounded Marines. Many of them.

Near the top of the finger, Cannon came upon Lieutenant Schworm and three other Marines clustered together. "Schworm told me he and the others were the only ones to make it that high," Cannon recalled. "Two of the four had been hit. I told him I was glad to be able to pay him back for the help he'd given me six days earlier."

Marden came upon Lieutenant Carroll farther down the hill. "We'll get you outta here as fast as we can," Marden assured him.

"Forget about me," Carroll responded. "I've got other wounded down there. Get to them."

As Marden continued on, he saw that the finger ended in a steep drop-off. A dense tree line sat behind the drop-off. "I could see where NVA had lain up against the end of the finger," he recalled. "From there they could easily pick off the Marines higher up."

Several of Marden's men sprayed the tree line with M16 fire. "Hey, don't shoot," someone called. "We've got wounded in here." Some Foxtrot Marines had taken refuge in the trees. Marden sent one of his squads and a corpsman to help them. Then he set up a defensive perimeter around the bottom of the finger.

By this time Lieutenant Elliott's platoon had left the plateau on its way to help Foxtrot. The platoon descended into the vegetation-choked ravine that separated them from Hill 778's finger. The thickness of the jungle surprised the Marines. "It was the worst I'd seen in the hills," LCpl. Wayne Ithier recalled.

The terrain had benefits, though. Halfway across the ravine, Elliott's point man signaled a halt. "Gooks" came the word down the line. He had heard Vietnamese voices crossing from his right to his left and immediately crouched down. After a few minutes the voices grew fainter, then disappeared. The point man signaled the patrol forward.

After the linkup with Corporal Monahan, Elliott's platoon proceeded across the high side of the finger, then swept down into the ravine on its opposite side. They found no NVA. Elliott set up a perimeter to provide an outer ring of defense for the battle site.

Cannon's corpsmen were busy treating Foxtrot's wounded. Most of the casualties did not know who their rescuers were, but they all felt great relief when these new Marines suddenly appeared. "I wasn't sure who they were, but I was mighty glad to see them," Lieutenant Carroll remembered. One of the corpsmen knelt by Carroll and treated him. Then helping hands carried him to an LZ.

Captain Sorensen was carried to the LZ, too, but he does not remember much about it. "I just knew a helicopter was there and I was getting on it," he said. His radioman, Cpl. Joseph O'Connor, helped place him aboard the chopper, then turned to help others.

The few able-bodied Foxtrot Marines, aided by some Echo troops, commenced the grisly task of policing up their dead. Private First Class Lance Campbell helped lay out the bodies in neat rows. "Some of the guys were unrecognizable since they'd been shot in the head at close range, execution style," he said. "It was very gruesome."

Private First Class James Mason of Sergeant Marden's squad also saw several Marines who had been shot in the head. They were at the low end of the ridge finger where Mason had taken up a defensive position. Intermingled with them were a number of dead NVA, some killed by M16s and grenades, others obvious victims of Cannon's M60 fire.

While Foxtrot's casualties were being medevacked, NVA on the crest of Hill 803 opened fire on the command group. Mortar rounds fell on them first. A few minutes later, AK-47 fire drove the small force of Marines to cover. Lieutenant Colonel Delong, aided by his S-3, Captain Lemon, directed 106mm recoilless rifle fire and countermortar fire on the enemy position. This return fire proved effective. The enemy quickly withdrew after killing one Marine.

All of Foxtrot's casualties were evacuated by 1700. Twenty-four Marines died in the fight; another nineteen were wounded. Helicopters carried the survivors back to Hill 881N. When Private First Class Campbell debarked, a buddy came up to him. "Lance, where's the rest of your platoon?"

"This is it," Campbell responded, indicating the dozen or so men around him.

Miraculously, Cpl. Albert Potts and his M60 team escaped unscathed. How, he could not imagine. "I didn't think any of us were going to make it out," he said. "The rounds passed so close they popped as they went by. It was the worst experience of my whole tour. Only Lieutenant Cannon's M60 fire saved us."

At the Foxtrot Company's perimeter on Hill 881N, Lieutenants Koehler and Chritton spent several hours reconciling the company roster before they concluded they had one man, Pvt. Robert J. Todd, missing in action. Now the company commander, Koehler had to report the bad news to Lieutenant Colonel Delong. Delong reacted with fury. "A missing Marine is unacceptable," he said. "Find him."

Lieutenant Chritton recalled, "I closely questioned Todd's squad leader and, though he vividly remembered putting Todd's body on a helicopter, the remains hadn't shown up anywhere. We feared he had been left behind.

"Delong told us, 'We've got a missing Marine and we're going out and not coming back until we find him.'"

No one wanted to go back into hostile territory, but Koehler and Chritton prepared their men. Before they set out, word came that the search mission was canceled. What happened to Todd remains a mystery.

Helicopters returned to Hill 778 late in the evening to carry out Cannon's and Elliott's men. Originally they had headed for Hill 881N, but a fog developed and forced the aircraft back to Hill 803. There, Cannon joined with Delong and his CP group to set up a night defensive perimeter.

Sergeant James Marden waited patiently with his men as the others boarded the choppers and flew off. His concern increased as it became dark and he had no word about the extraction of his men. He radioed Lieutenant Izenour to ask when he could expect to be lifted out.

"Are you shitting me?" Izenour exploded. "Is this some kind of a joke?"

Marden assured him it was not. He and his squad were still in the field. Izenour radioed for a chopper, and a short time later an old H-34 chugged in to Marden's position. He and his squad hastily climbed aboard for the short flight to Hill 803. They dug in and passed an uneventful night. The next morning, after Delong and his staff flew out, the grunts humped back to Hill 881N.

On 11 May, Colonel Lanigan issued the necessary orders to turn the Khe Sanh area of operations over to the 1st Battalion, 26th Marines. Late that morning helicopters landed on Hill 881N to ferry Echo and Foxtrot Companies back to Khe Sanh. There the Marines boarded C-130s for the short flight to Dong Ha and further movement out to the SLF's ships.

Golf and Hotel Companies had to hump back to the combat base, a decision that thoroughly irritated them. They spent the night along the airstrip, then were flown to Dong Ha. From there they joined the rest of the battalion on the ships.

Charlie 1/26 replaced the four companies that had been on Hill 881N. The enormity of the previous day's battle immediately became apparent to the new Marines. Second Lieutenant James Epps, a Charlie Company platoon leader, could not believe what he saw. "We set in among a jumble of trees blown off at knee level," he remembered. "We noticed details attesting to the ferocity of the battle. And I don't mean just the giant trees tossed about like matchsticks, but the debris of big military units in a desperate battle: ammunition wrappings, rocket and mortar cardboard shipping tubes, piles of spent brass mixed with machine gun links, ragged battle dressings, food garbage, abandoned web gear, an NVA bush hat in the low branches of a denuded tree, loose rounds, and empty wooden ammo boxes."

Overpowering everything was the sickening aroma of death. Violent death.

Just before 1700 on 11 May, an H-34 resupply helicopter crashed on departure from Hill 881N. It ended up right in the middle of Echo BLT 2/3's 3 May perimeter. None of the passengers or crew was injured and they were quickly lifted out. Epps's platoon was ordered downhill to protect the metal carcass.

"It was obvious a big fight had occurred there," he said. "The stench was incredible."

Epps's men attempted to occupy some of the existing bunkers but found that many of them contained the putrefied remains of NVA who had been dumped there by Echo and Hotel Companies ten days earlier. Epps's men spent a miserable night and day waiting for the recovery craft to arrive.

Alpha 1/26 arrived on Hill 881S at 1000 on 12 May. Kilo and Mike 3/9 were to have been lifted out, but an emergency order grounding all CH-46s because of a suspected structural deficiency forced them to hump all the way back to the combat base. On the way in, they picked up Sgt. Spencer Olsen's platoon of Echo 2/9, which was still guarding Hill 861. Once at the Khe Sanh Combat Base, Olsen rejoined Capt. William Terrill and the rest of Echo 2/9. The 3/3 survivors boarded the trucks of a Rough Rider convoy for the trip back to Camp Carroll. That same day, Charlie 1/26 departed Hill 881N, relinquishing the hard-won terrain to the NVA, and moved overland to garrison Hill 861.

At 1500 on 12 May 1967, Col. J. J. Padley, CO, 26th Marines, assumed responsibility for the area from Colonel Lanigan. The Hill Fights, or the First Battle of Khe Sanh, had officially ended.

The after-action report for the Battle of Khe Sanh submitted by the 3d Marines on 9 June 1967 lists a total of 168 Marine and Navy personnel killed in action during the fighting. Four hundred forty-three men were wounded in action, and two are listed as missing. The largest number of casualties came on 30 April, when 2/3 sustained 12 dead and 56 wounded and 3/3 lost 43 dead and 109 wounded.

The same report claimed 824 dead NVA by body count and another 551 probably killed. Although there is no doubt that the enemy units assigned the mission of taking the Khe Sanh Combat Base suffered grievous casualties, the numbers are suspect. The NVA did a thorough job of removing their dead from Hills 861 and 881S, so their actual casualties will never be known.

The intensity of the fighting in the Khe Sanh hills prompted Lt. Gen. Victor Krulak to acknowledge that, "It was the toughest fight we had in Vietnam." In recognition of the tenacity and bravery of the North Vietnamese soldiers, the Marines along the DMZ rarely employed their deeply ingrained "hey diddle-diddle, straight-up-the-middle" infantry tactic again. Instead, they settled into fixed defensive positions that forced the NVA to attack them, which they did with amazing regularity. When the Marines did launch offensive operations, the objectives were heavily prepped with air and artillery before the infantry went in. That helped, to be sure, but the NVA were a determined foe. Through months of bloody fighting between Route 9 and the DMZ, the Marines never conquered the North Vietnamese Army. At best, they managed a stalemate.

Generals Westmoreland and Walt considered the Hill Fights a victory. After all, the combat base had been saved. If they had had a crystal ball, neither commander would have left just three rifle companies at Khe Sanh.

Part Four: Aftermath

Chapter Thirteen

The 1st Battalion, 26th Marines, wasted no time in starting its new mission at Khe Sanh: saturation patrols in the TAOR within range of the supporting artillery. Battalion commander Lt. Col. Donald D. Newton began Operation Crockett on 14 May 1967. He stationed one rifle company each on Hills 861 and 881S, put a small detachment on Hill 950 to guard the radio relay station, and kept the rest of the battalion at the combat base for security and reserve. The infantry from the hilltop outposts patrolled continuously, ranging out as far as four thousand meters.

For the balance of May and into June, 1/26's patrols found plenty of evidence that the NVA 325C Division still roamed the area, but they rarely saw an enemy soldier. Then, at 0100 on 6 June, the security detachment on Hill 950 frantically radioed the base that it was under a ground attack. A reaction force saddled up at the airstrip, but the radio calls grew more desperate: The enemy was in the lines; the enemy was overrunning the position; please send help. Then silence.

By the time the reaction force arrived, the fight had ended. Of the seventeen Marines on Hill 950, six were dead and nine were wounded. If 1/26 needed a reminder that the NVA still held the upper hand in the Khe Sanh hills, they had it.

The next day the enemy repeated that lesson. About two kilometers west of Hill 881S, a patrol from Bravo 1/26 was hit by NVA mortars and small-arms fire. Before the Marines recovered from that attack, a strong force of NVA soldiers poured out of a nearby tree line. A desperate close-quarters fight raged across the hillside for several hours before a reinforcing platoon from Alpha Company reached the scene and forced the NVA to break contact. Eighteen Bravo Marines died; another twenty-eight were wounded. Sixty-six dead NVA lay among the Marine casualties.

As a result of these vicious contacts, Maj. Gen. Bruno A. Hochmuth, the 3d Marine Division commander, ordered Lt. Col. Kurt L. Hoch's 3/26 to Khe Sanh. It arrived on 13 June and headed into the hills.

There was little contact until the early morning hours of 27 June, when the NVA sent more than fifty 82mm mortar rounds flying into the combat base. The rounds killed 9 Marines and wounded 125. The combat base had barely secured from that attack when the NVA struck again. Just before dawn they launched fifty 102mm rockets at the base. Another Marine died and fourteen more were wounded in this attack.

At noon that same day, India 3/26, on a search west of the base for the enemy mortar positions, bumped into two NVA companies. The fight lasted all afternoon. Not until 1900, when Lima 3/26 arrived by helicopter, did the enemy flee. India lost eight killed, including a platoon commander, and thirty-five wounded; Lima lost its commander and thirteen others, plus fifteen wounded. An estimated twenty-five NVA died in the firefight.

After this action the enemy seemingly vanished. The two battalions continued their extensive patrols but found few NVA. As a result, 3/26 received orders on 16 July that sent it east, where enemy activity had heated up around Con Thien.

That left one battalion, 1/26, now under Lt. Col. James B. Wilkinson, the sole defenders of the northwest quadrant of Quang Tri Province. As had Lieutenant Colonel Wickwire of 1/3 before him, Wilkinson sent his men out on patrols every day. And just like Wickwire's Marines, Wilkinson's men rarely spotted the enemy. Throughout the rest of the summer and into the fall, the Marine patrols searched far and wide, but the NVA remained out of sight. Yet no one doubted they were out there.

In November, intelligence sources reported that two NVA divisions, the 325C and 304, had entered the Khe Sanh area. This convinced General Westmoreland that his long-hoped-for major battle with the North Vietnamese Army loomed just over the horizon. Determined to engage his foe in a decisive battle, the MACV ordered III MAF, now commanded by Lt. Gen. Robert E. Cushman, Jr., to reinforce Khe Sanh. Cushman passed the orders to the 3d Marine Division. That headquarters tapped

3/26 for a return trip to Khe Sanh. Three of its rifle companies landed at the improved airstrip on 13 December; the fourth arrived the next day. Operation Scotland began on 14 December, and the Khe Sanh hills once again felt the pounding of Marine jungle boots.

All remained quiet until just after dusk on 2 January 1968. In response to an alert Marine sentry's warning, a quick-reaction team shot and killed five enemy soldiers dressed in Marine utilities who had been reconnoitering the western end of the combat base. A search of the enemy bodies revealed that the team had slain an NVA regimental commander and members of his staff. The corpses yielded a rich supply of documents indicating that the enemy had planned a major attack on the base. Colonel David E. Lownds, CO of the 26th Marines since August, passed the data up the line.

When the intelligence reached General Westmoreland, it convinced him he had been right all along. In his mind, the NVA hoped to duplicate their stunning 1954 defeat of the French at Dien Bien Phu. Westmoreland ordered a major buildup for the base. Two more Marine battalions (2/26 and 1/9) arrived at Khe Sanh in mid-January; the ARVN sent its 37th Ranger Battalion. By the end of January, five full infantry battalions, three batteries of 105mm howitzers, a battery each of 4.2-inch mortars and 155mm howitzers, and a variety of track-mounted weapons defended the base and the nearby hills.

Fearful that the NVA would have an unobstructed invasion route into South Vietnam's two northernmost provinces if Khe Sanh did fall, Westmoreland shifted more infantry battalions north. By the end of January 1968, half of all U.S. combat troops—nearly fifty maneuver battalions—were in I Corps.

The Second Battle of Khe Sanh began on 17 January 1968 under circumstances deadly similar to those that triggered the first battle. A recon team on the southern slope of Hill 881N walked into an ambush. The patrol commander and his radioman died in the initial blast of fire; several more Marines were wounded. They and the others fell back and frantically called for help.

A platoon from India 3/26, which garrisoned Hill 881S, happened to be nearby. In response to the desperate radio calls, the platoon rushed to aid the recon team. When it arrived, the NVA fire stopped. Medevacs flew in and carried the wounded recon team members back to Khe Sanh. The India Company Marines returned to Hill 881S.

Two days later, another India Company patrol, sent to recover some radio codes left behind by the recon Marines, came under fire in the same area. After a brief firefight, the Marines withdrew.

These two contacts convinced Colonel Lownds that the NVA had re-occupied Hill 881N. Captain William Dabney, CO of India 3/26, received orders to conduct a company-sized reconnaissance-in-force of the hill. India set out at 0500 on 20 January, after Mike 3/26 replaced it on Hill 881S. The Marines moved in two platoon columns along parallel ridge fingers leading to Hill 881N's crest. To flush out ambushers, Dabney walked artillery up the hill in front of his men. It did not work.

Halfway up the hill, a vicious blast of automatic weapons fire and rocket-propelled grenades ripped into the right-hand column. Dabney ordered the left-hand platoon forward to flank the ambushers. That did not work either. The platoon made all of twenty feet when a flurry of hot lead erupted from a nearby tree line, decimating it.

For the rest of the afternoon, supported by artillery and air, Dabney continued his efforts to move up Hill 881N. Not until 1730, with seven dead and thirty-five wounded to care for, did Dabney throw in the towel. He ordered his battered company back to Hill 881S.

That same day an enemy deserter revealed that both the NVA 325C and 304 Divisions were, indeed, in the hills outside Khe Sanh. In fact, he said, his former comrades planned an attack on Hills 861 and 881S that night. Colonel Lownds immediately sent word to the outposts to be prepared.

At thirty minutes past midnight on 21 January, the first of several hundred NVA rockets, mortar shells, and rocket-propelled grenades slammed into Kilo 3/26's positions on Hill 861. When the barrage ended, bursts of enemy machine gun fire raked the hillside. Deep in their bunkers, Kilo's Marines gripped their weapons and prayed.

At 0100 more than 250 enemy soldiers started up Hill 861's southwest side. Despite the Marines' best efforts, the enemy soldiers breached their perimeter and poured into Kilo's positions. The CO, Capt. Norman J. Jasper, Jr., went down from a direct hit on his command bunker. Unable to continue, he turned command over to his exec. The close-quarters, ferocious fight drove the Marines from their prepared positions to higher ground along the hill's crest.

From his CP on Hill 881S, Captain Dabney watched the nearby battle unfold. Because he anticipated an attack on his position, he could only wait. However, after several hours of quiet around Hill 881S, Dabney decided he was not in the bull's-eye that night. He ordered his mortars to fire in support of Kilo.

Despite the beating they had taken, Kilo's Marines had a lot of fight left. At 0500 they counterattacked. Down the enemy-filled trenches they went, taking on the NVA in the most vicious hand-to-hand combat imaginable. The Marines won. At 0700 they radioed Colonel Lownds that they still held the hill.

Lownds had but scant minutes to savor the good news. From Hill 881N the enemy launched more than sixty 122mm rockets and one hundred 82mm mortar shells at the base. Dabney's Marines witnessed a rare spectacle, akin to a world-class fireworks display, as the rockets headed toward the Khe Sanh Combat Base, trailing showers of sparks across the morning sky. Seconds later, explosion after explosion erupted throughout the base. The blasts ripped the runway's steel matting to shreds, tossed helicopters about like toys, collapsed bunkers, destroyed tents, and zinged shards of red-hot shrapnel into human flesh.

Worst of all, one of the first rockets landed in the middle of the ammo dump. A colossal secondary explosion rocked the entire east end of the base as the bulk of more than fifteen hundred tons of pyrotechnics went up and sent flaming debris down on the base. To add to the destruction, numerous barrels of aviation fuel burst from the heat and poured rivers of fire onto the base.

That same night, NVA infantry attacked the South Vietnamese troops who garrisoned Khe Sanh village. Colonel Lownds had to turn down their plea for help. He told them to abandon the village and come to the combat base.

With the enemy now between the combat base and Lang Vei and in control of Route 9, Khe Sanh was truly cut off. The comparisons to the French defeat at Dien Bien Phu increased, but General Westmoreland remained optimistic. Indeed, he welcomed the presence of the NVA around Khe Sanh, for he had one advantage the French had not had: airpower. With the massive destructive power available from the sky, Westmoreland could easily destroy his foe. He also began to plan for the relief of Khe Sanh. He would leapfrog the U.S. Army's 1st Cavalry Division (Airmobile) down Route 9 from Ca Lu and reopen the highway. He would then send the cavalry into the hills and annihilate the NVA.

Then the Tet Offensive erupted.

On 30 January 1968, well-coordinated attacks by Viet Cong and North Vietnamese Army units were launched all across South Vietnam. Over the next two days, thirty-six of forty-four provincial capitals were attacked. Every major airfield was bombarded by mortars. And enemy sappers nearly overran the massive U.S. embassy complex in downtown Saigon.

About the only major allied base not attacked was Khe Sanh. None of the five NVA divisions that U.S. intelligence reported to be in western Quang Tri Province joined in the offensive. Westmoreland believed that he knew why. He explained the countrywide attacks by announcing, "This is a diversionary attack to take attention away from the north, from an attack at Khe Sanh."

It would be some weeks before Westmoreland accepted the truth—that the NVA movement on Khe Sanh had been the diversion. The NVA wanted to pull allied troops away from the cities and the populous coastal areas. Only then could their General Uprising–General Offensive succeed. That it did not is a testament to the valor of the individual American fighting man, backed by a nearly unlimited supply of supporting arms.

The relative quiet at Khe Sanh lasted until 2 February. On that date more rockets fell on the base. One hit an Army Signal Corps communications bunker, killed four, and temporarily cut the base off from the rest of the world.

Two days later, super-secret electronic sensors detected a large body of men near Hill 881S. By carefully calculating their route, the Fire Support Control Center (FSCC) at Khe Sanh identified a target box north of Dabney's position. On signal, five hundred high-explosive artillery shells pummeled the target box. When no attack developed against Dabney, the men of the FSCC congratulated themselves.

Shortly after 0400 on 5 February, the NVA dropped a tremendous volley of mortar rounds on Echo 2/26, newly ensconced on Hill 861A. As soon as the last of the 82mm shells erupted, an NVA force estimated at battalion size, about four hundred men, threw themselves at the freshly strung barbed wire barrier. Sappers blasted passageways through the wire, and enemy infantry poured through the gaps.

The Echo Marines gave ground as they fell back to the center of the perimeter. Echo's CO, Capt. Earle G. Breeding, called down massive quantities of artillery around his position. But the enemy kept coming. By 0500 they held a quarter of the hill.

The surviving Marines summoned a reservoir of courage few men knew they possessed, and they counterattacked. At close quarters, too close in most cases to use the M16, the plucky Marines stormed down the trenches and killed NVA with grenades, bayonets, and bare hands until they reclaimed the lost positions. By 0630 it was over. No less than 109 enemy bodies lay on the hill. Given the ferocity of the fight, Echo suffered relatively light casualties: 7 dead and 35 wounded.

At 2000 on 6 February, U.S. Army Special Forces sentries at Lang Vei heard the unmistakable rumble of approaching diesel engines. "Tanks in the wire!" The panicked cry echoed throughout the camp.

Seven enemy tanks supported by several hundred NVA infantry overwhelmed the Green Berets and their indigenous charges. At 0400 on 7 February, the camp commander radioed Colonel Lownds and asked him to execute a long-established relief and rescue plan.

Lownds refused. As far as he was concerned, a night movement to Lang Vei amounted to suicide because there were NVA between the base and Lang Vei. Also, the combat base had been under a mortar and rocket attack since 0100. Even if he had had a spare rifle company to send, dispatching it would have seriously weakened his own defenses. The Green Berets were on their own.

By late afternoon, the fight for Lang Vei ended in victory for the NVA. Of more than 500 defenders, only 175 survived. Only 14 of 24 Americans reached safety, and 11 of those were wounded.

Over the next seven weeks, the defenders of Khe Sanh endured daily artillery and rocket attacks. Each day at least a hundred shells, and on some days more than a thousand, hit the base or its outposts. Every day men died or were wounded. In the first four weeks of the siege, more than 10 percent of the defenders became casualties. Although soldiers in earlier wars had endured heavier shelling, the defenders of Khe Sanh suffered more because of the persistence of the barrages and their inability to stop them. Even B-52 Arc Light missions failed to halt the enemy artillery.

In early March, General Westmoreland concluded that the NVA no longer planned to capture the Khe Sanh Combat Base, and he so informed President Johnson. But Westmoreland continued to plan for the relief of Khe Sanh, code-named Operation Pegasus.

The operation infuriated the Marine commanders. They had not wanted to be in Khe Sanh in the first place, then they had been roundly criticized for not defending it well. General Cushman angrily insisted to Westmoreland that he did not want an "implication of a rescue or break-ing of the siege by outside forces." Thus, Operation Pegasus was officially touted as a joint Army-Marine operation to reopen Route 9 between Ca Lu and Khe Sanh.

At 0700 on 1 April 1968, two battalions of the 1st Marines—2/1 and 2/3—headed down Route 9 from Ca Lu toward Khe Sanh while elements of the 1st Cavalry Division (Airmobile) began their leapfrog movements, air-assaulting onto key terrain features alongside Route 9. One week later the cavalrymen linked up with a patrol from the 26th Marines. The siege was over.

The Second Battle of Khe Sanh ended where it began. Three com-panies of 3/26—Kilo, Lima, and Mike—attacked Hill 881N on Easter Sunday, 14 April. The enemy-occupied hill had been a thorn in the Marines' side for weeks; when the 3d Battalion, 26th Marines, finished, the hill would be free of enemy soldiers.

The pre-assault bombardment began at 0400. Dozens of howitzers blasted the hill with hundreds of rounds. Marine jets roared in to drop dozens of canisters of napalm. For nearly two hours, a frightening array of high explosives blanketed the hill.

At 0540 the infantry started their attack. A short time later the point elements encountered the first enemy outposts. Quick bursts of rifle fire killed the defenders. For the next six hours, the Marines fought and clawed their way up the side of Hill 881N. By noon they had reached the crest. The mopping up of stubborn pockets of resistance continued for several more hours. At 1430 the Marines declared Hill 881N theirs.

Marine casualties were surprisingly light: six dead and thirty-two wounded. One hundred six North Vietnamese had been killed. The next day 3/26 departed Hill 881N and left it free for the NVA to reclaim.

The 26th Marines departed Khe Sanh over the next several days as op-erational control of the TAOR passed to Col. Stanley S. Hughes's 1st Marines. On 15 April 1968, Operation Pegasus officially ended and Op-eration Scotland II began. For the next two months, the four battalions of the 1st Marines—1/1, 2/1, 2/3, and 3/4—patrolled a large TAOR that extended north of Khe Sanh to the DMZ, west to the Laotion border, and south of Route 9. Contact with the enemy was frequent and deadly. The Marines suffered about 300 dead during Operation Scotland II as compared to an official casualty count of 205 dead during the original Operation Scotland.

Almost immediately upon the second capture of Hill 881N, III MAF began to petition MACV to abandon Khe Sanh. Westmoreland rejected the proposal. In his opinion, the base was too large a symbol of American resolve in the divisive war to close it so soon after the siege. General Cushman, however, persisted. Cushman pointed out that with improved mobility due to the increased use of helicopters, there was no need to maintain a combat base so far removed from reinforcement. He argued that the new base at Ca Lu, south of the Rockpile, continued the Marine presence in northwest Quang Tri Province and sat comfortably beyond the range of enemy artillery batteries in Laos. It was also easier to supply and was not susceptible to the *crachin*.

Westmoreland eventually agreed. He had one condition, though. The base could not be closed while he remained as the MACV.

General Westmoreland departed South Vietnam on 11 June 1968. His successor, Gen. Creighton Abrams, allowed a grace period of one week before he issued the order to commence Operation Charlie: the destruction and evacuation of the Khe Sanh Combat Base.

The plan called for the Marines to withdraw all salvageable supplies and equipment and destroy everything else. Along Route 9, battalions of the 4th Marines occupied key terrain positions that would allow them to control the road and protect the many convoys that would move between Khe Sanh and Ca Lu. The 1st Marines guarded the base and garrisoned the surrounding hills. The 3d Battalion, 9th Marines, would provide the labor needed to dismantle the historic base.

The arrival of Kilo 3/9 at Khe Sanh on 19 June began with a near disaster. One of the troop-laden CH-46s whipped a discarded parachute into its rear rotor after it had been waved off from a landing. In an instant, the whirling blades disintegrated. Huge hunks of metal slashed through the aircraft's thin aluminum skin. One piece sliced through the pilot's right shoulder and leg as he futilely tried to keep the chopper from crashing. Fuel sprayed everywhere as the trapped Marines rushed to the exits. A few, such as nineteen-year-old LCpl. Jack M. McKenna, squeezed through a porthole. He became stuck in the little opening, but several of his buddies pulled him through. When he looked back at the burning wreckage, McKenna felt grateful to be alive.

The Marines of 3/9 were divided into working parties to tear down the base. It was hard, physically demanding work. The troops toiled eight to ten hours a day in the blazing sun as they destroyed bunkers, emptied sandbags, knocked down standing structures, tore up runway matting, and burned what could not be carried off. Captain Gary E. Todd, the CO of India 3/9, later said the effort required the "working parties to move around exposed and 'non-tactical' in what was still very much a tactical situation."

Lance Corporal McKenna, a fourteen-month veteran of Kilo who had missed the Hill Fights a year earlier because he had been severely bitten by a rat on his first night there, could not have agreed more. "Every day we ripped open sandbags with machetes and poured the dirt into the bunkers or trenches," he recalled. "We were all very concerned because we became more exposed as the trenches filled up. Sniper rounds and mortar shells came in as our cover disappeared. All we could do then was run to the nearest remaining bunker, which was often a good distance away."

Some of the structures were too big to be torn down with entrenching tools. McKenna remembered, "We had this huge command bunker to destroy. We packed it with six hundred pounds of TNT. It blew up in a huge explosion. There was nothing left of the bunker. Nothing."

The NVA rarely missed a chance to pound the base and the work parties with artillery shells. On some days as many as 150 enemy rounds fell on the base; most caused casualties. One round on 29 June wounded twelve Marines, six seriously enough to be evacuated.

Lethal danger also came from all the unexploded ordnance that littered the base and lay hidden in the bunkers. Nineteen-year-old Indiana Marine Pfc. John Bosley remembered what happened to another Mike 3/9 work party on 4 July: "One of the men swung his entrenching tool down to tear open a sandbag and hit a dud round buried in the wall. The explosion blew him up and wounded four others working with him. I was in the next bunker and the blast threw me ten feet."

Other dangers presented themselves to the Marines, too. Private First Class Bosley remembered the hordes of rats. "We used our e-tools to rip apart the sandbags and our bayonets to kill the rats," he said. "The rats were everywhere. Every bunker we went into seemed to be filled with them. And they were big, too. About half the size of a house cat. Some of the guys started keeping score of how many they'd kill. I can still see one guy marching around, two rats impaled on his bayonet, laughing hysterically."

Although the Marine command tried to keep its intentions for Khe Sanh quiet, an overeager reporter broke the news. On 27 June 1968, John S. Carroll's scoop on the closure ran in the *Baltimore Sun*. Besides costing Carroll his MACV press credentials, the story also allowed the North Vietnamese to claim a substantial victory. To lend credence to their claim, the local NVA commander struck several of 3/4's rifle companies.

A particularly strong attack hit India 3/4 at its position three kilometers southeast of the base before dawn on 1 July. After a four-hour barrage of mortars and 130mm artillery, a full company of NVA charged the Marines. India held its position and easily drove them off. Later that morning, the Marines spotted the enemy swarming nearby and attacked them with the help of helicopter gunships and jets. The fight continued into the late afternoon before the enemy again fled, leaving two hundred of their comrades behind. Two Marines died in the fight.

Enemy ground activity persisted over the next several days. Incoming artillery and mortar shells hit the hill positions, and each night small groups of sappers probed Marine perimeters. Although none of these reached the intensity of the 1 July attack, the Marines on the hills outside the combat base suffered casualties. And despite the best efforts of the Marines, enemy artillery continued to pummel the base, even on its last day.

Captain Michael Joseph, the air liaison officer for 2/1, spent most of 5 July on his belly at the bottom of a shallow trench along the remnants of Khe Sanh's airstrip. During breaks in the enemy artillery barrages, he would direct in helicopters to pick up some of the remaining materiel. This was not only dangerous work but tricky, because Joseph never knew when the enemy would unleash its cannon anew.

"One pilot radioed to ask if it was all clear," Joseph remembered. "Since no shells had hit for several minutes I thought it would be safe. I responded, 'Looks clear to me.' The guy came in and no sooner did he touch down than a shell went off nearby. He pulled pitch and flew off, all the time demanding to know, 'Who the hell told me it was clear down there?' I never responded."

Joseph had been at Khe Sanh for three weeks, his assignment a result of his desire to take a more active role in the war and some ill-chosen words. A highly skilled radar intercept officer, the twenty-six-year-old Stanford graduate had felt useless during his first five months in-country as he rode around in the backseat of an F-4 and called out altimeter and altitude readings to the pilot. He wanted to do more to help win the war. One night in early June, while he imbibed in the air-conditioned comfort of the Da Nang officers' club, he loudly announced, "I'd rather be a FAC than a backseater in an F-4." Someone heard him.

"Two days later I was jumping off a helicopter at Khe Sanh, carrying my sea bag in one hand and my rifle in the other as some guy's yelling, 'Get out! Get out! Incoming!' I ran as fast as I could and rolled into a trench as shells started exploding all around me. I kept asking myself what the hell I'd gotten into."

By the evening of 5 July 1968, Khe Sanh had been reduced to a flat plain. Nothing of value to the enemy remained. Along the once busy runway, the remaining 2/1 headquarters people, including Captain Joseph, waited in trenches, anxious for the order to go. They would walk out because it was too dangerous for helicopters to come in and get them. Not far away, the last trucks at the base maneuvered to form a final convoy. They took too long and gave an NVA forward observer in the hills too good a target to pass up.

Artillery shells dropped out of the evening sky and walked back and forth across the desolate base. Captain Joseph and the other headquarters personnel hunkered down as far as their holes allowed. Shells hit several of the trucks and sent cargo flying everywhere. The situation appeared to be out of hand until someone yelled for the trucks to just roll, the hell with organization. When the last truck disappeared down the road, the shelling stopped.

The remaining 2/1 Marines spent a nervous two hours as they waited for the darkness to deepen. Finally, they started out. They snuck down the runway toward a break in the wire at the eastern end of the base. As the point man reached the barrier, the black night exploded into day.

"A flare ship, off course and thoroughly confused, had dropped his ordnance and illuminated all of Khe Sanh," Joseph remembered. "We were standing there as exposed as could be."

Fortunately, the enemy did not take advantage of this golden opportunity. When the flares burned out, the column started to move again. It faced a brutal fifteen-kilometer hump over rocky terrain in pitch darkness to the pickup zone. The fifty-plus-pound packs carried by most of the Marines made the march even more difficult. Whenever the order to "take five" came down the line, most of the men collapsed where they stood, desperate for a few minutes of sleep. "The five-minute breaks stretched into twenty or thirty only because it took so long to wake everyone up. And we had to make sure we didn't leave anyone behind," Joseph said.

More than four hours after it started, the column reached the pickup zone. Utterly exhausted, the Marines managed several hours' sleep before the choppers arrived to carry them away.

In a letter home, Captain Joseph paid tribute to all Khe Sanh veterans when he told his wife, "I think a lot of these troops. They are loaded with courage and pride. If anyone asks you where America's best are, you tell them right here."

At midnight on 6 July 1968, Operation Charlie ended. The Marine Corps was finally free of Khe Sanh.

Epilogue

The weary survivors of BLT 2/3 returned to their ships after the Hill Fights burdened with the sorrow of so many lost buddies and anger at being sent into combat with a defective weapon. Fueling this bitterness was their superiors' insistence that any problems with the M16 were solely the fault of the individual. You don't keep it clean enough, the NCOs insisted. The troops knew better. (Marines of the rifle companies assigned to 3/3 for the Hill Fights also experienced problems with the M16. However, because those four companies were widely dispersed after they left Khe Sanh, and the 3/3 Marines did not have the opportunity to discuss the failures with one another, they had to believe that the problem was theirs alone.) Many of them had been worried about the rifle's tendency to jam ever since they had fired their first magazine on Okinawa. Private First Class William Ryan, Foxtrot 2/3, a machinist in civilian life, was so concerned that, on the trip back to South Vietnam, he had the ship's machine shop fashion lengths of steel rod for him. Ryan then passed these out to his squad mates. They went into combat with these rods taped to their rifle's stock, readily available if the rifle jammed.

Corporal Jerry Pett, Hotel 2/3, realized there was a serious problem with the weapon when orders came down that no one was to discuss the M16 situation with anyone. Period.

Lance Corporal Thomas Rice, Echo 2/3, remembered that the NCOs had tried to prove their point by ordering all the Marines to bring their M16s to the ship's fantail. Fresh magazines were passed out. The men were ordered to fire their weapons. If anyone experienced a jam, he was to hold his rifle upright, the butt on his shoulder.

Almost as soon as the firing began, rifles started going up. That brought down the fury of incensed NCOs on the hapless troops. Shouting and screaming worse than any boot camp drill instructor, the NCOs blatantly accused the Marines of failing to properly maintain their rifles. Under the watchful gaze of battalion and company-level officers, the NCOs berated the troops. But it did not work. The effort, in fact, backfired. Not only did the exercise confirm there was a problem with the rifle, the incident lowered the troops' confidence in their NCOs and officers.

"I lost whatever faith I had in my leaders at that point," Private First Class Ryan said. He recalled that a number of men actually talked about refusing to return to combat with the weapon. But they also knew that the system would deal harshly with them for their mutiny. They had no real choice. "You cannot imagine the sense of horror and helplessness I felt at having to go back to war with a weapon I had no confidence in," Ryan said.

Others wondered why the Marine Corps took the extraordinary step of grounding the entire fleet of CH-46s until an alleged defect was confirmed and corrected but scoffed at the riflemen's claims that their new weapon had an inherent defect. A number of the young Marines, and a few of the junior officers, tried to carry their concerns to higher levels through the chain of command but were rebuked. Fortunately, some of the Marines decided to go outside the system. They wrote letters.

On 22 May 1967, New Jersey congressman James J. Howard read to the assembled House of Representatives excerpts from a letter a combat Marine had written home.

Referring to the Hill Fights, the unidentified Marine told his parents: "We left [Okinawa] with close to 1,400 men in our battalion and came back with half. We left with 250 men in our company and came back with 107. We left with 72 men in our platoon and came back with 19.

"Believe it or not, you know what killed most of us? Our own rifle. Before we left Okinawa [we] were all issued this new rifle, the M16. Practically every one of our dead was found with his rifle torn down next to him where he'd been trying to fix it."

The letter created a furor. Missouri representative Richard Ichord, chairman of a House Armed Services subcommittee, coincidentally set up just days earlier to investigate Army procurement irregularities involving the M16, announced that he and several other congressmen would travel to South Vietnam to investigate the problem. To the surprise of many, Ichord admitted at the outset that he had already accepted the military's explanation that there was nothing wrong with the weapon that a little proper care and training would not cure.

On 26 May, the same day Ichord departed on his fact-finding mission, the commandant of the Marine Corps, Gen. Wallace M. Greene, Jr., held a news conference. He announced that although the new weapon sometimes did malfunction, charges that it had jammed in combat with disastrous results were isolated and misleading.

"The M16 rifle has proved to be a reliable, hard-hitting lightweight weapon for our troops," the top Marine flatly stated.

Greene laid the blame for any malfunctions squarely on the back of the individual Marine. The reasons, he said, included an occasional faulty round, a broken part, dirt, or excessive carbon in the firing mechanism. "At times," he also observed, "it [the malfunction] could be the result of battle stress on the individual firing the weapon."

General Lewis W. Walt entered the fray with his own press conference on 7 June. Having just returned from his two years as the commander of all the Marines in the combat zone, Walt lent considerable weight to opinions about the weapon. "I think the M16 is the finest weapon the troops have ever had," Walt announced unequivocally.

He said he had personally spoken to the commander whose unit took and held Hill 881S in one of the bloodiest battles of the war. "If we had not had the M16 in my company, we could not have held that hill," General Walt quoted the officer as saying.

"How many malfunctions did you have?"

"'None,'" he answered, according to Walt.

(Although this officer was never identified, Walt had to be referring to Captain Bennett, Mike 3/3, which makes Walt's claim suspect. Bennett's company did not take and hold Hill 881S. It was thrown off and never went back. If Bennett did claim that none of his troops experienced a malfunction, that might have been because he never asked or because he did not know, because he had been at the foot of the hill away from the actual fighting all day, then left the company soon afterward. Captain Jerry Giles could not have been the officer, because his Kilo 3/9 did not take and hold Hill 881S either. By the time Kilo 3/9 went up the hill on 2 May 1967, the NVA had abandoned it.)

General Walt went on to state that "a recent survey showed that of more than thirteen million rounds fired from 12,676 rifles, there were only 1,243 malfunctions. That is remarkable."

How Walt arrived at these numbers remains unanswered. And although he might have felt that a 10 percent failure rate was "remarkable," there was no one to speak for any of those who died as the result of an M16 failure.

The controversial M16 evolved from the Army's desire to arm soldiers with a weapon that would register more hits on the enemy. A post–World War II study had revealed that although aimed fire was significant in the defense, the opposite was true in the assault. The Army determined it needed a weapon that released a salvo of small-caliber projectiles with a light recoil, which allowed more control for a tighter dispersion pattern.

While various agencies searched for such a weapon, the United States agreed with its NATO allies to adopt a standardized 7.62mm cartridge for its basic infantry weapon. After it evaluated a number of test weapons using that round, the Army approved the Springfield (Massachusetts) Armory's–designed M14 on 1 May 1957, but the weapon was really only a stopgap measure until something better came along.

At the same time, the Continental Army Command (CONARC) decided to sponsor the development of a .22-caliber (5.56mm) military rifle. Officers of CONARC had been impressed with the killing power of the smaller cartridge (as early as 1928, tests had indicated that the lighter bullet tended to tumble upon striking a human, doing more damage than a heavier, more stable round). Also, an infantryman could carry more of the lighter rounds. Finally, the reduced recoil of the .22 round gave the rifleman more control over the weapon during automatic firing. In a break with the traditional small-arms development process, CONARC sought commercial assistance for the design of a .22-caliber rifle. This change resulted from the dissatisfaction that many senior Army officers had with the M14.

During CONARC's search for a new NATO weapon, the ArmaLite Division of Fairchild Engine and Airplane Corporation had submitted a weapon designated the AR-10. Though the M14 won, the AR-10 had left a favorable impression on the Army. As a result, in 1958 CONARC asked ArmaLite to develop a .22-caliber rifle.

Eugene M. Stoner, who had helped design the AR-10, did most of the design work on the new weapon, dubbed the AR-15. Stoner delivered ten prototypes to the Aberdeen Proving Ground in Maryland on 31 March 1958. The weapon did not fare well in the subsequent tests. For one, the barrel had a tendency to rupture if there was any water in it. Regardless, the test board recommended the purchase of 750 rifles for extended trials. Army Chief of Staff Gen. Maxwell Taylor said no. He was concerned that the NATO allies would react negatively to this change in cartridge size.

Thoroughly discouraged by this rejection, Fairchild sold its design and marketing rights to Colt's Patent Firearms Manufacturing Company in December 1959. Six months later Colt asked the Army to reevaluate the rifle. Dr. Fred H. Carten, chief of the Army's small-arms research and development office and the spiritual father of the M14, refused. Colt was incensed. As far as they were concerned, the Army's refusal was vested in their inherent "Not Invented Here" philosophy. Colt elected to seek approval for the weapon outside normal procurement channels. They invited Air Force vice chief of staff Gen. Curtis LeMay to a personal demonstration. LeMay came away so impressed that he authorized the purchase of 8,500 AR-15s to rearm air base sentries.

As a result of this purchase, Colt convinced the Department of Defense's Advanced Research Projects Agency to send some AR-15s to be field-tested in that little war in far-off South Vietnam. One thousand of the new rifles went over in the summer of 1962. The results were impressive, and all the comments made were favorable. The Department of Defense ordered another round of tests.

The Army still resisted, though. After a wide variety of tests personally ordered by defense secretary Robert S. McNamara, the Army concluded that "only the M14 is acceptable for general use in the U.S. Army." Army secretary Cyrus Vance rightly suspected that the AR-15 had not fared well due to the Army ordnance department's reluctance to accept a weapon designed by a civilian firm. He ordered an investigation. The investigating officers concluded that many of the tests had been constructed to reflect adversely on the AR-15.

Secretary McNamara reviewed all the data and terminated procurement of the M14 as of the end of fiscal year 1963. He authorized the purchase of 85,000 AR-15s (now designated the M16) for the Army and 19,000 for the Air Force. But these were to be one-time-only purchases to fill the gap until Army designers at the Springfield Armory completed their work on the special purpose individual weapon (SPIW), a new rifle that would fire both conventional ammo and launch grenades.

By late 1964 it was apparent the SPIW would not be ready in any reasonable time frame. The Defense Department then decided to use a combination of the M14 and M16. Troops deployed in support of NATO commitments would be armed with the M14. Those sent to Southeast Asia would be armed with the M16 as it became available. But availability became a serious problem as American involvement in South Vietnam accelerated at an unbelievable rate.

Even though the Army signed two additional contracts to manufacture the M16, one to Harrington & Richardson and the other to the Hydramatic Division of General Motors, supply could not keep up with demand. Many troops trained with the M14, then were issued the unfamiliar M16 when they arrived in the war zone. Only a few units— the 1st Cavalry Division, the 173d Airborne Brigade, and the 199th Light Infantry Brigade—deployed to South Vietnam with the M16. All other combat units, including the Marines, arrived in-country with the M14. When the new rifle became available, it was swapped for the M14. And that is when the troubles began.

Representative Ichord and his team spent nearly two weeks in South Vietnam investigating problems with the M16. They spoke to scores of individual riflemen. What they heard horrified the congressmen. Story after story of failed rifles and dead Americans were told to the officials. But not everyone believed the troops. Marine brigadier general Louis B. Metzger, the 3d Marine Division's assistant commander, flat out accused the troops of lying. He described taking the congressmen around the DMZ area to talk to some riflemen: "If it weren't so serious it would have been laughable. They insisted on questioning individual Marines with no officers or NCOs present, I suppose to ensure they got the truth, without command influence. The result was they were fed the most awful line of 'hog wash' imaginable. Tall tales of heroic action, patrols wiped out, etc. all due to the M16, but which according to the sergeant major of one unit involved, had never taken place. The young Marines had a field day."

Despite such open skepticism, Representative Ichord's team thoroughly researched the M16 and reached a shocking conclusion. On 26 August 1967, the Missourian reversed himself. "I believe . . . that one of the major causes of excessive malfunctioning of the M16 rifle in Vietnam can be directly traced to the type of powder used in the ammunition."

In the course of his investigation, Ichord learned that Eugene Stoner had designed the AR-15 to use improved military rifle (IMR) powder because it was cleaner burning than the ball-type propellant preferred by the Army. When Stoner discovered that the Army had arbitrarily switched to the ball-type powder, he was dumbfounded. He strongly advised against the change. But because the ball-type powder was cheaper and was produced by longtime military contractor Olin Matheson, the Army made the change. Ichord's final report said this decision by the Army "borders on criminal negligence."

The propellant change had two negative results. First, the new powder changed the cyclic rate from 850 rounds per minute to between 850 and 1,000. To slow the rate, the Army increased the weight of the recoiling parts. Second, because the ball-type powder burned less efficiently than the IMR powder, it left a residue in the chamber and on other moving parts. In the chamber this residue caused pitting. These pits, in turn, held the expended cartridge tight in the chamber. When the extractor mechanism attempted to remove the spent cartridge, it sheared off or jumped the cartridge's rim, leaving the cartridge in the chamber. When a new round was pulled from the magazine and fed into the chamber, it jammed behind the spent cartridge.

Although some experts felt that installation of a chromed chamber would eliminate the pitting problem, others said no. The reworked chamber did nothing to protect other moving parts from the residue, according to the opponents.

Eventually, Pentagon armament experts worked in concert with Colt's engineers to arrive at a solution. In addition to a chromed chamber, existing M16s would be retrofitted with a newly designed buffer mechanism to slow the rate of fire. New weapons, of course, would have both.

Beginning in late 1967, the modifications were made in South Vietnam. In III MAF, the Force Logistic Command set up assembly lines to install the new parts. It was a massive undertaking that extended into the new year. When it was over, and coupled with the arrival of factory-modified weapons, America's military at last had an infantry weapon comparable to the venerable AK-47. But that was no solace to those who had died in Khe Sanh's hills as a result of a failed weapon.

Appendix

Artist Austin Deuel retained vivid memories and intense visions of the combat he had witnessed during his six months in South Vietnam long after his release from active duty in the summer of 1967. From these mental images he created dozens of paintings that depicted the combat Marine at war. One of the few official artists to serve in the combat zone, Deuel developed a well-deserved reputation for accuracy and authenticity in his work. These qualities and his credentials caused a fellow Vietnam veteran to call Deuel's Scottsdale, Arizona, studio in 1981.

"Dick Stranberg, who had commanded a navy river boat in the delta, called me," Deuel said. "He was looking for professional artists who were also Vietnam veterans to put together a show for Veterans Day that year in Minneapolis–St. Paul. I don't know how he found me but he asked if I'd be interested in the event and I said yes."

Deuel wanted to create a special piece for this unique show, so he searched his memory for an image that realistically depicted both the brutality of the war and the frustration experienced by those who fought it. He mentally returned to the foot of Hill 881S. Once again he saw the string of wounded Marines as they staggered and stumbled downhill. Their haunted faces revealed the anguish they felt for lost comrades and the bitterness of their defeat. As Deuel played the scene over in his mind, the image he sought came together.

Deuel titled his piece *For What? Hill 881 South*. The small sculpture captured a Marine radio operator hopelessly scanning the sky for a helicopter as he kneels protectively over a dying comrade. The creation of the sculpture caused Deuel considerable stress. "At one point I called

Dick and said I was having great emotional difficulty with the project; in fact, it was the first time I'd cried about the war," he recalled.

With Stranberg's support and encouragement, Deuel overcame his emotions and finished the sculpture.

The art show, "The Vietnam Experience," proved to be a great success. After strong reviews in the Twin Cities, the exhibit moved to New York. Once again the show was well received. Favorable publicity, which included a plug on Walter Cronkite's network news program, resulted in a flood of visitors. As a result, a photo of Deuel's sculpture appeared in a veterans' magazine.

In Kalispell, Montana, a police detective happened to pick up that magazine one day. Former Marine radio operator Donald Hossack's pulse quickened when he spotted the photograph of Deuel's sculpture. The statue depicted his futile attempts to save Pfc. James A. Randall on Hill 881S. He had to talk to the artist. Hossack soon had Deuel on the telephone. He explained who he was and what he had experienced atop Hill 881S that terrible day. "The fact that Deuel, whom I'd never met, had so vividly captured the scene with Randall amazed me," Hossack said. The coincidence astonished Deuel as well. The two spoke by phone several times over the next few years and closed each conversation with a vow to someday meet in person. Events beyond their control arranged that meeting.

In 1985, San Antonio, Texas, businessman John D. Baines, a two-tour veteran of the war, chaired the local committee created to erect a Vietnam War memorial. Baines's mission was to find a simple sculpture that dramatized the battlefield courage displayed by those who fought their nation's most controversial war. When he saw a photograph of Deuel's piece, he knew immediately that his search had ended. Baines contacted Deuel and commissioned the statue.

Austin Deuel went to work on the twice-life-sized statue in January 1986. He toiled daily for months in a hangar at the Scottsdale airport. In all, he welded more than five thousand feet of cold rolled steel and applied more than twenty thousand pounds of plaster to form the 170 pieces of bronze that made up the work.

The dedication ceremony took place on 9 November 1986 at San Antonio's Vietnam Veteran's Memorial Plaza, near that other Texas shrine to personal valor, the Alamo. Thousands of local citizens and veterans from across the country attended the ceremony. Donald Hossack, former Mike 3/3 radioman, stood among the honored guests.

After the requisite speeches, a squad of combat-laden, active-duty Marines removed the sculpture's cover. Then a flight of Huey helicopters passed overhead, as if in response to radioman Hossack's plea. The emotions proved too much for many observers, and their tears flowed openly.

The day after the ceremony, former artillery FO David Rogers read reports of the event in the Dallas newspaper. The mention of Hill 881S flooded his mind with long-suppressed memories of the carnage he had witnessed that day. Then he suddenly remembered the poem he had written that terrible evening nearly twenty years before. Though he had never shared it with anyone, he knew the time had come for others to read it.

Rogers wrote to Baines and included a copy of his poem. "He was moved," Rogers said, "and quickly wrote back to ask if I would give the committee permission to inscribe it on the base of the memorial."

On 30 April 1987, accompanied by several surviving members of Mike 3/3, Rogers watched solemnly as the bronze plaque bearing his words was dedicated.

Death at My Door

Day is over as danger hastens
Young Marines at their battle stations
Instruments of war outline the sky
Means of death are standing by.

Can it be true on this high hill
Forces will clash only to kill?
Silence fills the near moonless night
Restless thoughts of a bloody fight.

Endless memories for those awake
Meaningful discussion experience would make
Though silent world in which we live
Permits only God's comfort to give.

Somewhere through the darkness creeping
A date with death is in the keeping

> Alone I sit and question why
> Life itself, to be born merely to die?

Until then Rogers had never understood what had compelled him to jot down those lines. Now he knew.

In late January 1997, an air-conditioned, modern tour bus turned off the paved two-lane Route 9 and drove up the Khe Sanh plateau. Since the Communist government opened the country to outsiders a decade earlier, Vietnam has become a mecca for U.S. veterans of the war. Some come to grieve lost comrades, some to recapture their lost youth, others to revisit old battlefields under less strenuous conditions, still others to seek closure for the tragic events that defined their postwar lives. A few come for all those reasons and more. Whatever the reason, among the more popular tourist spots is the former Marine combat base at Khe Sanh.

On top of the plateau, the passengers filed from the bus and moved in silence across the hallowed ground. Little evidence of the once powerful base remained; the Marines of 3/9 had done a thorough job. Most of the old base was covered with coffee plants in a government-sponsored program to revive the tradition of the French planters from decades earlier. A wide, cleared swath of red dirt cut diagonally across the plateau, but it did not mark the original runway; that lay hidden by the coffee plants. This one had been started by the Communists but was never finished.

The veterans walked through the dusty red dirt and recounted to one another what they knew of the great battles that had raged there. Though low clouds covered the surrounding hills, the land's vivid green color and complete lack of battle scars impressed the men. One said, "Thirty years of tropical jungle growth can cover a lot of damage."

Near the western end of the new runway stands a memorial that commemorates the last days of the Khe Sanh Combat Base. The memorial was erected by the Vietnamese government. The inscription tells how the valiant North Vietnamese soldiers overran the base and killed and captured hundreds of American Marines in their victory. Though all of the American veterans knew the truth about the closing of the Khe Sanh Combat Base, one of them knew it more personally than the others.

Former Marine captain Michael Joseph chose that spot to relate to the others his adventures during the base's final hours. He read from the letter he had written nearly thirty years earlier, recounting the events that occurred that hot July night in 1968. Joseph's voice cracked several times as he read his account of the brave Marines, but when he tried to read the last paragraph, he could not continue. Another veteran stepped forward and read it for him:

"I think a lot of these troops. They are loaded with courage and pride. If anyone asks you where America's best are, you tell them right here."

JOHN P. ADINOLFI (E/2/3) died on Christmas Eve 2000.

STEPHEN W. AMODT (F/2/3) was wounded twice during his tour but was medevacked with a badly twisted ankle in April 1968. Discharged in September 1969, he earned a college degree hoping to become a lawyer. However, the negative attitude of his professors and fellow college students toward Vietnam War veterans soured him, and he reenlisted in January 1974. He retired as a captain in 1991. He battled alcoholism for years but finally achieved victory. He served as an alcohol abuse counselor in the Marines and later worked with the homeless and veterans after his discharge but quit due to burnout. Today he is a supervisor in a manufacturing plant and lives in Oceanside, California, with his wife. They have three children and seven grandchildren.

JAMES ANDERSON (F/2/3) was posthumously awarded the Medal of Honor for his self-sacrifice.

JOSEPH W. ASCOLILLO (3d Engineer Battalion attached to 1/3) left South Vietnam in May 1967 after being wounded for the third time. He voluntarily returned for a six-month tour in September 1967 and was discharged in August 1968. He works as a security consultant and lives in Malden, Massachusetts, with his wife and their twins.

RAYMOND H. BENNETT (M/3/3) is deceased.

FRANCIS A. BENOIT (E/2/9) was posthumously awarded a Navy Cross for his valor.

DONALD G. BIGLER (K/3/3) left South Vietnam in July 1967, still mourning the loss of his friend Tom Miller. He was discharged a sergeant in January 1969. He earned his college degree at Eastern New Mexico University, then became an over-the-road truck driver. He retired in 1994 after he injured his back. He lives in New Braunfels, Texas, with his wife. They have three sons and two grandchildren. In late 1998, through the Internet, Bigler learned that Tom Miller had survived the war and was living in Maryland. They have been in frequent contact since then.

JOHN BOSLEY (M/3/9) was wounded twice during his tour. Discharged in July 1969, he joined the Indianapolis, Indiana, police department. Six years later he became a U.S. Customs special agent. Retired after twenty-one years of service, he now works for the Military Order of the Purple Heart in Indianapolis. He and his wife make their home in Carmel, Indiana.

RICHARD R. BRAMMER (B/1/12 attached to 2/3) spent a month on the hospital ship *Repose,* then reinjured his leg the day he was released. After more time on the *Repose* he rejoined 2/3 in South Vietnam, but because he then had less than three weeks remaining on his tour, he was assigned to the 3d Marines headquarters. He received a promotion to captain before he rotated. He spent his remaining six months at Camp Lejeune, where he was presented a Bronze Star for his heroism on 28 February–1 March. He was discharged in December 1967, later earned his master's degree, and has worked in sales and marketing his entire career. Married with two children and one grandchild, he lives with his wife in Huntington, West Virginia.

LEON R. "LEE" BURNS (B/1/9) received a Bronze Star for his actions at Khe Sanh and earned a Navy Cross for his valor when two-thirds of Bravo Company was wiped out on 2 July 1967 near Con Thien during Operation Buffalo. He completed his tour and remained in the Marine Corps until his retirement in February 1976. He then worked in industrial security until he retired again in 2000. Widowed since 1995, he lives in La Puente, California.

STANLEY C. BUTTERWORTH (K/3/9) earned a Bronze Star and his second Purple Heart on Hill 881S. He was wounded a third time on 20 May 1967 and was medically evacuated. Discharged in June 1967, he joined the Warwick, Rhode Island, police department. He retired after twenty years, then joined the attorney general's office as an investigator. He is married, has two children and two grandchildren, and resides with his wife in Barrington, Rhode Island.

LANCE M. CAMPBELL (F/2/3) was wounded during Operation Buffalo on 7 July 1967 but returned to duty and completed his tour. He is a customer service representative in the printing paper business and lives with his wife in Rancho Cucamonga, California.

JAMES R. CANNON (E/2/3) received a Silver Star for his valor on 3 May 1967. He retired from the Marine Corps as a major. He later moved to New Mexico and entered the real estate business. Diagnosed with post-traumatic stress disorder (PTSD), he is now 100 percent disabled. He resides with his wife in Las Lunas, New Mexico.

CLIFTON H. CANTER (E/2/3) was medically retired as a captain in August 1969. He returned to his Florida home, earned a master's degree, became a certified public accountant, then organized and operated two lead fabrication companies. He was married with four daughters when he was killed in the crash of his ultralight aircraft on 7 July 2001.

PATRICK G. CARROLL (F/2/3) spent fourteen months in the hospital recovering from his wounds. He then entered flight training, becoming the first disabled combat veteran to do so. He graduated near the top of his class, thus earning a coveted assignment as a jet fighter pilot. He flew A-4s for VMF-214 (the Black Sheep Squadron) until he resigned his commission in December 1973. Married with two sons, he resides in Lynwood, Washington, where he owns and operates a real estate development and multi-family unit construction company.

JAMES D. CARTER, JR. (B/1/9) was killed in action on 7 June 1967. He is survived by his wife and son, Scott, whom he never saw.

JAMES L. CHASE (E/2/9) spent more than a month in the hospital recovering from his wounds. He was discharged in September 1968 and went to work for the postal service. In 1997 he suffered a breakdown and was diagnosed with PTSD. He now receives 100 percent disability. He resides with his wife in Oceanside, California.

CHARLES P. CHRITTON (F/2/3) remained with Foxtrot and served as its executive officer and commander. He took command of Echo 2/3 in December 1967. He was due to rotate home on 30 January 1968, but the Tet Offensive delayed his departure for several hectic weeks. He was discharged a captain in May 1969 with a Bronze Star and two Purple Hearts. After two years of corporate management, he entered Notre Dame Law School and graduated in 1974. He lives in Lakeland, Florida. He is married and has three children and one grandchild.

JOSEPH CIALONE (M/3/3) was wounded in action in July 1967 but soon returned to the company. He commanded M/3/3 from November 1967 until he rotated in February 1968. He was awarded a Bronze Star and a Purple Heart. Discharged a captain in 1970, he graduated from the University of Texas Law School in 1972. A senior partner in the firm of Baker Botts, he is married and has two sons; he lives in Houston, Texas.

EDWARD F. CRAWFORD (H/2/3) spent a month in the hospital before he returned to Hotel. Wounded again on 30 June, he received his fifth Purple Heart and returned to the States. He then reverted to reserve status and eventually retired as a Marine gunner in 1982. He also returned to the police department; he retired from there in 1985. He has since been employed as a Pennsylvania state constable. A widower, he has three children, nine grandchildren, and one great-grandchild. More than thirty-five members of his family have served in the Marine Corps. His two sons retired from the Marine Corps and he currently has three grandsons on active duty with the Marines. His nephew, J. M. Reid, who motivated Crawford to return to active duty in 1966, was killed in action on 30 May 1967 and posthumously awarded a Navy Cross for his gallantry in action that day.

BILLY D. CREWS (M/3/3) remained with the company until July 1967, when he became the S-2 officer for the battalion. He filled that slot until he left South Vietnam in January 1968. He continued his career in the Marine Corps, reverting to enlisted status in 1971. He retired as a sergeant major in 1985. He ran a hazardous waste company in Atlanta, Georgia, for five years before he retired again. Married with two stepchildren and three grandchildren, he resides in Cullowhee, North Carolina.

HAROLD A. CROFT (K/3/3) earned a Bronze Star for his action on 25 April 1967. He was medically evacuated from South Vietnam in December 1967 due to a severe case of malaria and arrived home in time to celebrate Christmas. He then returned to Villanova University, joined the Vietnam Veterans Against the War, earned his undergraduate degree in December 1969, then earned his master's in English from Salem State College. Married with four children, he lives in Reading, Massachusetts. He taught English and coached the track team at Reading Memorial High School until his retirement in 2002. His track team was undefeated since 1972. As a result, he was profiled in *Sports Illustrated* in 1995. In 1996 he was selected as the National Track Coach of the Year, and that same year was named the Athletic Coach of the Year by Disney-McDonalds at their annual teacher awards ceremony.

PHILIP G. CURTIS (M/3/3) spent several weeks aboard the hospital ship *Repose* before he rejoined M/3/3. Wounded again in June 1967, he completed his tour in January 1968 and was discharged one year later. He drifted from job to job for a number of years before he sought counseling. Diagnosed with PTSD, he received a disability rating and now works for the postal service. He is married and has two daughters and five grandchildren. He lives in Madisonville, Kentucky.

DANA C. DARNELL (B/1/9) was posthumously awarded a Navy Cross for his valor.

EARL R. DELONG (2/3) is deceased.

AUSTIN DEUEL (III MAF) finished his active duty tour as a combat artist in July 1967. He is a successful commercial artist in Scottsdale, Arizona.

ORD ELLIOTT (H/2/3) was medically evacuated from South Vietnam in August 1967. After a stay at Bethesda Naval Hospital, he completed his tour of duty at Headquarters, U.S. Marine Corps, and took his discharge in June 1969. He attended graduate school and earned his Ph.D. in management. Divorced with one daughter, he runs his own management consulting firm in Woodside, California.

JAMES EPPS (C/1/26) died in January 2000.

GORDON J. FENLON (K/3/9) spent several weeks in the hospital before he returned to Kilo. He was seriously wounded again on 20 May 1967. Hospitalized in the States, he was discharged in May 1968. When he returned home, he purchased a milk collection business but had to give it up in 1976 after he was badly injured in a collision with a seventeen-year-old drunk driver. Married with two children, he lived in Sturgeon Bay, Wisconsin, until his death in June 2001.

ROBERT E. FRENCH (2/3) retired from the Marine Corps as a master sergeant in 1985. He then went to college. Semi-retired, he lives in Madison, Kansas, and is a fine antiques and militaria dealer.

CURTIS L. FRISBIE, JR. (K/3/3) ended up in Brooke Army Hospital in San Antonio, Texas, so he could be near his expectant wife; she gave birth to their second son in a room just down the hall from his. After numerous operations he regained use of his arm. Discharged in 1969 with a Bronze Star for Hill 861, he earned his law degree. He lives in Dallas, Texas, with his wife and is a partner in a major law firm.

ARTHUR GENNARO (K/3/9) rotated from South Vietnam in August 1967, one of only a handful of Kilo members not to be wounded during their tours. After his discharge in April 1969, he joined the Passaic, New Jersey, police department and retired in 2001 as a captain. He is married with four daughters; he and his wife moved to Las Vegas, Nevada, upon his retirement.

MICHAEL G. GIBBS (K/3/3) was posthumously awarded a Silver Star for his gallantry in action.

JERRALD E. GILES (K/3/9) saw additional combat action with Kilo and earned a Bronze Star for a sixteen-hour fight at Hill 70 near Con Thien on 20 May 1967 and a Silver Star during Operation Buffalo on 4 July 1967. He rotated from South Vietnam a short time later. He returned for another tour in 1970–71. He retired from the Marine Corps in 1979 as a lieutenant colonel. He resides in Grass Valley, California, and is a self-employed motivational speaker.

THOMAS GIVVIN (H/2/3) remained with Hotel Company until October 1967. He then extended his tour for six months to serve as an aerial observer flying out of Da Nang. He was shot down three times and earned an Air Medal. He left South Vietnam after nineteen months in September 1968. He was discharged a captain in May 1969 and remained in the reserves for five years. After he earned his MBA, he purchased a retail garden center in Marina Del Ray, California, which he and his wife continue to operate.

BRUCE E. GRIESMER (H/2/3) returned to South Vietnam after he spent three months in the hospital, joined 2/9, and remained with them until he completed his tour in May 1968. He received the Bronze Star with a "V" for valor for his actions on 30 April as well as a Purple Heart. He retired from the Marine Corps in 1986 as a major. He resides in Jacksonville, North Carolina, with his wife and three children; he works in real estate and automobile sales.

WILLIAM GRIGGS (M/3/3) retired as a major and today is a mechanical engineer for the postal service. The father of four and grandfather of three, he resides with his wife in Fredericksburg, Virginia.

DAVID S. HACKETT (H/2/3) was posthumously awarded a Silver Star. Each year Princeton University awards an athletic trophy in his name.

ROBERT D. HANDY (CIA with H/2/3) was killed on 26 August 1969 near the Cambodian border northwest of Saigon.

DAVID J. HENDRY (B/1/9) was badly wounded during Operation Buffalo in July 1967 and was medically evacuated to the States. Married three times, he has two children. He retired from the postal service and lives in Medford, Oregon.

PETER M. HESSER (G/2/3) departed South Vietnam in February 1968 with three Purple Hearts, a Silver Star, and a Navy Commendation Medal. He retired from the Marine Corps as a lieutenant colonel in 1988. He and his wife, a Navy admiral, live in Annandale, Virginia, where he is a CPA with Johns Hopkins Applied Physics Laboratory.

DONALD E. HINMAN (E/2/3) spent twenty days in the hospital at Da Nang, then rejoined Echo. He remained with it until he was medically evacuated in January 1968 due to a knee injury. Honorably discharged in July 1968, he returned to his home in Medina, New York, and joined the Albion, New York, police department. He retired in 1998. He and his wife have one son and two grandsons.

RANDALL J. "JOSH" HOFFMAN (M/3/9) transferred to the 3d Medical Battalion at Phu Bai in September 1967. He rotated from South Vietnam two months later. Discharged in September 1968, he earned a degree in economics from California State University. He then worked as a logger and a surveyor in northern California and southern Oregon before he joined the U.S. Bureau of Reclamation as a planner. He is married with one daughter and one grandchild. He resides in Sacramento, California.

DONALD A. HOSSACK (M/3/3) spent three months in the hospital. He returned to South Vietnam to complete his tour and rotated in December 1967. Discharged a sergeant in June 1968, he returned to college at the University of Wyoming, where he earned a degree in business administration. He joined the Kalispell, Montana, police department in 1973 and retired as the assistant chief of police in 1998. Married twice and now single, he has three children and two grandchildren.

MICHAEL A. HOUSE (M/3/9) received a Silver Star for his gallantry on Hill 881S. He was badly wounded on 3 June 1967 when a sergeant near him stepped on a land mine. House spent four months in stateside hospitals before he returned to duty. He was discharged in November 1967. Married for twenty-six years, he lives with his wife in Taunton, Massachusetts, where he is a director agent for the Massachusetts Veterans Service.

TOM HUCKABA (G/2/3) was wounded on 3 September 1967 but returned to Golf. Wounded again in January 1968, he did not have to return to the war zone. He was discharged in January 1969 as a sergeant with the Bronze Star and three Purple Hearts. He returned to his job as a letter carrier, entered the postal department's management training program, and is today an area manager for the postal service. He is married, has two children and four grandchildren, and resides in Joliet, Illinois.

RICHARD HUFF (B/1/9) retired from the Marine Corps as a first sergeant in 1981. He worked as the police chief of Pilot Knob, Missouri. Now completely retired, he has an address in Greenville, Missouri, but spends most of his time traveling throughout the United States.

WAYNE L. ITHIER (H/2/3) never did receive the Bronze Star he was promised for his rescue of the wounded on 30 April 1967. He left South Vietnam after being wounded twice more on 18 and 30 June 1967. He reenlisted in February 1969 but soon began to experience the early symptoms of PTSD. He was honorably discharged in January 1970. He spent the next twenty years as a recluse in the mountains of western Pennsylvania until he connected with a veterans outreach program. He went into therapy for his PTSD, was declared 100 percent disabled, and is now recovered. He is married, lives in Fort Wayne, Indiana, and devotes his time to helping other veterans.

FRANK IZENOUR (E/2/3) died in 1988.

BRIAN R. JACKSON (B/1/12 attached to G/2/3) remained with Golf until December 1967, when the battalion left the SLF. He then became the artillery liaison officer for 2/3 until he rotated in May 1968. He was awarded a Bronze Star and a Purple Heart. Discharged in June 1969, he worked in accounting for the Veterans Administration until his retirement in 1999. He is married and resides with his wife in Indianapolis, Indiana.

WILLIAM H. JANZEN (G/2/3) rotated from South Vietnam in August 1967. He returned for a brief second tour in 1969 but already had his retirement papers submitted. He retired in March 1970. He then worked for the Xerox Corporation for eighteen years before he retired a second time. He resides in Lake Forest, California.

IRA G. "RICKY" JOHNSON (M/3/9) was seriously wounded during an enemy rocket attack on 2 September 1967 at Dong Ha while he awaited the completion of his paperwork to return to the United States. He spent five months in the hospital, then was discharged while in a body cast. Two months later he was married, still in the body cast. He worked in the construction industry in Oklahoma until 1990, when he and his family moved to Florida. In 1999 he became the facilities manager for the Bradenton Missionary Village. He and his wife of thirty-three years have two sons and two grandsons.

MICHAEL JOSEPH (2/1) completed his tour as a forward air controller in September 1968 and returned to the 1st Marine Air Wing at Da Nang. He rotated from South Vietnam in December 1968 and finished his tour at Beaufort, South Carolina. Discharged in the fall of 1970, he joined the family business. Today he is chairman/CEO of DACOR, the kitchen appliance manufacturer. A father of four and a grandfather of three, he lives in Oceanside, California, with his wife.

HAROLD E. KEPNER (M/3/3) completed his tour in November 1967. He spent ten years in the Parma, Ohio, police department, then moved to Florida and joined the Miami-Dade metro police department. He retired as an armed robbery detective in 1999. He is married with two children and three grandchildren and lives in St. James City, Florida.

THOMAS G. KING (B/1/9) was killed in action on 2 July 1967, when Bravo was overrun by the NVA near Con Thien.

RICHARD D. KOEHLER (F/2/3) remained with Foxtrot until September 1967 and served several times as its commander. He earned a Bronze Star in July 1967 for his personal heroism during Operation Buffalo. He served three months as an aide to the commander of the 9th Marine Amphibious Brigade before he rotated home in January 1968. He was discharged as a captain in 1969. He lives in Lexington, Kentucky, with his family and is an investment banker.

EDWARD J. KRESTY (M/3/9) completed his tour and rotated from South Vietnam in December 1967 after he received his fourth Purple Heart. He retired in 1971 as a captain. He and his wife settled in Jacksonville, North Carolina, where they opened an upscale restaurant and lounge. Sixteen years later he sold that business and opened a gun shop. He sold that and retired in 1996.

JOHN A. KROHN (K/3/9) was seriously injured on 22 May 1967 during Operation Hickory along the Demilitarized Zone when an enemy mortar round landed in his hole; it killed one man and wounded him and another Marine. He spent five months at Great Lakes Hospital, then was discharged in January 1968. He lives in Chicago with his wife and three children and works as a union electrician.

KENNETH LEASE (B/1/9) was wounded by friendly artillery fire ten days after he left Khe Sanh. He spent four months in stateside hospitals, then was assigned as a brig guard on Guam until his discharge in September 1969. He has a master's degree in counseling, lives in Crawfordsville, Florida, and works for the state of Florida as a mental health therapist.

CATHERINE LEROY (civilian) received a number of prestigious awards for her dramatic photographs of Hospitalman Wike. The series of photographs has appeared in numerous books and magazines dealing with the Vietnam War; the images are among the most recognizable war photos of all time. She covered wars around the world as a photojournalist for the next twenty years before she settled in Los Angeles, California. She now runs a fashion photography Web site.

ALFRED E. LYON (E/2/3) was not allowed to return to South Vietnam due to his three wounds. He finished his tour on Okinawa. He returned to the United States in August 1967 and was discharged in December 1967. He then went to graduate school, earned his master's degree, and went to work for Pacific Bell. He retired in 1991. He now lives in Stagecoach, Nevada. In July 2001 he was awarded a Silver Star for his heroism during the Hill Fights.

RAYMOND C. MADONNA (H/2/3) returned to South Vietnam for a second tour in 1970 as commander of Charlie 1/5. He retired as a colonel in 1983. He is employed in business development for the Motorola Corporation. He is married with two children and resides in Manassas, Virginia.

ROBERT J. MARAS (G/2/3) was badly wounded in the leg on 22 May 1967 and spent two months in the hospital. Wounded again on 30 August and for a fourth time the next day, he spent several more months in the hospital. Upon his discharge in December 1968, he joined the Tulsa, Oklahoma, police department. He also joined the Army reserves and learned to fly helicopters. He retired from the police department in 1989 and the National Guard in 1997. After being cast by Francis Ford Coppola for a small role in *The Outsiders,* he obtained his Screen Actors Guild card and moved to Hollywood in 1990. He appeared in several motion pictures and television shows as an actor and a stuntman. He returned to Tulsa and is now employed by the U.S. Marshall's office. He is single with one son.

JAMES J. MARDEN (E/2/3) rotated from South Vietnam at the end of his enlistment in January 1968. He returned to Boston, where he went to work for the telephone company. He retired, then started his own communications business. Married for more than thirty years, he and his wife have a son (a Marine Corps veteran of the Gulf War), a daughter, and one grandchild. He lives in Gaylordsville, Connecticut.

JAMES R. MASON (E/2/3) remained with Echo for the rest of his tour. He rotated from South Vietnam in December 1967. After an early discharge in July 1969, he returned to St. Paul, Minnesota, and became a meat cutter. He divorced after being married for twenty-seven years. In 1994 he was declared 100 percent disabled with PTSD. He resides in Inver Grove Heights, Minnesota. In July 2001 he was presented a Bronze Star for his heroism in July 1967 during Operation Buffalo.

ANDREW B. McFARLANE (G/2/3) rotated from South Vietnam in October 1967, then returned for a second tour in 1970. He retired as a captain in 1971, having earned two Bronze Stars and the Navy Commendation Medal during his career. He then worked in law enforcement until 1991, when he retired again. He lives with his wife in Saddle Brook, New Jersey, and works part-time as a scout for major league baseball.

JACK M. McKENNA (K/3/9) rotated from South Vietnam in September 1968 and was discharged in May 1970. He returned to his hometown of Dothan, Alabama, and went to work in the civil service at nearby Fort Rucker. He retired in March 1999 after being injured in an automobile accident on his way to work. He is married and has two children.

DOUGLAS W. McKESSON (M/3/3) completed his tour in August 1967. Discharged a sergeant in January 1968, he worked in the restaurant business for several years before he moved to Sonoma, California. He and his wife purchased a bicycle shop there and still own and operate it. They have two children.

TERRANCE L. MEIER (M/3/3) was awarded a Silver Star for his valor on Hill 881S. He was posthumously awarded a Navy Cross for his gallantry above and beyond the call of duty on 21 July 1967, when his platoon was ambushed by the NVA on Route 9 just west of Ca Lu.

DAVID L. MELLON (B/1/9) was evacuated from South Vietnam and spent several months in stateside hospitals before he returned to active duty. He was discharged in December 1968. He pursued a career in chemical sales and retired in 1999. Married, he and his wife have two daughters and two grandchildren. He lives in Laguna Niguel, California.

JOHN R. MEUSE (E/2/9) was posthumously awarded a Navy Cross for his valor.

FREDERICK G. MONAHAN (E/2/3) received the Navy Cross for his gallantry in action on 3 May 1967. He also received two Purple Hearts during his tour. He was discharged in February 1968. He lives in Holland, Pennsylvania, with his wife and two daughters and is retired from the construction industry.

HARRY MONTGOMERY (B/1/9) completed his tour in August 1967 and was discharged from the Marine Corps in January 1968. He then enrolled at Kent State University in Ohio. Present during the student riots protesting President Nixon's invasion of Cambodia, he was so distraught by the murder of four fellow students by members of the Ohio National Guard that he dropped out of school and wandered around Europe for more than a year before he returned to the United States. He is employed as a cable repairman for Ameritech and lives in Sandusky, Ohio, with his wife and three sons.

JOHN A. MOORE (B/1/9) was badly wounded on 7 June 1967 when two enemy hand grenades landed near him. He spent several months in hospitals before being discharged in July 1968 with three Purple Hearts. He served as a police officer in Richmond, California, and Reno, Nevada, for ten years, then moved to Cour d'Alene, Idaho, and joined the fire department. He retired from there in 1995. He lives in Cour d'Alene with his wife.

MICHAEL R. MORGAN (M/3/3) was posthumously awarded a Silver Star for his valor.

ROBERT L. MORNINGSTAR (E/2/9) was killed in action on 5 July 1967.

DESMOND T. MURRAY (H/2/3) was severely wounded on 22 May 1967. He spent nearly one year in the hospital before being medically discharged in April 1968. He completed college, attended law school, and is a real estate lawyer. He resides in Fairport, New York, with his wife and daughter.

ERNEST M. MURRAY (M/3/9) left South Vietnam in July 1967. After his discharge in 1969, he joined the Marine reserves. Several years later he returned to active duty. He retired as a master gunnery sergeant in 1991. He resides in Oceanside, California, with his wife and five children and works in auto sales and auto auctions.

JOSEPH P. O'CONNOR (F/2/3) completed his tour in August 1967 with a Purple Heart for wounds received in a later action. He is an investment banker.

HARRY J. O'DELL (K/3/9) spent thirty days aboard the hospital ship *Repose* before he rejoined Kilo. However, embedded shrapnel made it too painful for him to carry his equipment, so Captain Giles ordered him back to the hospital. After six more weeks on the *Repose,* he again returned to the field. He was seriously wounded near Gio Linh on 30 July 1967 by an enemy mortar round. Suffering a broken left arm, broken jaw, and shrapnel wounds in the hand, leg, and arm, he ended up in the Great Lakes Hospital, where he spent ten months recovering from his wounds. Discharged in June 1968, he returned to Michigan, married his girlfriend, raised three children, and worked as a brick mason until his retirement in 1995. He resides in Three Rivers, Michigan, where he and his wife enjoy their seven grandchildren.

SPENCER F. OLSEN (E/2/9) earned a Silver Star for his heroism on Hill 861. He was hospitalized for three weeks, then returned to E/2/9. He left South Vietnam in July 1967. He continued his career in the Marine Corps and retired as a sergeant major in 1983. Married and the father of one son, he lives with his wife in Fowler, Colorado.

GERALD C. PETT (H/2/3) rotated from South Vietnam in August 1967. He was honorably discharged in November 1967 to attend college. A salesman in the precious metals recovery industry for most of his career, he is now involved in software development. Married for more than twenty-six years, he and his wife have three children and one grandchild and recently adopted a child. They live in Newman, Illinois.

DANIEL W. POLLAND (B/1/9) was transferred from B/1/9 in June 1967 to an engineer unit near Phu Bai. He completed his tour with them and was discharged in October 1967. He earned a degree in pharmacology from the University of Colorado in 1973, then took a degree in osteopathic medicine from the University of Kansas City in 1977. In 1982 he became an anesthesiologist. He is married, has three children, and resides in Grand Junction, Colorado.

ALBERT W. POTTS (F/2/3) completed his tour in August 1967. He was honorably discharged in December 1968. He went to work in a manufacturing facility in his wife's hometown until 1982, when he became a mold repairman with another firm. He joined the Marine Corps reserves in 1971 and retired as a master sergeant in 1993. He and his wife live in Ellwood City, Pennsylvania.

CLARENCE S. POWELL (F/2/3) ended up on Guam for treatment of his wound. He was ordered back to South Vietnam while his arm was still in a cast, but a sympathetic officer on Okinawa suggested he call his family. His father contacted their congressman, who had the orders changed. Powell finished his tour in Hawaii. He was discharged in May 1969. He returned to Burlington, Iowa, where he was employed as a welder for twenty years before he retired. He now operates heavy equipment. Single, he has one son and one grandson.

LARRY J. PRATT (B/1/9) was wounded by friendly fire in May 1967 and by the NVA on 2 July 1967, just four days away from rotation, when Bravo 1/9 lost two-thirds of its members near Con Thien during Operation Buffalo. He spent three months in the hospital, then was medically discharged, unable to pursue his dream of a career in the Marine Corps. He became an electrician, then went to work for the Disabled Veterans Outreach Program as the Illinois state representative. He resides in Springfield, Illinois.

IVORY PUCKETT (E/2/9) was wounded twice before he rotated from South Vietnam in December 1967. After his discharge in June 1968, he went to work for Mobil Oil as a pipe fitter. He remains there and lives in Los Angeles, California.

JAMES H. REEDER (Khe Sanh SOP) retired as a full colonel in 1973. He died on 13 November 2002.

ALFREDO V. REYES (B/1/9) was killed in action on 2 July 1967 when Bravo 1/9 was overrun by the NVA near Con Thien.

ALFONSO RIATE (K/3/3) was captured by the NVA and repatriated in 1973. He was one of a handful of American POWs accused of collaboration. The charges were later dropped. His present whereabouts are unknown.

THOMAS E. RICE (E/2/3) left South Vietnam in November 1967 and was discharged two months later. He earned a degree from California Polytechnic State University at San Luis Obispo. He resides in Lincoln City, Oregon.

DAVID M. ROGERS (C/1/12 attached to M/3/3) rotated from South Vietnam at the end of his tour in October 1967. After his discharge as a captain in 1968, he pursued a career in aviation and earned numerous pilot ratings. He then went to work as an air traffic controller for the Federal Aviation Administration. Eventually he became a data systems specialist in the agency. When it privatized in 1986, Rogers became an employee of Diversified International Sciences Corporation. Married with one daughter, he resides in Arlington, Texas.

THOMAS F. RYAN (B/1/9) was transferred to India 3/3 two weeks after Khe Sanh and completed his tour with them in March 1968. Discharged in September 1969, he worked in a variety of jobs until he finally received counseling and was awarded a 30 percent disability for PTSD. He now works for the postal service in Philadelphia and is married with two children.

WILLIAM A. RYAN, JR. (F/2/3) left South Vietnam in September 1967 due to a spinal injury suffered when he dove into his hole atop Hill 881N on 5 May. He was honorably discharged on 1 April 1969. After a year in college, he entered law enforcement. He retired from the Lake Worth, Florida, police department in 1996. Married with two children, he and his wife reside in Weare, New Hampshire.

CHARLES B. SALTAFORMAGGIO (K/3/9) completed his tour in South Vietnam in December 1967. After his discharge in February 1969, he joined the Louisiana State Police. Shot four times in 1971, he found police work more dangerous than service in South Vietnam. He retired as a lieutenant in 1999 and worked as a tour guide for veterans visiting Vietnam. He lives in Metarie, Louisiana, and is married and has two children.

MICHAEL W. SAYERS (B/1/9) finished his tour as the assistant S-3 for the 9th Marines. He left South Vietnam in October 1967 with a Bronze Star and a Purple Heart. He retired as a major in 1979. He then worked as the vice president of a bank in Fort Smith, Arkansas, before he started his own human relations consulting firm. He is retired and lives with his wife in Greenwood, Arkansas. He has always felt bitter that neither he nor his men received more recognition for their role in the Hill Fights.

ROBERT J. SCHLEY (M/3/3) was posthumously awarded a Navy Cross for his valor.

JAMES P. SHEEHAN (G/2/3) was wounded in July 1967 during Operation Buffalo and earned a Silver Star and a Purple Heart. He later transferred to a battalion staff position. He extended his tour after being promoted to major and served until December 1968 with the 4th Marines. Married to the Navy nurse he met while hospitalized, he retired in 1989 as a full colonel and resides in Silverdale, Washington.

CHARLES R. "DICK" SHOEMAKER (K/3/3) departed South Vietnam on schedule with a Bronze Star with "V" for his service. He was appointed to the warrant officer ranks and designated a Marine gunner in 1970. He retired from the Marine Corps seven years later, then worked in retail management and managed several political campaigns before he fully retired in 1996. He is married and resides with his wife in Prescott, Arizona.

ROBERT SLATTERY (E/2/9) rotated from South Vietnam at the end of his tour in June 1967 with a Purple Heart. After his discharge in November 1967, he joined the New York City Police Department. He retired as a crime scene detective in 1989. He now works in the security department of Merrill Lynch. Married with four children, he resides in Lynbrook, New York.

MERLE G. SORENSEN (F/2/3) returned to South Vietnam after one month in the hospital recovering from his wound. Denied the opportunity to return to Foxtrot, he became the assistant S-3 for the 9th Marines until his rotation in February 1968. He retired a major in 1979. He then worked in property management but is now retired and lives in Escondido, California.

BAYLESS L. SPIVEY (K/3/3) completed his tour in July 1967. He remained in the Marine Corps until 1981 when he retired as a lieutenant colonel. He then entered the real estate business. He is married with four children and runs a KOA campground in Myrtle Beach, South Carolina.

GEORGE STERNISHA (E/2/3) completed his tour and rotated from South Vietnam in October 1967. He was honorably discharged in March 1968. He returned to Crest Hill, Illinois, and the construction industry. Today he is a construction superintendent. He is married and has two sons.

ROBERT W. STEWART (F/2/12 attached to K/3/9) spent six weeks in the hospital recovering from his wound. The Marine Corps then made him take his thirty-day leave for extending his tour and his thirty-day convalescence leave concurrently. He returned to South Vietnam in July 1967 and served until December 1967. Discharged in May 1969 with 50 percent disability, he attended the University of Alabama, where he earned a business degree in 1972. A certified public accountant (CPA), he spent several years with a Big Eight international CPA firm, then became the chief financial officer for several large corporations. Diagnosed with PTSD in 2000, he is now retired with 100 percent disability. He lives with his wife and two children in Largo, Florida.

ROBERT W. SWIGART (M/3/3) was relieved of command in June 1967. He was killed in action on 4 July 1967.

WILLIAM B. TERRILL (E/2/9) finished his tour in South Vietnam as the battalion S-3. Upon his return to the United States in August 1967, he took his discharge. He returned to his hometown of San Angelo, Texas, and joined the family cabinetmaking business. Now semi-retired, he lives in Mertzon, Texas, with his wife.

WILLIAM VAN DEVANDER (K/3/9) spent two weeks in the hospital, then returned to the field. During this time his family received an erroneous notice that he had been killed in action. He left South Vietnam in June 1967. He was discharged in September 1968 with three Purple Hearts. He drifted for the next fifteen years, working odd jobs, drinking heavily, and fighting. He was eventually diagnosed with PTSD and given 80 percent disability. He was injured in an automobile accident in 1992 and forced to go on disability from his job with the General Service Administration. Married with three children and six grandchildren, he owns a farm near Huntington, West Virginia, and raises Tennessee walking horses.

KENNETH D. VERMILLION (B/1/9) received two Purple Hearts before he rotated from South Vietnam in June 1967. He was discharged in September 1967. He was employed as a sheet metal worker for ten years, then became a car salesman. He lives in Upper Marlboro, Maryland, with his wife and child.

THOMAS A. VINEYARD (K/3/3) had his left thumb amputated at the medical station at Phu Bai. He then was sent to Letterman General Hospital in San Francisco, where he remained until he was medically retired in November 1967. He earned his degree and became a CPA. He worked for Peat Marwick for many years, then opened his own firm. Today he is semi-retired and lives in Palm Desert, California.

LEWIS W. WALT (III MAF) left South Vietnam in June 1967. He retired as a four-star general. He died in 1989.

THOMAS C. WHEELER (M/3/3) spent forty-two days aboard the USS *Repose* recovering from his wounds. Instead of accepting a return to the States for medical reasons, he volunteered to return to M/3/3. He finally left South Vietnam in September 1967. After his honorable discharge in March 1969, he entered the construction business. He is now retired and lives in Tampa, Florida.

PETER A. WICKWIRE (1/3) retired as a full colonel in 1980. He then began a second career as a custom home contractor. He resides in Townsend, Georgia.

VERNON WIKE (G/2/3) remained with Golf until September 1967, when a hip injury forced his medical evacuation. After five months' hospitalization he was discharged. He returned to Phoenix, where he worked as a respiratory therapist and in retail management. His hip injury worsened and in 1979 the Veterans Administration declared him 100 percent disabled. He now resides in Prescott, Arizona.

GARY WILDER (3/3) completed his tour of South Vietnam in July 1967. He retired as a colonel in 1977 to care for his wife, who had been badly injured in an automobile accident. Upon her death in 1992, he went to work for the University of Central Florida as a designer of war games for the Marine Corps. He resides in Longwood, Florida.

ISAMU S. "SAM" YOSHIDA (K/3/3) spent several months in hospitals in South Vietnam and the United States. He eventually recovered his eyesight. He completed his tour at Camp Pendleton, California, and was discharged in December 1968. He then attended the University of California at Berkeley and earned an engineering degree and a law degree. He resides in Redwood City, California, with his wife and works for the General Services Administration as a real estate specialist.

Bibliography

Bowman, John S., ed. *The Vietnam War Almanac.* New York: World Almanac Publications, 1985.

Dougan, Clark, and Stephen Weiss, *The Vietnam Experience: Nineteen Sixty-Eight.* Boston, Massachusetts: Boston Publishing Co., 1983.

Esper, George, and the Associated Press. *The Eyewitness History of the Vietnam War, 1961–1975.* New York: Ballantine Books, 1983.

Ezell, Edward C. *The Great Rifle Controversy.* Harrisburg, Pennsylvania: Stackpole Books, 1984.

Krulak, Victor H., Gen. *First to Fight.* Annapolis, Maryland: Naval Institute Press, 1984.

Maitland, Terrence, and Peter McInerney. *The Vietnam Experience: A Contagion of War.* Boston, Massachusetts: Boston Publishing Co., 1983.

Nolan, Keith William. *Operation Buffalo.* Novato, California: Presidio Press, 1994.

Pisor, Robert. *The End of the Line.* New York: Ballantine Books, 1982.

Prados, John, and Ray W. Stubbe. *Valley of Decision.* Boston, Massachusetts: Houghton Mifflin Co., 1991.

Stanton, Shelby. *Green Berets at War.* Novato, California: Presidio Press, 1985.

Westmoreland, William C., Gen. *A Soldier Reports.* New York: Doubleday & Co., 1976.

Zaffiri, Samuel. *Westmoreland.* New York: Wm. Morrow & Co., 1994.

I consulted the official command chronologies for all the major units involved in the Hill Fights. Although these do not contain much detail, they are valuable for dates, times, and locations. The after-action report for the Battle of Khe Sanh, prepared by the 3d Marines S-3 and dated 9 June 1967, provided the most useful contemporary information regarding the Hill Fights. In addition, I used accounts of the battles and the M16 controversy as reported in newspapers and news magazines including the *New York Times, Life Magazine, Time Magazine,* and *Vietnam.*

Index